MICROPROCESSOR SYSTEM SERVICING

To Lyn, to Anita and to Susanne

MICROPROCESSOR SYSTEM SERVICING

JOHN D. FERGUSON
Computer Science Department
Strathclyde University
(formerly MEDC)

LOUIE MACARI
Senior Electronics Engineer
James Howden & Co., Glasgow
(formerly MEDC)

PETER WILLIAMS
Director
Microelectronics Educational Development Centre (MEDC)
(Paisley College)

Prentice / Hall PHI International

Englewood Cliffs, NJ   London   Mexico   New Delhi
Rio de Janeiro   Singapore   Sydney   Tokyo   Toronto

Library of Congress Cataloging-in-Publication Data

Ferguson, J. D. (John D.)
  Microprocessor system servicing.

  Includes index.
  1. Microcomputers—Maintenance and repair.
  2. Microcomputers—Maintenance and repair.
  I. Macari, L. II. Williams, Peter, 1937–
  III. Title.
  TK7887.F47 1986   621.391'6'0288   86–21246
  ISBN 0–13–581132–5 (pbk.)

British Library Cataloguing in Publication Data

Ferguson, John D.
  Microprocessor system servicing.
  1. Microprocessors —— Maintenance and
  repair
  1. Title II. Macari, L. III. Williams, P.
  (Peter), *1937–*
  621.391'6   TK7895.M5

  ISBN 0–13–581132–5

© **1987 John D. Ferguson, Louie Macari & Peter Williams**

Prentice-Hall Inc., Englewood Cliffs, *New Jersey*
Prentice-Hall International (UK) Ltd, *London*
Prentice-Hall of Australia Pty Ltd, *Sydney*
Prentice-Hall Canada Inc., *Toronto*
Prentice-Hall Hispanoamericana S.A., *Mexico*
Prentice-Hall of India Private Ltd, *New Delhi*
Prentice-Hall of Japan Inc., *Tokyo*
Prentice-Hall of Southeast Asia Pte Ltd, *Singapore*
Editora Prentice-Hall do Brasil Ltda, *Rio de Janeiro*

Printed and bound in Great Britain for
Prentice-Hall International (UK) Ltd,
66 Wood Lane End, Hemel Hempstead, Hertfordshire, HP2 4RG
by A. Wheaton & Co. Ltd, Exeter.

1 2 3 4 5   90 89 88 87 86

ISBN 0-13-581132-5

Contents

Preface

Servicing a microprocessor system requires a different base of knowledge from that for conventional electronics servicing. It does not demand a different attitude. The same questioning attitude, the same logical process of elimination holds good. Designers and technicians alike can have confidence that the good habits they have acquired, whether in analog or digital circuits, or in an earlier electromechanical era, will transfer to the microprocessor and its systems.

It would be foolish to deny the problems implicit in this new technology, but with the right attitude they can be kept in perspective. In this book we start from the assumption that the reader has a general knowledge of electronics, including digital techniques, with a logical approach to problems. We do not assume a detailed knowledge of microprocessors but a good appreciation of their principles will be helpful.

It is the purpose of Part I to bring these themes together so that readers with differing backgrounds can appreciate the new techniques presented in the body of the book. The aim is not to teach digital electronics nor to provide yet another 'Micros for Beginners'. Rather, it is to review these topics from a servicing standpoint in order to place the known facts in a new framework. For the practicing electronics engineer much in this first section will be familiar, though the viewpoint may be less so. Readers with a programming background may find these hardware ideas strange at first but without them the route to microprocessor servicing is blocked.

Part II looks at the techniques available for tackling the servicing problem. At each stage from development through production to user maintenance there will be common difficulties to which these techniques can be applied. The kind of information generated by any one method will vary in how helpful it will be to the individual. A designer needs to know why a system is not behaving as expected, while a serviceman working to tight time and cost budgets will give priority to the method that pinpoints a quick cure.

The ideal would be for each user to have a full range of professional equipment. Part III looks at simple designs that can be constructed to cover straightforward tasks and to offer cost-effective training tools. Because each user will have different priorities, the designs are presented in outline form suitable for adaptation by experienced electronics engineers and technicians.

Chapter 1 reviews the characteristics of digital devices and the appropriate fault-finding techniques. Microprocessor systems are considered in Chapter 2, emphasizing those aspects that help the understanding of servicing ideas. In Chapter 3 the characteristics of the interface between microprocessor systems and peripherals is considered from the same standpoint. An introduction to fault finding in Chapter 4 looks at those general points that can be checked without special equipment. Self-testing, discussed in Chapter 5, assumes that the system functions sufficiently to allow it to generate test patterns to probe suspect sections. A logic analyzer (Chapter 6) monitors the sequential bit patterns on the system bus lines to reveal both straightforward component faults and the more subtle effects of timing errors. Once data transmission takes place there are additional sources of faults, and Chapter 7 introduces the characteristics and appropriate testing procedures for serial interfaces. In-circuit emulation is a technique available on development systems as a design tool but Chapter 8 looks at its role in fault finding. Chapter 9 covers signature analysis in which a system is first documented running a pre-defined routine: the bit-pattern at any point results in a unique code, any departure from which siginifies a fault. Automatic test procedures for production lines can have application in fault finding but, as Chapter 10 shows, the actual equipment may bear little resemblance. Part III provides ideas for test equipment based on microcomputers and user-designed test boards. Chapter 11 illustrates this approach with a simple in-circuit emulator based on a standard microcomputer. Signature and logic analyzers can be implemented as low-cost single board devices for training purposes (Chapter 12). The serial interfaces between computers and their peripherals can be tested by using the serial analyzer and character generator of Chapter 13.

J.D.F., L.M., P.W.

PART I

Microprocessor Systems

1

Digital Devices and Systems

Microprocessors need other circuits and devices to form a complete system. Logic circuits of different families differ considerably in their behavior, even when performing similar functions. An outline of these differences is given. Test devices are available that can trace a fault to a specific pin on a device, and their advantages and limitations are discussed.

*   *   *

The best servicing aid to any system is a well-written manual. As in all other topics covered in this book, the reader should exhibit that true spirit of optimism without which servicing tasks can be so difficult – assume that the manual will be helpful until proven otherwise.

For the moment we ignore those unfortunately too frequent occasions when the manual is missing or hastily put together. It should give clear diagrams of the layout, and with luck a number of critical test points. A typical problem it can help avoid is in the measurement of clock frequency. A counter or oscilloscope may present sufficient loading to disturb the frequency of an oscillator if tapped onto a high-impedance port. Any manufacturer-designated test point should be well buffered, avoiding this risk.

The manual may contain a set of test procedures to trace the main categories of faults anticipated by the designers. Only the foolhardy would ignore such help, though in fairness there may be limited fault information available to the designers at the time of writing the manual.

It is important to realize that just because a pcb is part of a microprocessor system, any standard logic circuits behave in *exactly* the same way from a servicing standpoint as in older logic systems. Although the functions may be more complex, the electrical and mechanical faults are the same – track shorts, solder bridges, open-circuit gates. It may be more difficult to track down the area of the board where the fault occurs, but once narrowed down to one or two chips, all the well-known tests can

1

be used. In this section we shall review these tests: there are many books dealing with these techniques more fully.

When would these simpler methods be used, and when the advanced techniques discussed later? If automatic or semi-automatic tests are available, use them. They will have been implemented by professionals having considerably more experience and thinking time than you will have under pressure on an unfamiliar system. If by good fortune the fault is one that advertises itself, that is different. Symptoms visible on a display or output port may suggest a driver chip, and a quick test with a pulser and logic probe may identify the fault quickly. Equally, bad fortune may leave the service engineer without the appropriate analyzer or emulator tools at the critical moment. To fall back on these traditional approaches is then the only choice.

Let us identify some characteristics that can be picked up by suitable probes.

Static	Logic 0
	Logic 1
	'Bad' level (intermediate between 0 and 1)
	Open circuit
	Short circuit
Dynamic	Short duration pulses
	Transients
	Low repetition-rate pulses
	Reverse polarity pulses
	Current flow

Logic levels should be either 0 or 1. As noted above, the precise levels at which these states are guaranteed varies between device families. Taking the usual TTL values, the voltages below 0.8 V are recognized as logic 0 and above 2.4 V as logic 1. Intermediate values imply a circuit fault, and a logic probe should give a separate indication. An open circuit usually leaves the probe in the same state, i.e. there is no distinction between an open-circuit condition and a 'bad' logic level. Similarly a short circuit to either of the supply lines will ensure a level that will be unambiguously interpreted as a true logic level. A voltmeter (or oscilloscope) will distinguish between a TTL logic/output and a short circuit to the supply line.

A single light-emitting diode with suitable driving stage can provide three states to represent the three groups of possibilities:

'off'	Logic 0 (or s/c to common)
'dim'	Open circuit or bad (intermediate between level 0 and 1)
'bright'	Logic 1 (or s/c to positive supply)

Fortunately we are not restricted to static testing. By adding a transient detector and a monostable circuit to the LED driver, an output pulse of fixed duration is obtained on an input transition. If the probe is connected to a point at logic 1 which experiences a narrow negative pulse of as little as 10 ns, the LED is pulsed off for a fraction of a second. A second time delay inhibits its response to repetitive transitions such that a flashing output at ~10 Hz is obtained for pulse rates from this frequency up to many MHz.

Thus with a single indicator LED, single short transients of either 0–1 or 1–0 can be detected as well as a continuous pulse train (Fig. 1.1).

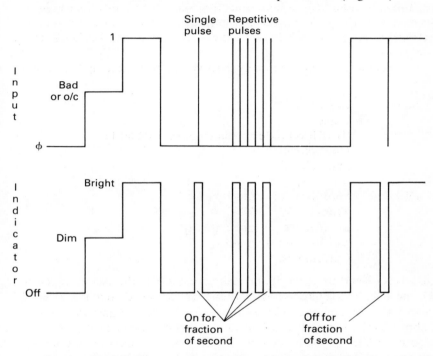

Fig. 1.1 Single indicator monitors static and dynamic logic states

High indicator on }
Low indicator off } True logic 1

Low on }
High off } True logic 0

Neither on Bad or open circuit
Both flashing Low frequency pulse train
Both dim High frequency pulse train (relative brightness indicates mark/space ratio)

A third LED is added, flashing for a pulse train but off for any static condition. No information is provided on the mark-space ratio of any such pulse train. If separate LEDs are used to indicate logic 0 and 1 levels with appropriate threshold detectors, more information can be provided (Fig. 1.2).

These alternatives can be extended by, for example, having a latched mode in which an LED is held on following the receipt of a single pulse, even of short duration. Each manufacturer adopts different specifications too for the pulse timings. The probes may respond to minimum pulse widths between 10 and 100 ns with output pulse widths between 50 and 300 ms. They may have switched threshold levels to make them compatible with different logic families. Check the manual to make sure you are getting the best possible use out of your probe.

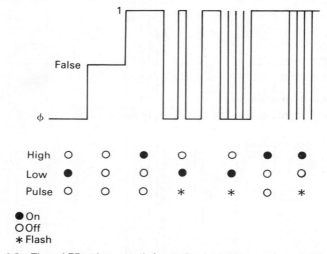

Fig. 1.2   Three LEDs give more information including mark-space ratio

CURRENT PROBE

Some faults cannot be identified by voltage probes no matter how complex the probes become. A short circuit may be distinguishable at a given node, but not the particular device, connected to that node, which is causing it. Similarly, a short circuit between two points might be within an IC or between pairs of tracks serving these points. We need to know where the current flows are being diverted to, without breaking tracks or removing ICs if at all possible. Though in the last resort this often has to be done, it is both time consuming and risky. It is so easy to introduce other faults in the process.

To detect a direct current is difficult though possible: Hall-effect devices are one possibility. It is difficult to achieve sensitivities appropriate to the levels in modern digital systems. Pulsed currents are somewhat easier and the current probe is a powerful tool. By aligning the tip of the probe along the conducting path, the field generated by the pulse is detected and the sensitivity is adjusted to keep an indicator on. The probe is then moved along the expected current paths until the indicator goes off, identifying the start of an unexpected conducting path. Note that it is a noncontact measurement, requiring close proximity to the conductor but not a direct electrical connection.

To see the different capabilities of voltage and current probes, consider Fig. 1.3. A pulse train at A should result in an inverted version at B, with the original recreated at D (ignoring propagation delay). No pulse activity should be present at C and E. A voltage probe at D might show no pulses, the output being at logic 1. This could be a fault in this gate, an output short circuited to the supply externally or that B is held at logic 0. Transfer the voltage probe to B. If a pulse train is present, that confirms a fault in the output gate or a short at D. No pulse train could mean:

1   the input inverter is faulty;
2   a short circuit at B to ground, supply line or other track.

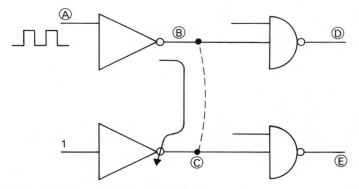

Fig. 1.3   Current probe traces short circuit current

If B is stuck at logic 0 this would check with the logic 1 state of D, suggesting the output gate as 'good'. A current probe at B should show a pulse train if the input inverter is functioning. Adjust the sensitivity so that the indicator is just on. Move the probe towards the output until the indicator goes out. This shows the point on the track at which a short circuit occurs. Inspection of the board should show up a solder bridge or other fault. Failing this, a check of neighboring points such as C might identify where the current is being diverted to, if not directly to ground, pinpointing the physical location of the dotted short circuit.

If a gate is used to drive multiple inputs the design will normally ensure comparable currents for the inputs, e.g. for the four inputs of Fig. 1.4 a pulse current of 8 mA from the driver would be needed to provide each with ~2 mA. This is not to suggest any precision in this sharing: the currents will only be approximately equal, but the probe in turn can only distinguish gross inequalities as under fault conditions. Set the probe to respond to the pulse output at A (if none is present, either the inverter is faulty or *all* the following inputs are open circuit!). Move the probe to each input in turn. If only one of them keeps it illuminated, this is strong evidence for a short circuit. If none of them do it, this is unsurprising – the individual currents may be too small. If the sensitivity can be increased sufficiently these lower but approximately equal currents should be detectable.

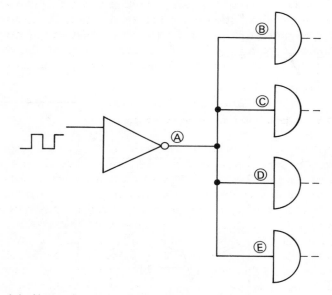

Fig. 1.4   Unequal currents pinpoint s/c input

LOGIC PULSER

The above examples assume that the circuit has a suitable pulse train driving it. If this is not so we have to be able to inject a signal. This can be done by physically breaking into the circuit – cutting a track, removing ICs, etc. The same objections apply to this procedure for current sensing. We may have to, but would prefer not to.

What is needed is a device that can be applied to any point in the system and *safely* override its existing condition, injecting a pulse train into a node regardless of whether it is resting at logic 0 or 1. A square wave pulse generator with an output impedance much lower than that of the point being driven would not do. Excessive current and hence dissipation would be imposed on the output of any gate so driven. For example, a square-wave voltage generator applied to a TTL output normally driven to logic 0 would result in excessive dissipation for 50 percent of the time (corresponding to shorting the output to the positive supply for that portion, Fig. 1.5).

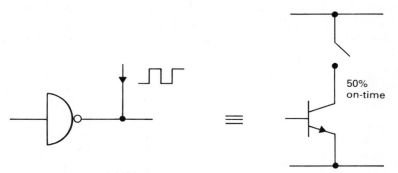

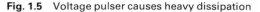

Fig. 1.5   Voltage pulser causes heavy dissipation

If instead that action can be restricted to, say, 1 or 2 percent of the time though the peak currents remain high, the average dissipation should not cause problems. The trick is to devise a pulser that adjusts its drive waveform to the static condition of the point under test. For a point at logic 0 it should force a logic 1 only briefly and vice versa. Thus between every pulse the generator should check the new condition of the node under test, changing the nature of the following pulse if necessary. This implies a tristate output from the generator. In the open-circuit state an internal detector determines the logic level of the test point, and conditions the next pulse accordingly. This copes with the outputs of flip-flop systems in which each pulse may reverse the state of that output via the feedback paths.

The pulser can be used to detect short circuits to ground. Having a current-limiting action internally, it is designed to override standard outputs such as TTL, and a voltage probe would display the presence of these pulses. For a short circuit (or a lower-than-usual impedance to ground) no voltage pulses would be detected (Fig. 1.6).

Replacing the voltage probe by a current probe, the track can be scanned in either direction from the pulser to determine the path of the current flow. Disappearance of that current pulse train indicates the short-circuit point. It also provides a quick test for a faulty gate in wired-OR systems (Fig. 1.7). These effectively consist of a series of parallel transistors, the conduction of any one of which changes the logic state of the

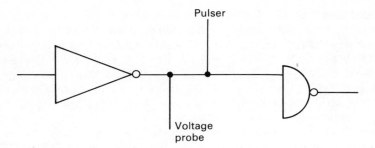

Fig. 1.6   Current pulser monitored by voltage probe

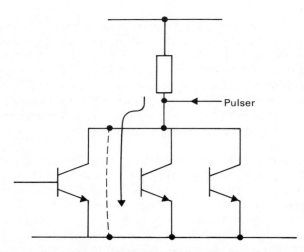

Fig. 1.7   Current pulser and probe test wired-OR gates

output. If one of them is permanently on, it is not possible to use input pulses to detect which. Pulsing the output and moving a current probe towards the individual gates should identify which of them is stuck in the on condition.

The pulser is likely to have both single-shot and repetitive pulsing capability – the former offers even less risk of dissipation problems, but the latter may be needed, particularly in flip-flop, counter or time-delay systems. Output pulse width varies from 10 ns to 10 μs for TTL and MOS use, with current limits from 100 mA to less than 50 mA respectively. With CMOS circuits it is necessary for the pulser to cope with voltages up to 18 V, though such levels are unlikely in microprocessor systems.

During all these pulsing tests it is assumed that internal clocks are inactive – either from a fault condition being investigated or deliberately – so as to ensure that only the controlled test pulses are being monitored.

LOGIC CLIPS

These are multipoint monitors that clip over ICs, giving a mimic diagram of the status of the pins on a set of LEDs. They have monitoring circuits capable of sensing the highest voltage present, presumably the +ve supply, and using that to provide for the internal display devices and circuitry.

If the effective clock rate applied to the test chip is slow enough, its function can be viewed dynamically. Of considerable value in logic systems, the usual restriction to 14/16 pins makes them less useful with microprocessors. They could be used with 16-pin support chips but give little information with, for example, multiplexed buses, even if accessible on these chips.

Logic comparators suffer from the same disadvantages. They are used to compare test and reference ICs having paralleled inputs, and can check even transient differences in performance. It is unlikely that they will be widely used in microcomputer systems now that the newer techniques of logic and signature analysis, in-circuit emulation and the like are available. The very philosophies are different. All of the test methods discussed in this chapter are chip oriented: a step up from component level testing but different in kind from the thinking necessary with bus-oriented systems. They will still have a place in testing peripheral boards, and where other tests have narrowed down a fault to a physical area. They can then pinpoint the precise location of a fault for visual inspection.

LOGIC FAMILIES

Faults may occur in isolated gates and digital circuits on the periphery of microprocessor systems. The symptoms will depend on the particular family of logic used. A brief description of these families and their characteristics is included, but there is no substitute for a study of manufacturers' data sheets. Many text books on digital circuits cover this subject.

The most common logic families are:

TTL
ECL
I^2L
PMOS
NMOS
CMOS
Dynamic MOS

(For peripheral devices, TTL and CMOS are the most common and their structure warrants a closer study.)

Earlier logic forms such as RTL and DTL are most unlikely to be found in microprocessor systems.

Each family has advantages, with ECL outstanding for speed, though pressed very hard by special versions of TTL. Both PMOS and, more recently, NMOS have been used in microprocessors, with CMOS favored for low power operation. Dynamic MOS is used for large scale memory circuits, having a simple structure in which the logic state is determined by charge stored on the natural gate capacitances. I^2L has been used in custom designed circuits.

TTL

This has perhaps the greatest variety of forms – because there has been more time to find the limitations and ways of overcoming them. The basic inverter of Fig. 1.8 is found in a 14-pin dual-in-line package as a hex-inverter. The maximum voltage at the base of Tr1 is ~2 V, being the sum of three forward-biased pn junctions (b-c of Tr1 and b-e of Tr2, Tr3). If the emitter of Tr1 is raised to within ~0.6 V of that value, the current in the emitter drops towards zero. All the current in the 4 K resistor flows throught the collector of Tr1 into the base of Tr2, driving Tr2 and Tr3 into

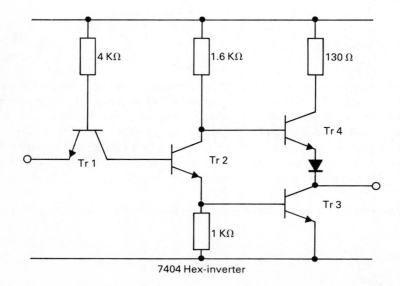

7404 Hex-inverter

Fig. 1.8 Standard TTL inverter

conduction. This pulls the base of Tr4 below 1 V (the saturated collector-emitter voltage of Tr2 plus the base-emitter voltage of Tr3), insufficient to keep Tr4 in conduction because of the diode in its emitter. With Tr3 ON and Tr4 OFF the output is at logic 0. Typically, Tr3 can sink up to 16 mA without its collector voltage rising above 0.4 V. The significance of this point is assessed later.

Because the connecting paths to inputs have distributed inductance and capacitance, high-speed pulses can produce ringing with substantial negative transitions. Diodes from each input to ground are integrated into many TTL gates as in Fig. 1.9. Any negative transitions are clamped to ~−0.7 V, preventing damage or unreliable operation.

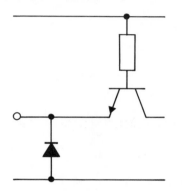

Fig. 1.9   Diode protection on gate input

The output circuit of the basic form is often called a totem-pole stage, and can switch with almost equal rapidity in either direction. It is not possible to parallel output stages safely – if they are driven into opposing states a damaging current flow could result, with Tr4 of one and Tr3 of the other, both trying to act as short circuits. We would like to parallel outputs in some cases to obtain a so-called wired-OR action.

In Fig. 1.10, only Tr3 is present at the output and any number of these outputs can be paralleled. If any one of these transistors conducts, the output is held at logic 0. Normally a resistive or other passive load will be present between the collectors and the positive supply line. The speed of response is slower, particularly for the logic 0–logic 1 transition.

Another variation is found in high-speed versions of TTL. Firstly the resistor values are reduced so that the higher currents can charge internal capacitances faster. Transistor Tr4 at the output is replaced by a Darlington pair for increased current drive into load and stray capacitances (Fig. 1.11). A reverse compromise is found in low-power TTL in which the resistor values are raised, trading-in speed of response against reduced operating power. A mixture of these facilities can be used, with the high-

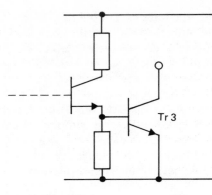

Fig. 1.10   Open collector output

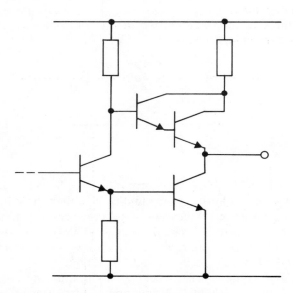

Fig. 1.11   Darlington output stage of high-power TTL

speed power-hungry devices restricted to critical areas of the system. Mixing brings problems in that low-power circuits cannot drive multiple high-speed circuits with their larger input current requirements. Each family has a specified fan-out, i.e. the number of standard inputs it can drive simultaneously. The figure is typically 10:1, but a low-power TTL operating at one-tenth of the power of standard TTL would have its fan-out reduced by that factor if driving a standard TTL input. It would barely be able to drive a high-speed TTL circuit. To get around this new techniques are needed. It is worth noting, as in Fig. 1.12, that the configurations available in IC form may be quite different from those in discrete circuits. The AND/OR functions follow from the multiple emitters that can be produced in a single transistor. Taking any one of them to logic 0 bypasses the drive current from Tr2, switching it off. Similarly we find multiple collector structures in the I²L family. The new technique devised for increasing speed came by isolating the reason for the slower response of TTL – it is a saturated-logic family. Transistors are driven heavily into conduction, with the base-emitter junction forward biased such that there is substantial charge stored in the junction. When the drive to the transistor is removed that stored charge keeps the transistor conducting for tens of nanoseconds. Other families such as ECL have a structure in which current is diverted from one part of a circuit to another without any transistor being saturated. The delays are reduced by an order of magnitude, but with various other disadvantages such as higher quiescent power consumption and smaller noise margins (i.e. the gap between the voltage at an output and the critical voltage at which the following input may fail to recognize the correct logic level).

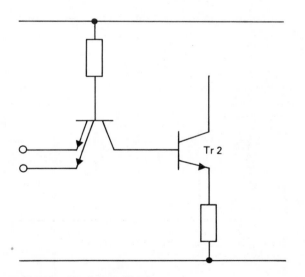

Fig. 1.12 Multi-emitter input of logic gate

The addition of a special diode called a Schottky diode is shown in Fig. 1.13. It is a metal semiconductor junction that can be formed automatically during the production of the IC by modifying the process. It has a forward-conduction voltage substantially lower than that of the silicon pn junctions (~0.4 V). Consider a source of bias current driving the

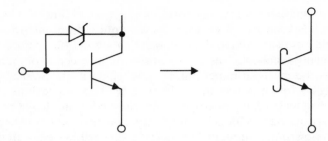

Fig. 1.13   Schottky diode clamped transistor avoiding saturation

transistor base. The base voltage rises towards 0.7 V and the collector conduction increases. More current flows in the collector load resistance and the collector voltage falls towards its saturation level. As soon as the collector falls to ~0.4 V the Schottky diode becomes forward biased sufficiently to conduct. This begins to divert any excess base current into the collector and minimizes the stored charge. The net effect is that the form of the circuit is unaffected, the logic levels are comparable but the transistors no longer saturate. The speed is considerably increased for no increase in power consumption (or the speed can be maintained while cutting that power). A typical circuit Fig. 1.14 is the Schottky equivalent of Fig. 1.8, part of a hex-inverter package.

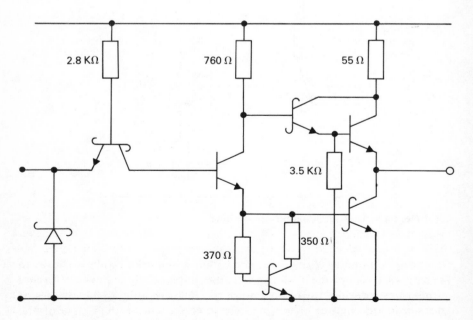

Fig. 1.14   Schottky clamped transistors increase speed of TTL

A comparison of the characteristics of some of these variants is given in Table 1.1 'Characteristics of TTL families'. To see how these current levels can be estimated, look at Fig. 1.15 (a). If a TTL input is grounded, then allowing for ~0.7 V across the input junction, we can expect ~4.3 V across the resistor assuming a 5 V supply. The resistor value in the first example was 4 K, giving a current of <1.1 mA. This figure is reduced (Fig. 1.15(b)) when the logic 0 is provided by a preceding TTL stage whose logic 0 might rise as high as 0.4 V depending on how many circuits it is required to drive. So a logic 0 input current of ~1 mA is a reasonable guess for such a stage. The tolerance on resistor values is loose – to maximize yield and keep down costs it could hardly be otherwise. So for safety, manufacturers specify that the driving stage may have to sink up to 1.6 mA for each input it drives. Other families of TTL may have input requirements varying by more than 10 : 1. When the input is driven to logic 1 it should require negligible current since the input junction is reverse biased. A leakage current of 40 A is assumed to cover the worst case and this is well within the capability of any likely output stage.

Parameter	Standard	Low-power	High-speed	Schottky
+V	5 V	5 V	5 V	5 V
'0' current	5.5 mA	0.46 mA	10 mA	9 mA
'1' current	1.3 mA	0.18 mA	4.2 mA	4.25 mA
Fan out	10	10	10	10
Gate dissipation	10 mW	1 mW	22 mW	20 mA
Output delay '1' to '0'	8 ns	30 ns	6 ns	3 ns
Output delay '0' to '1'	12 ns	30 ns	6 ns	3 ns
Noise margin '1'	400 mV	400 mV	400 mV	700 mV
Noise margin '0'	400 mV	400 mV	400 mV	300 mV
V_{INmax} '0'	800 mV	700 mV	800 mV	800 mV
V_{INmin} '1'	2 V	2 V	2 V	2 V
V_{OUT} '0'	400 mV	300 mV	400 mV	500 mV
V_{OUTmin} '1'	2.4 V	2.4 V	2.4 V	2.7 V
I_{IN} '0'	1.6 mA	0.18 mA	2.0 mA	2.0 mA
I_{IN} '1'	40 μA	10 μA	50 μA	100 μA
I_{OUT} '0'	16 mA	2 mA	20 mA	20 mA

Table 1.1   Characteristics of TTL Families

The output characteristics can be assessed from Fig. 1.16. In the logic 0 state, only a single transistor is involved, saturated for normal TTL, held out of saturation for Schottky TTL. A maximum of 0.4 V is specified. When driven to logic 1, there are two pn junctions involved: the base emitter of Tr4 and the diode in its emitter. If the load current is high, the resulting base current causes a substantial voltage drop in the base resistor. The values indicated suggest a voltage drop of up to 1 V in the resistor for a heavily loaded output. Then the output might fall to 2.4 V, while into a virtual open circuit it might rise to 3.6 V.

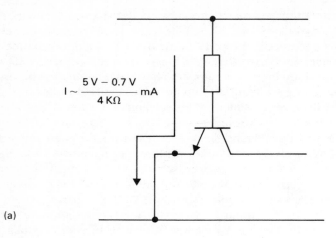

$$I \sim \frac{5\,V - 0.7\,V}{4\,K\Omega}\;mA$$

(a)

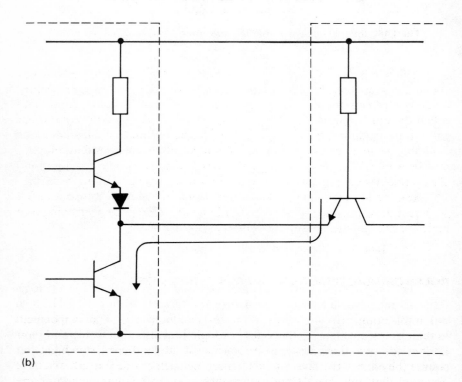

(b)

Fig. 1.15 (a) Input current in logic 0 state
                (b) TTL output pulls input low

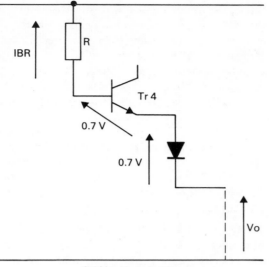

Fig. 1.16 Internal voltage drops limit maximum output voltage

The input of a TTL stage is guaranteed to respond to all voltages above 2.4 V as logic 1, even under the worst combination of temperature loading, etc. This gives a safety margin of $(2.4-2.0)$ V $= 0.4$ V, commonly called the noise margin. Any noise pulse of <0.4 V injected into that input will fail to produce a false zero. In practice the output may be well above 2.4 V in the quiescent state and the minimum input recognized as a logic 1 may be well below 2.0 V, widening the *practical* noise margin considerably. This cannot be guaranteed and should not form part of a design procedure.

For the logic 0 condition an output is guaranteed not to rise above 0.4 V. The following input will recognize all voltages below 0.8 V as being true logic 0, again giving a minimum noise margin of 0.4 V.

PULSE CHARACTERISTICS: CURRENT TRANSIENTS

All of this points to some very obvious tests on logic stages that can be held in their quiescent state. If the logic 0 or logic 1 levels are at or beyond their limit conditions, they are excessively sensitive to transients from whatever source they arise. Unfortunately TTL can be such a source itself. We have assumed that only one of the totem-pole transistors is conducting at any one time. During logic transitions this assumption breaks down. With the output at logic 0 the bottom transistor of the totem pole is saturated. At the transition to logic 1, the upper transistor begins to conduct. Charge storage in the base of the bottom device holds it in conduction for a further 10 ns or so, and during this time both transistors conduct, drawing a brief but intense pulse of current from the supply.

Even if the main supply is adequately decoupled, the distributed reactances of the printed circuit tracks would result in transient voltage swings in response to this pulse current. It is generally accepted practice to incorporate decoupling capacitance throughout the PCB so that no IC is more than a few centimeters from a capacitor. The accepted value is ~2000 pF for each totem-pole output, leading to a total capacitance of 100 nF for a board with 50 totem-pole outputs distributed over ten packages. An additional larger capacitance of, say, 10 μF tantalum might be found across the power supply leads at the point of entry to the board. For all these capacitances to be effective they must:

1   be good RF types with low self-inductance, e.g. ceramic disc;
2   have short connecting leads;
3   be connected as close as possible to the chips they serve.

SLOW TRANSITIONS

In most cases the input transitions to a gate will be rapid, and the output will be driven at full speed. Sometimes, perhaps where the signal is derived from an analog source, the transition may exceed a microsecond. Then the TTL stage is within its linear region for a short time, i.e. it has a definite voltage gain, with each millivolt change on the input, causing several millivolts change on the output. With stray coupling and phase shifts at very high frequencies, it is perfectly feasible for instability to occur. Instead of the output having a smooth transition it may exhibit ringing, with rapid multiple transitions through the threshold of a following circuit. The cure is to insert a buffer stage with internal regenerative feedback that provides a snap action. The slow input transition is ignored until a critical level is reached, when the output of the buffer suddenly switches between logic levels. Hysteresis is incorporated so that no further change in output occurs until the input has returned well past the original trigger point. This protects in turn against false triggering on any input ringing.

TRISTATE TTL

For bus systems, many outputs are connected to a common line, but only one should be active at any given time. The principle is familiar within microprocessor systems; Fig. 1.17 shows a simple implementation within a TTL gate, with Tr5 as an enable input. A logic 0 on this enable terminal keeps Tr5 OFF and the TTL gate operates normally. Raising it to logic 1 brings Tr5 into conduction, pulling the base of Tr4 to ground and cutting it off. Tr2 collector is simultaneously grounded and all of Tr3 drive current is bypassed (including that from Tr1, shunted to ground via the base-collector junction of Tr2). With both Tr4 and Tr3 non-conducting the output is effectively open circuit and only small leakage currents have to be allowed for. A typical failure mode would leave one or other of these transistors in the ON state, with the bus line connected to that gate jammed at 0 or 1. If a bus line is stuck at one logic level, a current probe may be able to detect the point at which current is being directed through a faulty gate.

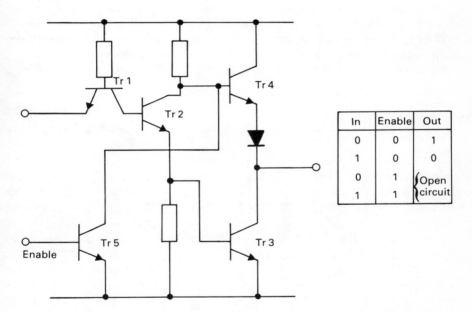

In	Enable	Out
0	0	1
1	0	0
0	1	⎰Open
1	1	⎱circuit

Fig. 1.17   Tristate logic allows output to go open circuit for bus connection

FAULT TRACING

The following routine checks are worth carrying out.

1   Check the power supply lines both for quiescent and transient conditions at various points on the board (make sure the oscilloscope

has a good enough response, a 50 KHz response may be barely adequate for high speed pulses).

2   If any gates can be held in the static condition, check for logic levels which may be reducing noise margins.

3   Under dynamic conditions a carefully calibrated oscilloscope can be used for logic level checks.

ECL Emitter Coupled Logic

This is normally found only in the high-speed sections of a system. Inputs A, B and C (Fig. 1.18) have emitters commoned with that of a reference transistor in a configuration related to the long-tailed pair. The tail current set by the 1.2 K resistor remains substantially constant but can be diverted to either side of the circuit, depending on whether all of ABC are below V REF. If any or all of them become more positive than V REF the current is diverted into the 270 resistor. The logic convention is unusual with logic 0 at ~ -1.7 V and logic 1 at ~ -0.8 V. The logic level swings are

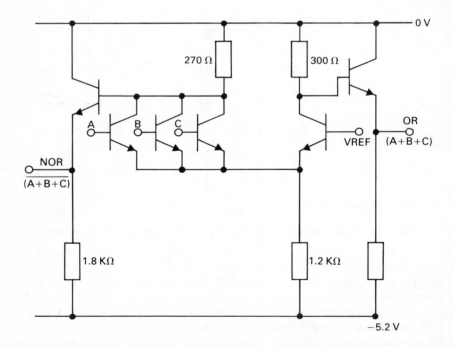

Fig. 1.18   ECL logic provides higher speed but increased power

small: this has the advantage of speeding up response at the expense of reduced noise margins. On the other hand, because no transistor saturates and the current is merely channeled to one side or the other, the speed is basically very high and there are no current transients to disturb the supply.

The fan-out is large (25:1) because of the light loading by each base on the emitter follower outputs. Complementary outputs are automatically available, eliminating the need for inverters. Special circuits are needed to change levels when coupling between ECL and TTL or CMOS. Standard ECL can operate at almost twice the clock rate of even Schottky TTL (200 MHz as against 125 MHz).

I²L INTEGRATED INJECTION LOGIC

The inverter is reduced to its simplest form – a single transistor with multiple open-collector outputs (Fig. 1.19). No internal resistors are required and this improves the packing density remarkably, resistors

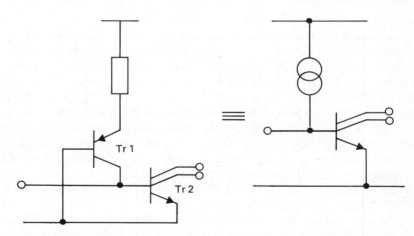

Fig. 1.19 I²L, an economical configuration for large-scale custom designs

normally occupying ten times the space of a transistor. The current drive for the base (Fig. 1.20) is provided by Tr1 and an external resistor. An open-collector transistor Tr2 connected to a following stage bypasses that current to ground when in the ON condition. The voltage swings are small and, combined with the ability to vary the quiescent current, a range of speed-power combinations is possible that makes I²L competitive with TTL and MOS families.

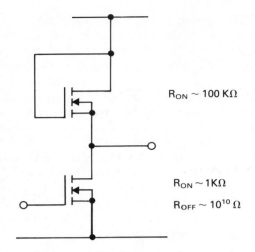

$R_{ON} \sim 100\ K\Omega$

$R_{ON} \sim 1K\Omega$

$R_{OFF} \sim 10^{10}\ \Omega$

Fig. 1.20   MOS circuits use active device as load

NMOS/PMOS/CMOS

The structure of these two forms of MOS logic are similar, with Fig. 1.21 showing the NMOS version. Each of the MOS devices is enhancement mode in which the gate has to be forward biased with respect to the source to bring it into conduction. This is convenient for the active devices (Tr1, Tr2), but less so for the passive load (Tr3). To keep this load conducting, gate and source are connected. Unfortunately the load current changes strongly with logic level because of the change in gate-source voltage of the load device. This is a severe penalty to set against the simplicity of a single device type. It is no better to base logic entirely on depletion-mode devices. These conduct unless the gate is reverse biased with respect to the source: with a positive supply for the drain circuit we would need a separate negative supply for the gate drive.

Ideally the active devices would be enhancement mode and the passive loads depletion mode as in Fig. 1.21(b). This makes the IC processing more complex to get the different doping levels for the two types of device, but the performance is better. N-channel is preferred to P-channel. Tighter packing density is found to be possible, and the speed is higher because of the greater mobility of electrons in the N-channel as against the holes in the P-channel.

Inverters could use either enhancement of depletion mode devices as loads. The depletion mode device is preferable because the current is self-limiting once the gate-drain voltage rises above the so-called pinch-off level.

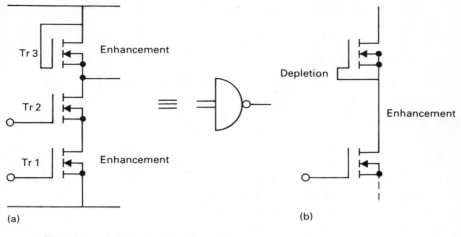

(a)   (b)

Fig. 1.21 (a) NAND gate using NMOS devices
(b) Improved performance if both enhancement and depletion mode
devices available

Another competing logic family which is now of major importance is
the complementary metal-oxide semiconductor or CMOS logic. In its early
development only the originating company, RCA, supported it. Now most
IC manufacturers include CMOS logic in their product range and for some
it is the dominant family.

CMOS logic was known to have many potential advantages. The
higher costs were treated as an acceptable penalty for special applications
where low power and high noise immunity were important. Gradually, as
production levels increased and manufacturing techniques improved, the
cost differences shrank and CMOS became increasingly important. It uses
N-type and P-type devices, both enhancement mode, and Fig. 1.22 (a)
shows a standard inverter. Additional diode protection networks across the
input are produced automatically during manufacture (Fig. 1.22(b)). This
gets over a problem with early versions of CMOS where static charges
combined with the high natural input impedance could result in voltages
sufficient to damage the thin insulating regions on which the circuit
depended. Now these diodes absorb such charges as well as any voltage
transients on the power supply lines. These protection networks play no
part in the circuits' normal operation and are not shown on functional
diagrams. Thus for normal operation, oscilloscope inspection of logic
levels should show pulse trains of almost 5 V and anything below 4 V peak–
peak is worth checking.

The high input impedance of CMOS can lead to problems with long
input lines. These should be properly terminated at input and output to

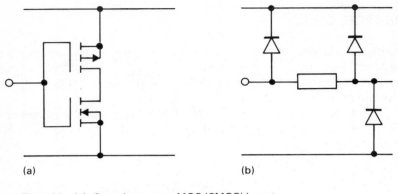

(a)   (b)

Fig. 1.22   (a) Complementary MOS (CMOS) inverter
                (b) Diode protection on input

match the natural impedance of the line (transmission line theory applies). With a low drive impedance and high load impedance, ringing will occur and at both the rising and falling edges of each pulse there will be transients that can be comparable in amplitude to the pulse itself. The internal protection diodes will normally prevent damage, but a single pulse can be recognized as multiple pulses under extreme conditions. The designer should take advantage of the high input impedance of the CMOS devices – the line can be resistively terminated with the correct value, the circuit itself offering negligible additional loading.

If the CMOS output limitations are ignored, the pulse amplitude will fall below the 5 V level, as the field-effect devices are driven into their current limited mode. Beyond this level the peak voltage will fall proportionally to the load resistance. Assume a given load resistance pulls the output below 4 V, at which any other CMOS input would still respond correctly. Dropping that load resistance by, say, 30 percent might reduce the output by almost the same amount. The resulting pulses of < 3 V amplitude could no longer be relied on to safely activate following circuitry. For higher outputs a CMOS stage can be buffered by a TTL stage, normally a low-power version.

Inadequately designed circuits can yield other faults. If unused gates do not have their inputs tied to one of the supply lines, their high input impedance can result in very high frequency oscillation via stray coupling. This in turn can be coupled into other gates on the chip.

These principles apply to other MOS-based digital circuits, but it is less likely that these will be involved in the input/output stages of systems. They are predominantly found in devices such as RAMs, ROMs and EPROMs which are buffered from external effects. Fault finding is not then carried out at chip level but at board level via the system interconnection buses.

HIGH-SPEED CMOS

Recently a number of the major semiconductor manufacturers have introduced high-speed CMOS devices* in a 74' series family of logic elements. They are available with LS TTL or B-series CMOS compatible inputs and outputs.

The devices have all the advantages of CMOS gates with additional features which make their performance characteristics closer to those of LS TTL. For example:

–   reduced propagation delays (of order 10 ns for 7400);
–   reduced power dissipation (frequency dependent but roughly equivalent to LS TTL at 10 MHz);
–   output source and sink currents of the order 4 mA.

High-speed CMOS is available with normal and tristate outputs and some devices are unbuffered for use in oscillator circuits.

Only one active device conducts at any one time for normal logic levels. If the input is at logic 0, the top device is in its conducting state because the gate-source voltage is large. The bottom device then has zero gate-source voltage and is nonconducting. This allows the output to be pulled up to logic 1 but with negligible quiescent current in the stage. A further advantage is that the output is very close to the positive supply voltage, leaving a big gap or noise margin between it and the level at which any following stage might register a change in apparent logic level caused by transients. A logic 1 at the input drives the bottom device into conduction, switching the top device off. During a voltage transition there is a brief instant when both devices conduct, drawing a pulse of current from the supply. This, together with the energy lost during successive charge and discharge of stray and internal capacitance, is the only way in which power is consumed for an ideal CMOS device. Under static conditions the power consumed is negligible. It only begins to approach that for TTL and other logic families at very high pulse rates corresponding

---

*Other logic families including ECL and I^2L have their own segments of the market; ECL for example is found in high-speed bit-slice microprocessor systems. Because of these high speeds, the testing techniques are more specialized and standard laboratory oscilloscopes would be inadequate to the task. Logic-level testing is straightforward but the low swings make it important that the scopes or logic probes are accurately calibrated. These logic families are comparatively rare in commercial and industrial equipment, and reference to manufacturers' data is recommended.

The other major memory family is dynamic logic. The principle is described in Chapter 2 and again it is not proposed to include fine details of the internal construction. They are only used in complete memory circuits for which testing will be via the system bus. To test an individual chip could be very difficult as the data in the devices needs to be repeatedly 'refreshed' on triggering from an external clock, or from the microprocessor itself.

to perhaps millions of transitions per second. Relatively few gates within a system operate at full speed, keeping the *average* power consumption low.

A typical transfer characteristic (Fig. 1.23) shows the output staying close to 5 V until the input is over 2 V, and falling close to 0 as the input reaches 3 V. This provides a noise margin about 2 V, i.e. a following stage would remain unaffected by stray pulses of up to 2 V in amplitude.

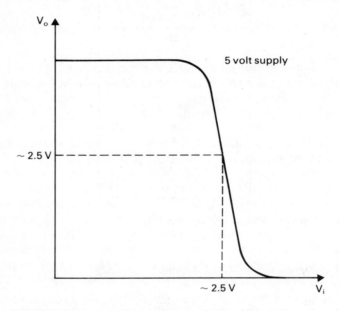

Fig. 1.23 Symmetrical characteristics lead to good noise margins

Gates of all the usual varieties are then composed of collections of series and parallel devices as in Fig. 1.24. CMOS technology is being increasingly used in analog circuits and can provide mixed analog and digital functions in such circuits as A/D converters.

Marginal failures of CMOS are less likely than straightforward open and short circuits. All internal devices are very lightly loaded by the high input impedances of the following stages. Logic levels substantially different from 0 and 5 V can only be expected where the circuit drives some external load.

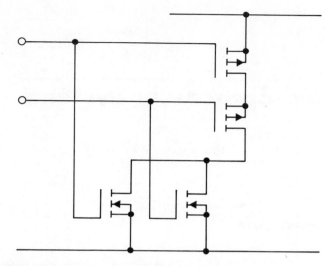

Fig. 1.24 Simple structure of CMOS logic gates

SUMMARY

Microprocessors need other circuits and devices to form a complete system. Logic circuits of different families differ considerably in their behavior, even when performing similar functions. An outline of these differences is given. Test devices are available that can trace a fault to a specific pin on a device, and their advantages and limitations are discussed.

2
Microprocessor Systems

SYSTEM COMPONENTS

Microprocessors are digital integrated circuits which are designed to perform, sequentially, different operations on binary data. The operation is determined by the data read by the processor as part of its sequential operation and can be, for example, an arithmetic operation on data which has been read and stored. The different operations which the microprocessor can perform are known as the instructions, and the sequence of instructions presented to it are known as a program. Microprocessors are the central elements of microcomputers and microcontrollers, which can perform a wide variety of functions.

The microprocessor, however, cannot exist in isolation, and needs to be connected to other devices to make up a microprocessor system. Read-only and read-write memory are required for the purpose of storing the program and data. Additional circuitry is required to permit peripherals such as keyboards, printers and displays to be connected to the system. In control applications, circuits are needed to exchange information between the microprocessor system and the system being monitored or controlled, where such interface signals are often a mixture of digital and analog. The devices used to control the flow of data between the system and its external environment are referred to as input/output devices.

The microprocessor system can be represented by the block diagram of Fig. 2.1. In addition to the processor, memory and input/output (I/O) devices, it is usual to have some random logic associated with clock signal generation, reset circuitry, device selection, and signal buffering. There are also single chip microprocessors which have processor, read-only and read-write memory, and I/O in the one package.

The microprocessor communicates with the different system components by activating and monitoring signal lines which can be considered in three main groups known as buses (or highways). These groups are:

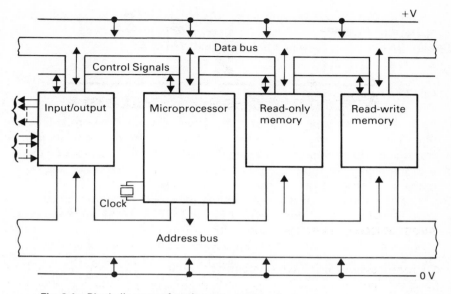

Fig. 2.1 Block diagram of a microprocessor system

1   the data bus;
2   the address bus;
3   the control bus.

In addition there are power supply lines, required to energize all the active components in the system. The clock circuitry provides a source of regular pulses to the processor to control its internal operating sequences. It is usual to have at least one buffered clock signal available for connection to other devices which need to be synchronized with the processor.

The different parts of the block diagram will be described in more detail later in this chapter.

THE SYSTEM BUSES

(a) The Data Bus

The data bus consists of a number of bidirectional signal lines which carry binary information in parallel (one line for each bit). The common microprocessors have an 8-bit data bus, while more recently introduced processors have 16- and 32-bit buses.

The number of lines used in the data bus (or the data bus width) determines the maximum size of the number which can be represented by the binary information on the bus, and hence makes it desirable to produce processors which can transfer as large a number of bits as possible in one operation. (8 bits can be used to represent numbers between 0 and 255, while 16 bits can represent numbers from 0 to 65535.)

(b) The Address Bus

The address bus is a group of signal lines which are controlled by the microprocessor to enable it to select a device to or from which data is to be transferred. Each binary number on the address bus can represent a unique location which, when selected, has a path opened to the processor via the data bus, so that the data transfer can take place.

A location can be a single memory location or a register in an input/output circuit. This is illustrated in Fig. 2.2. To make the microprocessor flexible, the number of locations which it can address needs to be large, and the number of address bus lines is, therefore, greater than that of the data bus. 8-bit microprocessors usually have 16 address lines and can address up to 65536 locations. 16-bit processors usually have 20-bit address buses, making the number of addressable locations more than one million.

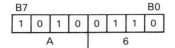

Fig. 2.2   Hexadecimal representation of 8-bit and 16-bit numbers

The address lines are usually unidirectional signal lines under control of the processor as it executes instructions. They determine the source or destination of the next data item to be transferred.

There are situations where another device can make more efficient data transfers by taking control of the processor's buses. It could be a second processor or an input/output device such as a disk controller.

It must be possible for the microprocessor to relinquish control of the data and address buses and the signals used to control data transfers. This is done using control signals which cause the necessary lines to go into a tristate condition.

This technique of data transfer is generally known as direct memory access (DMA). Some processors have the bus control signals to relinquish control of the buses on completion of the current instruction. Others would require additional logic and bus drivers to relinquish control of the processor lines at the correct point in the execution cycle.

DMA which is used on a cyclic basis to update data in memory can cause problems when running memory tests on the system. The test program usually writes patterns into memory and expects to find the same data later on. If DMA is running, then the data will be corrupted and a fault will be flagged. It is, therefore, essential to check that any DMA system is disabled before running such tests.

A common feature of microprocessors being produced today is the use of the address bus for more than one function by time multiplexing other signals on to the same lines. When this is done it is possible to use the address lines to carry data and other processor signals, thus releasing the corresponding pins for the other functions. The 8085, NSC800, 8088 and 8086 are examples of processors using multiplexed address buses. The operation of such buses will be discussed below in the context of signal timing.

Some processors have a facility for addressing input/output separately from memory, using special instructions called port operations, which do not necessarily use the full address capacity of the bus. Control signals are required to activate memory and turn off I/O when memory transactions are to be performed and vice versa.

When dealing with binary numbers with more than four bits it is useful to have a way of representing them not requiring them to be written as strings of 1s and 0s. One such shorthand system is the hexadecimal system, which gives a single symbol to each of the four digit binary numbers from 0000 to 1111. This is shown in Table 2.1, with the corresponding decimal equivalents.

Binary	Hexadecimal	Decimal
0000	0	0
0001	1	1
0010	2	2
0011	3	3
0100	4	4
0101	5	5
0110	6	6
0111	7	7
1000	8	8
1001	9	9
1010	A	10
1011	B	11
1100	C	12
1101	D	13
1110	E	14
1111	F	15

Table 2.1   Binary–Hexadecimal Conversion Table

When a binary number with more than four digits is to be represented, the number is divided into blocks of four digits, starting at the least
significant end, and each block is given its hexadecimal representation. Fig.
2.3 shows this for an 8-bit number and a 16-bit number. This system is used
when referring to both addess information and data.

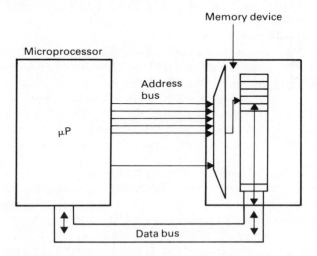

Fig. 2.3   Microprocessor selects a memory location for data to be transferred
              via data bus

Another system which is commonly used in 16-bit minicomputers,
and some microprocessors developed from them, is the octal number
system, which uses the decimal symbols for all possible 3-bit binary
numbers (i.e. 0, 1,. . .,7) and divides the binary number into blocks of
three instead of four. This means that the biggest 16-bit binary number,
which in hexadecimal is FFFF, is represented in octal as 177777. The
hexadecimal system will be used throughout this book.

(c) The Control Bus

This is a collection of different signals, some generated by the processor,
others generated by devices in the system. These signals are dependent on
processor type and can have a variety of functions. Those which are
processor outputs act as control lines for data transfer operations, and as
acknowledge signals for control inputs.

Control inputs are generally used to force or request a particular
processor action and include the following.

CLOCK SIGNALS – All processors have a clock input provided either by
a clock generator circuit or by a crystal oscillator connected directly to the

processor. The processor circuitry in turn usually produces one or two buffered clock signal outputs, which can be used by other components in the system. Fig. 2.4 shows three typical microprocessor clock circuit configurations.

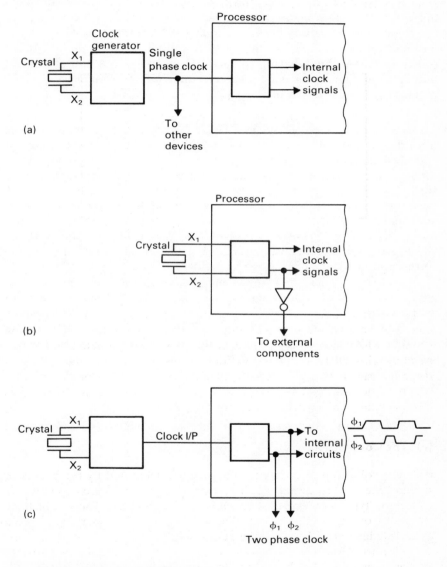

Fig. 2.4 Clock signal generators
    (a) Single phase external clock
    (b) Built-in clock generator
    (c) Two phase clock derived from single phase input

RESET SIGNAL – This line is used to reset the microprocessor to a known state from which it can then commence execution of a program. The end result of the application of reset is that the program counter is loaded with a value corresponding to the address of the first instruction.

It is usual to have a reset circuit external to the microprocessor which holds the reset line in its active state during power-up, removing the condition after all power lines have reached their steady-state levels. A push-button facility is usually provided to permit resetting the microprocessor system without having to turn off the power. A buffered reset output is sometimes provided for connection to other system devices which require to be initialized by this signal.

DATA TRANSFER CONTROLS – These consist of one or more signals from the processor system components to control the direction of flow of data. Data input to the microprocessor is normally called a read operation, whereas an output operation is termed a write operation. Sometimes a single line read-write ($R/\overline{W}$) is used to indicate which operation is to be performed. In this case the '1' state indicates that a read operation is to be done and a '0' indicates that the processor is about to write data. In other processors two signals are provided, RD and WR (or READ and WRITE) which are normally inactive. Only one of the two activates at any time corresponding to the operation to be performed.

In systems where more than one addressing technique is used it is necessary to provide control signals to select and deselect memory and I/O as appropriate.

If two signals are provided, e.g. MEMREQ, IOREQ, then only one would be active at any time. When a single line is used, e.g.$IO/\overline{M}$, the two states of the control line determine the nature of the transaction. (These situations will be treated in more detail in the section on timing.)

STATUS SIGNALS – These provide information on the internal operating cycle of the microprocessor, e.g. that an instruction is being fetched from memory.

INTERRUPT SIGNALS – These cause the processor to break its normal sequence of execution and carry on at a new address provided either by external hardware or by circuitry in the microprocessor itself. Interrupts permit events, which are asynchronous with the system clock and the current stage of the program, to be handled by the system.

BUS CONTROL SIGNALS – Some microprocessors have signals which can be used to slow down the processor, for example when dealing with slow memory. These signals usually cause additional integral clock cycles or wait states to be inserted in read or write operations to give the slow device time to respond.

When the processor has the facility to relinquish control of its buses to a second bus master, there are at least two signals needed for control. The first will be the release request line and the second the release acknowledge, signalling the second master to perform its data transfer.

BASIC SYSTEM TIMING

The operations, described briefly in the previous section, take place in defined sequences, with suitable delays between events to ensure that steady state conditions are attained before data is transferred from one device to another.

Consider a microprocessor with two data transfer controls $\overline{RD}$ and $\overline{WR}$. When the microprocessor has to read data from memory, the first action must be to place the address of the desired data on the address bus. The $\overline{RD}$ line can then be activated to place the data on the data bus. Some short time later, when the address information has settled and the data is valid, it can be latched into the destination register in the processor. Data lines are usually in a high impedance condition until activated. A similar situation arises when the microprocessor writes data, except that the data lines are set by the processor and will remain in that state during the latching transition of the' $\overline{WR}$ control line. Figs. 2.5 and 2.6 show typical timing diagrams for read and write operations.

In systems with I/O addressing capability, the read and write operations involving memory would also activate a select signal to ensure that the memory is selected. Fig. 2.7 shows a situation where a single select line is used and a memory read is followed by an I/O write. The clock signals are not shown in this diagram since their number and timing relation will depend on the processor.

One further technique, mentioned earlier, which gives rise to slightly different timing sequences, is that of multiplexing the address and data bus. Systems which use this technique require latches to hold address information during the time that the address lines are being used to carry data. These latches can either be part of the internal circuitry of memory and other system components, or are part of the random logic associated with the microprocessor. Microprocessors such as the 8085 and NSC800, which use multiplexed address buses, usually have a set of related devices which are compatible with this structure avoiding the need for additional demultiplexing components.

Fig. 2.8 shows the arrangement of a multiplexed bus system and the timing diagram associated with a data read operation. The control signal

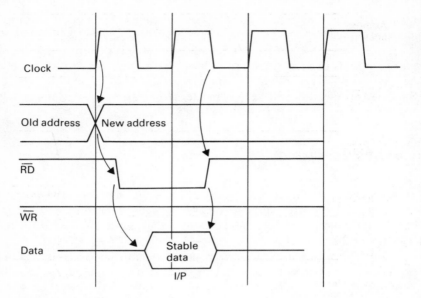

Fig. 2.5   A data *read* cycle

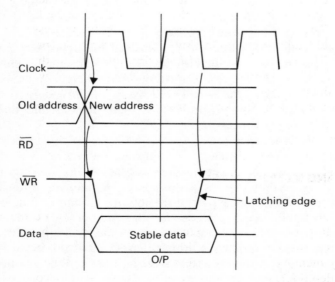

Fig. 2.6   A data *write* cycle

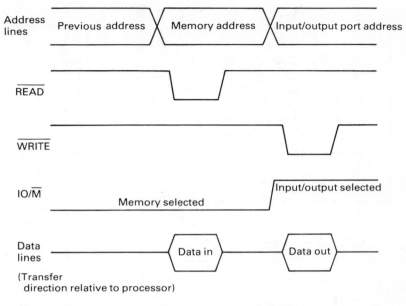

Fig. 2.7 Typical memory and input/output data transfers

'address latch enable' (ALE) is generated by the processor to act as a latch control for the address information which appears only for the first part of the sequence. The eight high address lines are set by the processor for the duration of the operation, while the low order eight bits are present only during ALE. The falling edge of ALE latches the data to the memory address latch, and following this the full 16-bit address is available for selection of a data location. The read operation causes the lines AD0–AD7 to become data inputs and the data is transferred from the memory to the processor.

MEMORIES AND MEMORY MAPS

Memory devices used in microprocessor systems fall into two categories: read-only and read-write. Semiconductor memories of both types are 'random access', since any data position can be selected with equal ease, but read-only memory is usually referred to as ROM, while read-write memory is called RAM (for random access memory). A more correct term would be RWM. Other storage devices such as magnetic tape, magnetic bubble, and floppy disks which may be used in a microprocessor system to

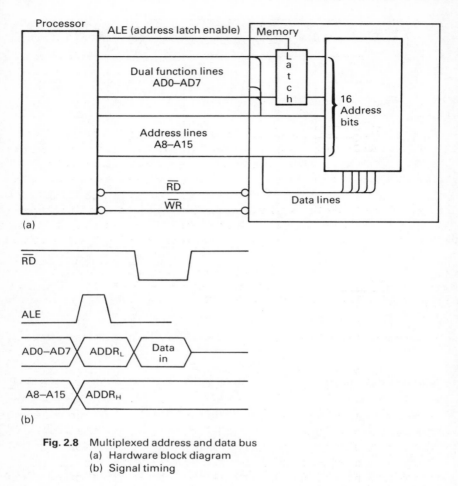

Fig. 2.8 Multiplexed address and data bus
(a) Hardware block diagram
(b) Signal timing

provide back-up storage are, on the other hand, 'sequential access' devices since the time to obtain or store data is location dependent.

Semiconductor memory consists of an array of storage elements or cells, each capable of storing one bit. The cells are grouped into words of one or more bits which can then be selected by applying a binary address to a decoder in the memory which ensures that only one word is selected for each binary pattern applied to the address lines (a 1 to 2^n decoder where n is the number of address lines). This is shown in Fig. 2.9 for a read-only memory. Large memories usually have a row and column decoder which selects a word when both row and column select lines are active as indicated in Fig. 2.10. It is usual to have, in addition, one or more control lines which must be active to select the memory device. When deselected, the tristate data lines are in the high impedance condition.

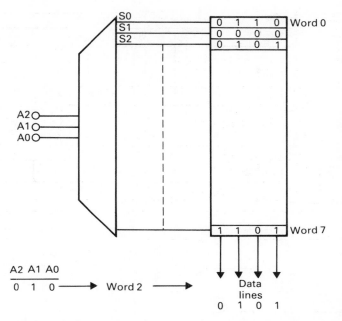

Fig. 2.9   Decoder in memory selects a word, connecting its cells to the data lines

A read-write memory requires control signals to set the direction of data transfer. This can be provided by a single $R/\overline{W}$ line which, when high, causes data in a selected word to appear on the data lines, and when low allows the data present on the data lines to overwrite that already in the location selected. In such an example the rising edge of the $R/\overline{W}$ signal would cause the data to be latched into the desired location. Fig. 2.11 shows a typical sequence on address, data and control lines.

Read-only memory can be mask programmed by the manufacturer when there is a sufficiently high volume requirement to justify the setting-up costs involved. At the development stage and where there are differences from system to system it is normal to use erasable memory. Programmable read-only memory (PROM) which can be erased and reprogrammed exists in two main types: one which is erased by exposure to ultraviolet light (EPROM), and one which is reprogrammable electrically (EAROM). Another type of read-only memory uses fusible links and can only be programmed once.

Read-write memory is available in two main types: static and dynamic. Static memory will hold its data as long as the power supply is maintained and can be used as non-volatile memory when low power, CMOS devices are used with a battery back-up supply. Dynamic memory requires to be refreshed by activating address lines on a regular basis, even when no data transfers are taking place.

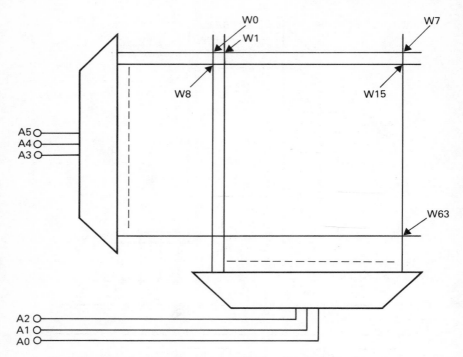

Fig. 2.10   Two decoders in *x* and *y* addressing for word selection

Most microprocessor systems require a mix of read-only and read-write memory. Read-only memory will be used for permanent program and data, while read-write memory will serve to store variable data generated by the program. When disk and tape are used to store programs, the information is usually transferred from them into read-write memory to be run.

Address Decoding

The use of a number of memories in a system requires some kind of circuitry to connect the memory devices to the address bus, to ensure that only one device is selected at a time. The circuitry is usually some form of decoder circuit connected to the most significant address lines, which allocates the memories to particular slots in the address space. The memory allocation can be described by a diagram, commonly known as a 'memory map' of the system.

Consider a small system which requires 2K of read-only memory to start at address zero, and uses one additional block of 2K read-write memory or RAM for variable data storage.

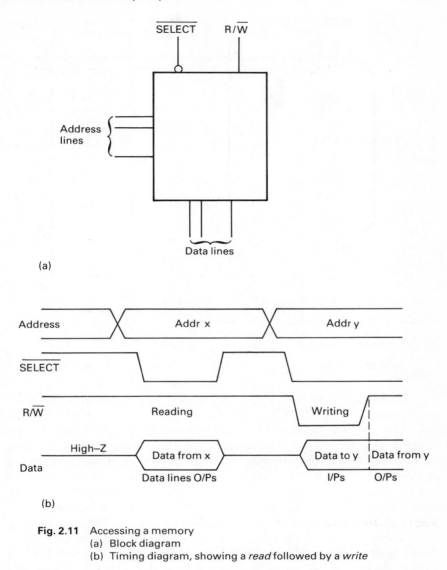

Fig. 2.11 Accessing a memory
    (a) Block diagram
    (b) Timing diagram, showing a *read* followed by a *write*

One solution to this is to connect the memories to the address bus as shown in fig. 2.12 where the inverter ensures that only one of the two memories is selected at any time. When A15 is '0', the ROM is selected, whereas the RAM is selected with A15 at '1'. Since both memories are 2K in size, the circuit will make the ROM appear at addresses in the range 0000–07FF and the RAM at addresses from 8000–87FF. These are not, however, the only addresses at which these memories appear.

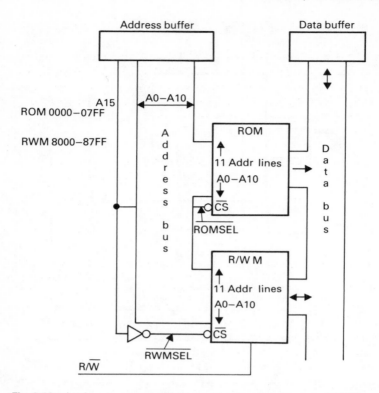

Fig. 2.12 A microprocessor with two memories showing use of A15 for memory selection

Consider the transition from an address of 07FF to 0800. Since A15 is still '0' the ROM will still be selected but since its eleven address lines are now at the '0' state the data placed on the data bus will be that from the first address in the ROM. Thus microprocessor address 0800 obtains the same data as address 0000. The address range 0800–0FFF will, therefore, obtain data which is the same as that from addresses 0000–07FF. This is termed 'foldback' and occurs for the ROM 16 times over the address range 0000–07FF, where A15 is '0'. The RAM data will also appear at 8000–87FF, 8800–8FFF up to F800–FFFF. The memory map for this system is as shown in Fig. 2.13. A circuit of this type is used in the Z80 single board system mentioned in Appendix 2.

Fig. 2.14 shows a memory decoding circuit which uses a 3–8 line decoder to select four blocks of memory. The decoder outputs are each active for a 2K range of processor addresses as indicated, so the first two ROMs have no foldback. The RAMs are only 1K in size and will appear twice in the address range of the corresponding select line. The memory map is shown in Fig. 2.15. This type of memory decoding is used in some single board microcomputers such as the AIM65 and the SDK85.

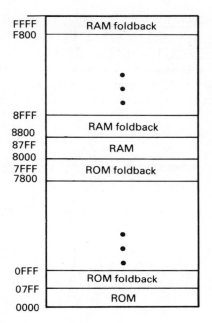

Fig. 2.13 Memory map for system in Fig. 2.12

Using Read-Only Memories for Address Decoding

Some systems use fusible link ROMs to perform the address decoding instead of a decoder. This provides additional flexibility since the output lines can be arranged to be active for different ranges of addresses. This is illustrated for a 32 word by 8-bit memory in Fig. 2.16, where a number of memory blocks of different size are set up.

As in any memory decoding arrangement, it is important to ensure that no two memory blocks are active at the same time. This means that the only valid data in an 8-bit ROM used for decoding is:

1111	1111 – FF	NO O/Ps ACTIVE
1111	1110 – FE	
1111	1101 – FD	
1111	1011 – FB	
1111	0111 – F7	ONE O/P ACTIVE
1110	1111 – EF	
1101	1111 – DF	
1011	1111 – BF	
0111	1111 – 7F	

This assumes that the memory select lines are active when low.

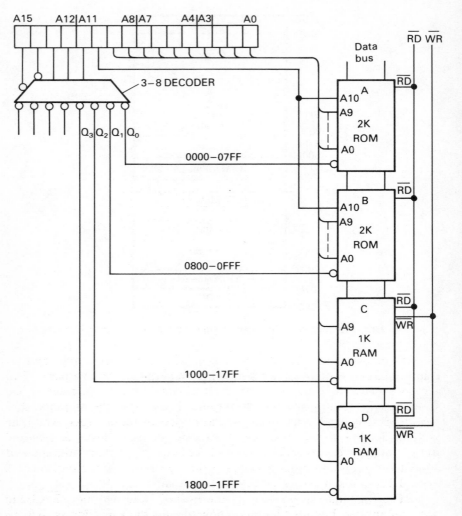

Fig. 2.14 A microprocessor with four memories

Special Requirements of Dynamic Memory

Dynamic memory has to be refreshed continuously to prevent loss of data. Each cell uses the charge on an internal capacitance to determine the state of the data in the cell. The cells usually consist of a single transistor, giving rise to memories with high storage density, high operating speed and low power dissipation. The refresh process is necessary to replenish charge lost by leakage.

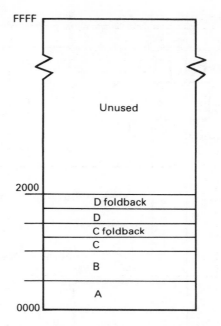

Fig. 2.15 Memory map showing repetition or foldback of the 1K memories in Fig. 2.14

Dynamic memories usually have multiplexed address lines and require the address of a storage location to be presented in two parts. Two strobe signals, row address strobe ($\overline{\text{RAS}}$) and column address strobe ($\overline{\text{CAS}}$) latch the appropriate address information into the memory. The row address is usually the least significant half of the address, while the column address is the most signifiant half. A multiplexer is required between the processor address bus and the dynamic memory address lines to switch the row and column addresses through in the correct sequence. A typical data transfer occurs in the following way.

The row address is active on the memory address lines. $\overline{\text{RAS}}$ and $\overline{\text{CAS}}$ are initially high. $\overline{\text{RAS}}$ is taken low to latch the row address. After a short delay the column address is active on the address lines and $\overline{\text{CAS}}$ is taken low to latch this address. If the memory is being read, the data appears when the address information has rippled through the decoder circuits in the device.

In the case of a write, data has to be valid and the write enable line active a short time after $\overline{\text{CAS}}$ has gone low. Note that $\overline{\text{RAS}}$ remains low during the active $\overline{\text{CAS}}$ period. It is usual to employ a delay circuit to generate $\overline{\text{CAS}}$ from $\overline{\text{RAS}}$, and to switch from row address to column address between the falling edge of $\overline{\text{RAS}}$ and that of $\overline{\text{CAS}}$. A typical circuit for this is shown in fig. 2.17. Note that this does not indicate how the refresh address is placed on the address bus.

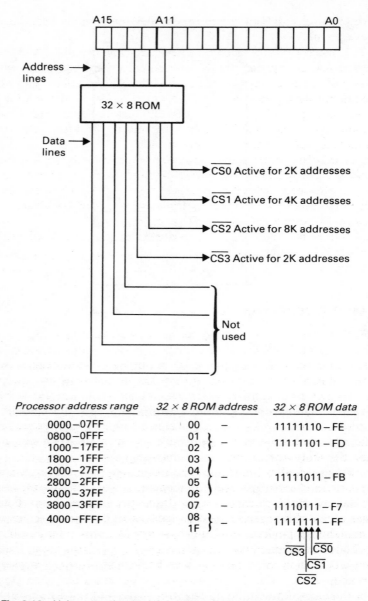

Fig. 2.16 Using a read-only memory to select memory devices in a microprocessor system

Refresh action also takes place every time data is read or written. All cells associated with a particular row address are refreshed (except the one being altered in a write operation). Additional refresh activity is, however, required to ensure that every cell is refreshed on a regular basis, usually at least every 2 ms.

It is usual to have some technique of scanning through all the row addresses, and of applying the $\overline{\text{RAS}}$ signal only. This must occur when the processor is not accessing the dynamic memory. This could be done using an additional multiplexer and a 7-bit binary counter in the case of the example in Fig. 2.17. The $\overline{\text{RAS}}$ signal must not generate $\overline{\text{CAS}}$, and additional logic is needed to prevent this and to block the refresh action when the microprocessor is accessing memory.

The Z80 microprocessor has features which facilitate interfacing to dynamic memory. An internal refresh register which increments automatically is placed on the address bus at the end of each instruction fetch (or its equivalent in block instructions). A signal RFSH, used to indicate this, can be used to activate $\overline{\text{RAS}}$ and block the generation of $\overline{\text{CAS}}$. An additional multiplexer is not required since this is effectively provided within the processor.

THE MICROPROCESSOR

It is not possible to obtain access to the internal circuits of the microprocessor to observe logic states or signal waveforms, or to repair faults. It is, however, necessary to be familiar with its internal structure, and how it functions. An understanding of the way a microprocessor works when no faults exist should precede a study of the faults and fault-finding techniques. This section describes the general structure of a microprocessor, how it functions, and how binary numbers stored in memory can act as a sequence of instructions which it can execute.

Microprocessors are large scale integration (LSI) digital devices designed to perform relatively simple operations or instructions, which are read and executed sequentially at high speed. The internal circuitry consists of multibit registers, parallel data paths, buffers to permit connection of external devices, multifunction circuits, and timing and control logic. The multifunction circuitry is designed to perform simple arithmetic and logic operations on binary numbers held in the processor registers, and to transfer data within the processor, and between it and connected external devices. The timing and control circuitry controls the sequence of the events in the processor, and requires a regular clock signal as its timing source.

Individual operations take place in a defined way over a number of clock cycles, varying with the complexity of the operation. The operations themselves are determined by data (the instructions) read by the microprocessor into a register known as the instruction register. This data is made

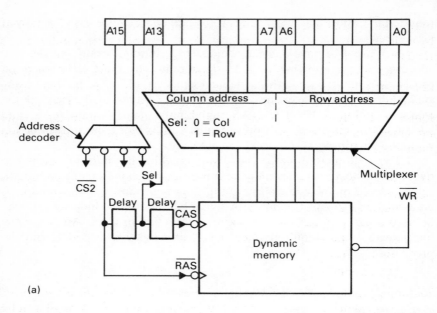

(a)

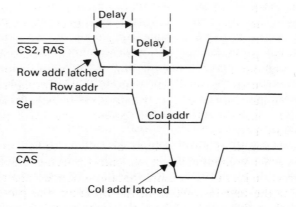

(b)

Fig. 2.17 (a) Block schematic of system with dynamic memory
            (b) Simplified timing diagram

available to a decoder connected to the control circuitry which determines
the nature of the operation and executes it.

An 8-bit instruction register can contain one of 256 different possible
numbers (from 00000000 to 11111111 in binary, or 00 to FF in hexadecimal), so 8-bit microprocessors will generally have up to 256 different
instructions. The Z80 microprocessor and its derivatives are the exceptions

to this rule, since these have some instruction codes which are a number of bytes in length (and therefore require more than one 8-bit number to be read from memory to determine the instruction).

The ability to perform many different operations in a sequence determined by data placed by the user in external memory is what makes the microprocessor such a powerful and flexible device. This is not, however, totally new for digital devices since many of the medium scale integration devices can be considered as capable of executing a limited number of instructions.

Consider, for example, a binary up/down counter with a reset line. This can be considered as a device which can perform three operations depending on the binary values supplied to the up/down control and the reset line, for example:

00 – counts down
01 – remains reset
10 – counts up
11 – remains reset

(assuming up/down = 1 to count up, and reset = 1 to reset the counter).

A sequence of data on these bits in association with a regular pulse train applied to the clock input will determine the output count pattern of the counter. This simple system can, therefore, execute 'instructions' but cannot fetch them as can the microprocessor. The description of the general structure of a microprocessor, introduced above, can be represented in a block diagram as shown in Fig. 2.18.

A fuller picture of the microprocesor includes an address bus and registers to hold address information. In 8-bit microprocessors these registers are usually 16 bits wide and are loaded in two operations using the internal 8-bit data bus. There are usually three registers associated with the address bus, namely the program counter, the stack pointer and the address register.

The program counter is used by the processor to keep track of addresses which contain instructions, and is incremented automatically as each instruction is read. To ensure that the system designer can use a given address for the first instruction in the program, the program counter is loaded with a fixed value when the reset signal is applied. The first instruction of the program is then read from this address, usually from a location in read-only memory.

Some processors load the program counter automatically with its starting value. Examples are the 8080 and related processors which reset to address zero. Others load the program counter from two fixed memory locations thus making it possible for the system designer to choose where his program resides in memory. The 6502 obtains its starting address from locations FFFC and FFFD, while the 6800 loads the program counter from FFFE and FFFF.

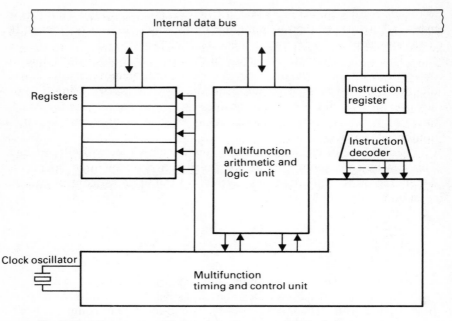

Fig. 2.18   Microprocessor internal structure – partial block diagram

The auto-increment feature of the program counter ensures that instructions are read in sequence. Additional flexibility is provided by instructions and input signals which can change the program counter value to alter this sequence. This makes it possible to have program loops, optional sections of code, and other code which can be called into operation by external events, known as interrupts, which are not necessarily synchronous with the processor clock.

A microprocessor not only reads an instruction but must also carry it out before reading the next. The sequence is known as a fetch–execute cycle and is shown in Figure 2.19. The stack pointer register is used to point to an address in read-write memory which can be used to store processor register contents temporarily. The contents of this register increment and decrement automatically, depending on whether data is being written to or read from the address pointed to. The memory area used by instructions which involve the stack pointer is known as the stack, and operates on a last in, first out basis. Care is required in programming to ensure that stack writes are balanced with stack reads, normally referred to as pushes and pops (or pulls) respectively.

Some instructions and signals 'push' the program counter on to the stack to save the address of the next instruction in a sequence which is about to be broken. The instructions are known as subroutine 'calls' and

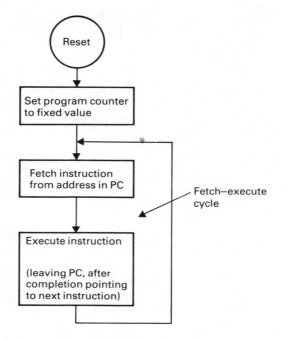

Fig. 2.19 Microprocessor *fetch-execute* cycle

are used to permit commonly used routines to be entered from different parts of the program.

The signals are known as 'interrupts' and permit subroutines to be entered as a result of events which are asynchronous with the operation of the program. A new instruction address is placed in the program counter as a result of subroutine 'calls' or 'interrupts'. Execution continues at this part of the program, which usually has a final instruction known as a 'return' to 'pop' the program counter back from the stack and resume the program at the point where the sequence was broken.

When 16-bit registers are saved or restored using stack operations, two data transfers are required. The address register is used when data transfers are required between processor and addresses not contained in either the program counter or the stack pointer. This increases the flexibility of the processor when it is storing or retrieving data. Sometimes facilities are provided for loading this register from other registers.

The diagram in Fig. 2.20 shows this fuller structure of a micropro-cessor with the computational circuitry in addition to the address bus and registers discussed above. An arithmetic and logic unit (ALU) is shown with one of the general purpose registers more closely associated with it – the accumulator or A-register. This usually holds the results of arithmetic operations in a similar way to the results register of a pocket calculator.

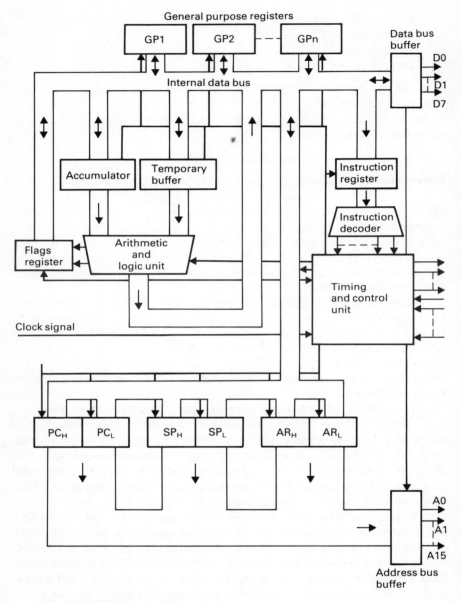

Fig. 2.20 Microprocessor structure

Another register, usually associated with the computational circuit, is the
flags register. This consists of a number of independently controlled flip-
flops which are set to indicate various features of a result such as

- – zero result
- – sign (positive or negative)
- – parity (even or odd)
- – carry or borrow

Some of the processor's registers can be loaded by instructions, and the data manipulated and transferred to other registers. These are the user registers. Others are not available to the programmer and are used as temporary storage buffers.

Microprocessor Operation

The description given of the fetch–execute cycle in the last section needs to be expanded to describe the different instruction types associated with 8-bit processors. These generally fall into three categories: single, two-byte and three-byte (although the Z80 and its derivatives use a slightly extended version of this where additional bytes of an instruction can be an extension of the instruction code).

The simplest type of instruction is one which uses information already in the processor's registers to manipulate information, for example to transfer data contained in one register to another, or to add the contents of one register to the contents of the A-register. These instructions are known as 'single-byte', since only the 8-bit code placed in the instruction register is required to define the instruction. Other instructions need one or more bytes of data to be read into processor registers before the instruction can be carried out and are known as 'two-byte' and 'three-byte' instructions.

The diagram in Figure 2.21 is a more detailed version of the fetch–execute cycle given earlier, covering the sequence for multi-byte instructions. The start of the fetch–execute process involves the reading of data by the microprocessor into its instruction register, the data being obtained from the address contained in the program counter. The instruction is then decoded, and can be considered to set up a byte counter in the control circuitry to determine how many more bytes have to be read to complete the instruction. The program counter is incremented by one to point to the next address. If the byte counter is zero, indicating that no further information is required, then the instruction is carried out. If the instruction itself does not alter the program counter, its contents will be the address of the next instruction in the program. When the byte counter is initially set to a nonzero value, the data contained in the address in the program counter is read to some temporary register or to one of the other registers, and the byte counter is decremented by one. The number of cycles round the left-hand loop, and hence the number of additional bytes read, will depend on the initial setting of the byte counter (as determined by the decoding of the first instruction byte). The program counter is

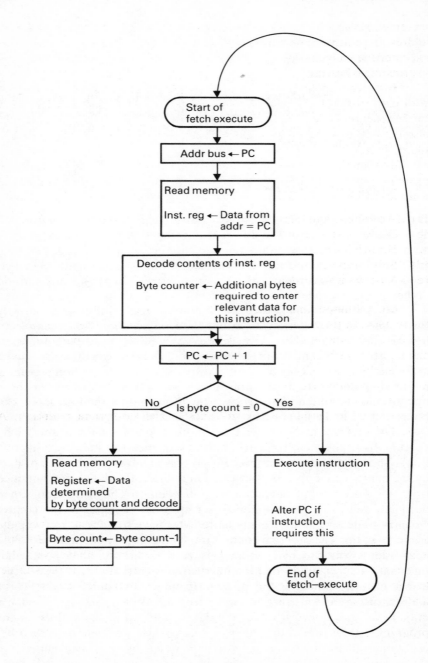

Fig. 2.21   The *fetch-execute* cycle in more detail

incremented at the correct point in the cycle so that it contains the next address in sequence. When the byte counter is zero again the instruction is executed, leaving the processor in the correct state to pick up the next instruction as before.

Instructions which alter the program counter can replace its contents: with data from other registers; with information read from memory after the instruction code (2 bytes required); or from the stack. The stack may also be used to store program counter contents before new information is placed in it.

To complete this overview of microprocessor operation, it is useful to examine some of the instructions. Those of relevance to the writing of test routines will be emphasized under the following headings:

(a)   Arithmetic and logic
(b)   Data transfer operations
(c)   Branch instructions
(d)   Subroutines, interrupts and the stack
(e)   Miscellaneous instructions.

(a) Arithmetic and Logic

Instructions in this category cover functions such as addition, subtraction, logical operations (AND, OR, EXCLUSIVE OR), comparison increments, decrements and rotates. The Z80 bit-check instructions can also be included.

Comparison is used to check a data value against a constant or data in a register. The original data is preserved in the operation. 'Compares' can thus be used in memory check routines to check for data retention. A typical sequence would be:

1   write data to memory;
2   wait a short time;
3   read data;
4   compare with original data.

Note: Some microprocessors have instructions which manipulate or use the contents of pairs of registers. Some of the examples below for the Z80 and 8085 refer to the H and L registers and the D and E registers as pairs (HL or DE). These are simply general purpose registers from the register set which can be treated together as a 16-bit combination. Examples of 'compares' are:

```
CMP #055H    ;6502, compares A register with 55H
CMP B        ;8085, compares A with B
CP (HL)      ;Z80, compares A with memory addr=(HL)
```

Note: When the result of the comparison indicates equality, the zero flag is set.

Single bits can be checked using AND or in the case of the Z80, the BIT operations. When using AND it is important to note that data is not preserved so the data must be saved before the operation.

AND #02   ;6502, will produce a zero result if bit 1 of A is
               ;not equal to 1

'Increments' and 'decrements' are used as counters and to provide moving memory pointers. Decrementing a register until the result is zero is one way to produce a delay.

EXAMPLES

DEX   ;6502, decrements X, the zero flag will be set
             ;when the result is zero
INX H   ;8085, memory pointer in HL incremented by 1
DEC DE   ;Z80, a 16-bit number in DE is reduced by 1

'Rotates' can be used to produce rotating patterns to be loaded into memory in memory tests. They can also be used to check bits by rotating them into the carry bit, which can then be checked. 'Rotates' are used in software routines to convert data from serial to parallel and the reverse.

(b) Data Transfers

These operations transfer data from one register to another; from a register to memory; or from memory to a register. Particularly useful data transfer operations are those which can be used to transfer data to or from sequential locations in memory. These include the indexed addressing modes of the 6502 and the register indirect modes of the Z80 and 8085.

EXAMPLES

;6502
    INX
    STA 0500H,X   ;stores the A register at an address 500+X

;8085
    INX H
    MOV M,A   ;stores the A register at an address pointed to
                    ;by the HL pair (one address on from the last
                    ;transaction

Input/output instructions are used to transfer data to or from ports when port addressing is available. Memory addressing instructions are used with those processors (6502/6800) with no separate port addressing and where the hardware has memory mapped input/output ports in other systems (8085/Z80).

EXAMPLES

OUT 20H   ;8085, output A contents to port 20H
OUT (PORTA),A   ;Z80, output A register to PORT A from A
                     ;register

The Z80 has useful block output facilities in addition to the simple input/
output of the 8085.

EXAMPLE

OUTI   ;the contents of the memory location stored in
         ;HL are output to the port number contained in
         ;the C register, and the B register is decremented

(c) Branching Instructions

These let the programmer take action depending on the result of tests, or
to produce loops in a program. The conditional branches use the state of
the flags to determine the next instruction in the program.

EXAMPLES

;6502
        DEX   ;decrement the X-register
        BNE LOOP1   ;The program will jump to LOOP1 until the
                           ;DEX produces a zero result

;8085
        RAR   ;rotate A right
        JNC LOOP2   ;The program jumps to LOOP2 until the
                           ;rotate right produces a carry

The 6502 conditional branches are limited in range, since they use relative
addressing. The 8085 and Z80 can jump conditionally to any location in
memory, but relative jumps are also possible with the Z80.

;Z80
        DEC B
        JR NZ, LOOP3   ;jumps to LOOP3 until the DEC B produces a
                       ;zero result

Unconditional branches are used to bypass sections of program and to
produce continuous loops.

(d) Subroutines, Interrupts and the Stack

A section of code which needs to be used many times can be written once and entered at different points in the program using the instruction which calls a subroutine.

        JSR address   ;6502, subroutine call
        CALL address   ;8085, Z80, subroutine call

This kind of instruction requires read/write memory since the address of the next normal instruction in sequence (contained in the program counter) is stored on the stack. The program then continues execution at the address referred to in the instruction. The subroutine has a COMPLE-MENTARY matching instruction to the 'call' to restore the program counter and cause the program to resume execution in its normal sequence.

        RTS   ;6502, return from subroutine
        RET   ;8085, Z80 return

Interrupts are input signals which cause the processor to go to a subroutine as soon as it has completed its current instruction. The subroutine is usually called an interrupt service routine and will include an instruction to return control to the interrupted program.

        RTI   ;6502, return from interrupt routine
        RET   ;8085, Z80
        RETI   ;Z80, return from interrupt
        RETN   ;Z80, return from nonmaskable interrupt

Some interrupts will only function when enabled by the appropriate instruction.

        EI   ;8085,Z80, enable interrupts
        CLI   ;6502, enable interrupts

There are corresponding instructions to disable interrupts, DI and SEI. Some interrupts cannot, however, be disabled and are known as nonmaskable interrupts. The maskable interrupts of the 8085 and the Z80 require information to be presented to the microprocessor to determine the address of the service routine.

Other instructions which use the stack are the push and pull operations. In the 6502 these place or retrieve one byte at a time, e.g.

        PHA   ;6502, push A register to stack
        PLA   ;6502, retrieve A from stack

The 8085 and Z80, on the other hand, transfer two bytes at a time, so

        PUSH PSW   ;8085, stores A register and flags on stack
        PUSH HL   ;Z80, stores H and L on stack

save on the stack the contents of A and the flags (using two stack locations).

(e) Miscellaneous Instructions

No operation (NOP) – each microprocessor has an instruction which does nothing but read the instruction and increment the program counter. NOPs are used in free run tests of the microprocessor by wiring the microprocessor data pins to supply this instruction, while keeping them disconnected from the system bus. NOPs are also used to produce short delays between operations and to equalize execution time in different paths of a program where required.

There are a number of instructions which affect only flags and the A register. Some which fall into the previous categories are also useful for this purpose.

EXAMPLES

CLC	;6502, clear carry
SEC	;6502, set carry
STC	;8085, set carry
CMC	;8085, complement carry
XOR A	;Z80, clear accumulator and carry flag
OR A	;Z80, clear carry

Both the Z80 and the 8085 have instructions to load the program counter with the contents of HL, causing a branch to the address in HL.

A useful instruction in the Z80 set is DJNZ which can be used for loops. This instruction uses the B register and, decrementing it, does a relative jump until the zero flag is set, when the loop terminates.

INPUT/OUTPUT CIRCUITS

The simplest type of circuit which can be used to input or output data in a microprocessor system consists of buffers and latches connected to the data bus. Suitable decoding circuitry connected to the address bus can then be used to select the device. An example of such a circuit is given in Fig. 2.22.

It is more common today to use purpose designed input/output devices which are produced by each manufacturer. These usually have registers to which data can be written to determine how the device functions. This facility to program I/O chips makes them more flexible than circuits built from discrete components.

A typical device consists of a number of buffered ports which can be configured as inputs or outputs by writing data to one or more control registers. Sometimes it is possible to mix inputs and outputs on the same port with a control register linked to it. Each bit of the control register determines the nature of the corresponding port bit. Such a control register is sometimes known as a data direction register.

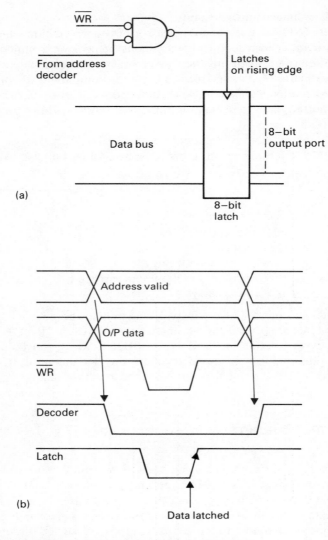

(a)

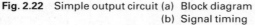

(b)

Fig. 2.22   Simple output circuit (a) Block diagram
                                        (b) Signal timing

Counters and timers can also be included in input/output circuitry to produce pulse trains derived from a clock source (which can be the system clock or a submultiple of it). Such timers are usually programmable and once started do not require processor intervention, so software delays are not required. If the processor needs to take action when the end of count is reached, the circuit can be arranged to interrupt the processor.

When serial data has to be output, programmable serial data handlers can also be provided in input/output devices. Input/output devices have developed in a similar way to microprocessors and new devices have many functions, whereas earlier devices were dedicated to a single function. Fig. 2.23 shows a block diagram of the typical structure of a combination chip which has serial and parallel I/O and counter/timers. More specialized devices in this area are used for such functions as keyboard, display and disk drive controllers.

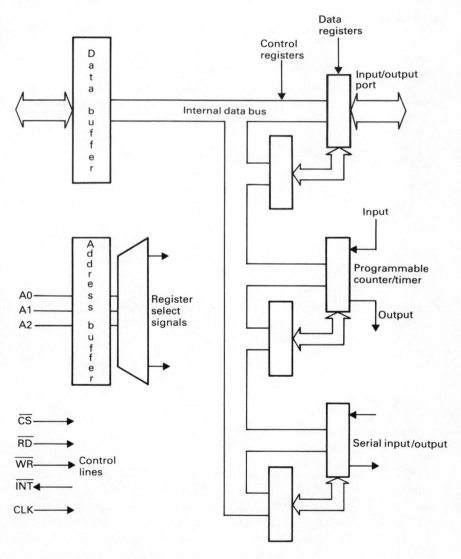

Fig. 2.23 Input/output device – general structure

Those microprocessors which use a multiplexed address/data bus usually have system components which contain memory and I/O. The IO/M control line (or lines) are used by the processor to select one circuit or the other. Single chip microprocessors have I/O circuitry built in and can be used in systems where a low chip count is important.

SUMMARY

These are bus-oriented, with data conveyed in parallel lines organized into groups known as buses. This external behavior needs new test approaches. The internal behavior of the microprocessor is treated from a servicing standpoint: register, memory and program activity is summarized as an introduction to the relevant techniques.

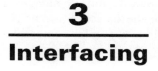

3
Interfacing

If the microprocessor is to perform a useful function in the real world, it cannot exist in isolation purely as a manipulator of binary data. It must, instead, be possible to enter data on which the program can operate and to output any results in a form which permits interpretation or control of the system of which the microprocessor is a part.

In the case where the microprocessor is required to interface with a human operator, input can be a keyboard which provides binary data for the microprocessor, and output can be a hexadecimal display which takes a binary number and presents it to the operator in an easily read form.

In more complex situations the microprocessor will obtain data from a number of sources including keyboards, sensors, data storage units and other microprocessors, while data will be output to devices such as displays, data stores, other computing units and control elements in the system.

Data transfer to or from the microprocessor can be effected in one of two ways – parallel transfer or serial transfer. In parallel data transmission, one physical line is used for each bit of data transferred, whereas serial transmission uses a single data line and sends the data down it one bit at a time.

Since both of these transmission methods connect the microprocessor to its external environment, malfunctions can occur on the data link, adversely affecting the operation of the systems at each end. Faults can also occur in transmitter and receiver logic or in one of the microprocessor system components. An understanding of the effects of faults in such situations is aided by an understanding of the interfacing techniques.

Each microprocessor manufacturer produces different parallel interface devices known by a variety of names such as peripheral interface adapter (PIA), parallel input/output (PIO), versatile interface adapter (VIA). Some chips combine memory and input/output circuitry, and some single chip microprocessors have input/output on chip in addition to read-only and read-write memory.

The distinguishing feature of parallel input/output hardware is that it will contain one or more registers known as ports, with connections from each bit position to pins on the package, which can then be connected to external devices. It is usual to have a number of additional registers to control the operation of the device, for example, to set the direction of data flow between the processor and the external device.

PARALLEL INTERFACING

In this form of interface the data is transferred to and from the microprocessor in a similar way to that used for the transfers between the processor and memory devices. In some instances the data bus has a number of 8-bit latches to which the external devices can be connected.

The interface between the microprocessor's address and data bus will consist of special hardware to or from which data can be transferred using read/write instructions (memory R/W or I/O R/W). Usually instructions will be required to set up the devices, determining the direction of data flow and other modes of operation.

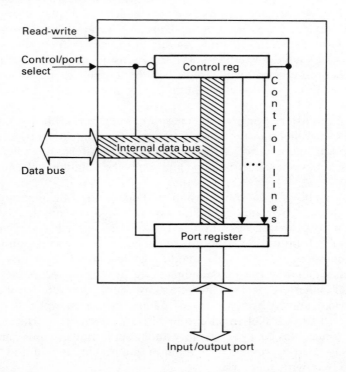

Fig. 3.1 A simple parallel input/output device

A block diagram is shown (Fig. 3.1) of the typical structure of a simple parallel input/output device, consisting of a control register and a single port. Data loaded into the control register determines whether each pin of the port is an input or an output. The control/port select determines whether data flow is between the processor and either the port or the control register. The device select is activated from decoder outputs connected to the address or I/O address bus, in such a way that two devices cannot be selected at one time. Such devices can be used to read the state of switches or to output to on/off elements such as indicators, relays and actuators.

In more complex data transfer it is usual to include handshaking control signals DR and ACK (data ready, acknowledge data received) in the input/output circuit. Fig. 3.2 shows such signals being used to control a transfer of data between two systems. The source changes the data on the output lines and after a short settling delay indicates that the data is ready by activating line DR. The receiver then accepts the data and indicates this by raising the ACK line for a short period. This signal can be used in the source hardware to clear the DR line and possibly generate an interrupt to the processor so that the next data item could be output.

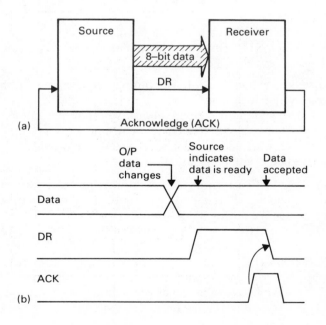

Fig. 3.2 Handshaking for parallel data transfers
(a) Block diagram
(b) Timing diagram

THE CENTRONICS INTERFACE

There is a standard parallel interface, known as the Centronics interface, used to transfer data from microprocessor systems to printers. This uses similar handshaking controls to those described above, except that the signals are active in the low state. In addition to the two handshaking signals there are control lines for other printer functions.

In its simplest form, however, it consists of seven or eight lines and two handshaking or control lines, strobe and acknowledge ($\overline{\text{STR}}$ and $\overline{\text{ACK}}$). Each signal line has its own associated OV return line, and is taken to a given pin on a standard connector. In this simple case the arrangement is as shown in Fig. 3.3. This permits twisted pair cables to be used for each signal to improve noise immunity.

The OV lines corresponding to the signals D0–D7 are 20, 21, . . ., 27 and to $\overline{\text{STR}}$ and $\overline{\text{ACK}}$ are 19 and 28 respectively. In the above example the operating sequence would be:

1   Data is set up on D0–D7 by the source.
2    $\overline{\text{STR}}$ is activated when the data is stable.
3   The rising edge of $\overline{\text{STR}}$ initiates the transfer to the receiver (via the receiver logic).
4   When the receiver is ready for more data the $\overline{\text{ACK}}$ signal is activated and a further $\overline{\text{STR}}$ signal can be initiated after the rising edge of $\overline{\text{ACK}}$.

This sequence is shown in Fig. 3.4. The timing requirements for the signals will vary from system to system.

The simple system described above will not be suitable for all situations, e.g. when the receiving device is off-line, or if a printer runs out of paper. The following additional control signals are provided on Centronics interfaces to deal with these situations:

1   BUSY – An active high signal which indicates that data cannot be received. This signal usually is activated, in systems with character buffers, when the buffer is full – pin 11.
2   PRIME – An active low signal which initializes the receiver logic – pin 31.
3   PAPER END (PE) – An active high output on a printer to indicate that paper has run out or that the print switch is OFF – pin 12.
4   SELECT – An active high signal which indicates that print switch is ON. This is sometimes called DESEL – pin 13.
5   FAULT – An active low signal which goes low on 'paper-out' or 'print-off' or safety switches open – pin 32.

The printer OV is usually available at pins 14, 16 and 33 while the +5 V supply is sometimes brought to pin 18. Pins 34, 35 and 36 are normally unconnected, but can in some cases be connected to nonstandard signals (even 23 V a.c. supplies as on one commonly used printer!). Table 3.1 and the associated diagram indicate in summary form the signal connections of the Centronics interface.

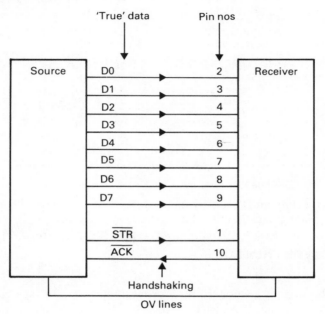

Fig. 3.3   Basic centronics interface

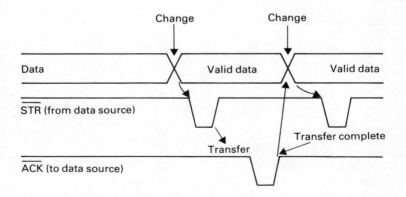

Fig. 3.4   Centronics interface timing

Pin No.	Signal	Pin No.	Signal
1	DATA STROBE	19	GND
2	Data bit 1	20	GND
3	Data bit 2	21	GND
4	Data bit 3	22	GND
5	Data bit 4	23	GND
6	Data bit 5	24	GND
7	Data bit 6	25	GND
8	Data bit 7	26	GND
9	Data bit 8	27	GND
10	ACKNOWLEDGE	28	GND
11	Busy	29	GND
12	Paper out	30	GND
13	Select	31	PRIME
14	GND	32	FAULT
15	Blank	33	GND
16	GND	34	
17	Chassis ground	35	NC.
18	+5 V	36	

Table 3.1 Centronics interface connections

IEEE 488 INTERFACE BUS

IEEE 488 provides a standard for a general purpose interface bus (GPIB) suitable for interfacing computers to each other as well as to devices such as voltmeters, logic analyzers, signature analyzers – in fact any instrument equipped to adhere to the standard. Hewlett–Packard played a major role in the development of the bus (sometimes called the Hewlett–Packard Interface Bus – HPIB) and hold a patent on the handshaking technique employed.

Devices connected to the bus can perform one or more of the following functions.

1   *Controller*: At power up only one unit is configured as the system controller. It is then said to assume the role of active controller managing the bus and only allowing one device at a time to 'talk'. It is possible for the system controller to pass the job of active controller to any other device capable of control. However, the system controller can reset the bus and regain its active state at any time. In the example shown in Fig. 3.5 the microcomputer performs the jobs of system and active controller.

2   *Talker*: Any device capable of transmitting data over the bus is termed a talker. Only one device can be talker active at any instant in time. In Fig. 3.5 the voltmeter, tape reader and microcomputer are all capable of talk activity.

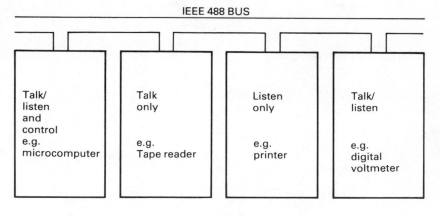

Fig. 3.5   Example cluster on IEEE bus

3   *Listener*: A device capable of receiving data is called a listener, e.g. the printer, microcomputer and voltmeter in Fig. 3.5.

Each device on the bus has a unique address that is used by the active controller to recognize and select who is talking to whom, i.e. to define the active talker and the active listeners as well as 'unlistening' all the devices not designed to receive the data message. The idea of unlistening might at first seem strange. Data transfers on the bus are asynchronous and occur at the speed of the slowest device involved. Unlistening all the devices not involved with the transfer ensures that information exchange is not slowed down unnecessarily by slow devices that do not require the data anyway, e.g. a printer and a disk are both examples of listeners, but if all accesses to the disk were slow enough for the printer to follow, the system would be inefficient.

The bus itself is made up of eight bidirectional data lines, three byte-transfer (handshake) lines and five general control lines that define the status of the information on the data lines (Fig. 3.6). The eight data lines transfer data as well as control and address information in a byte-serial, bit-parallel format.

The signals on the IEEE 488 interface (described above) are all active when in the low state. (Note that it would be ususal to designate such signals with complement bars over the names: this convention is not followed for the IEEE bus.)

Because some of the signals can be asserted by more than one device on the bus, they use open collector drivers, e.g. NDAC, NRFD and SRQ must always be open collector outputs. Similarly the data lines must be open collector when parallel polling is used in response to service request (SRQ).

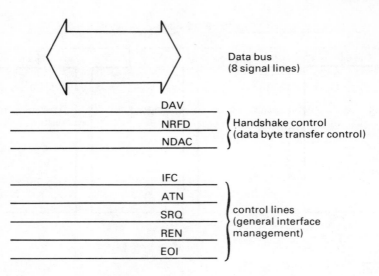

Fig. 3.6   IEEE 488/GPIB signal lines

The remaining handshake lines ATN, IFC, REN, EOI, DAV and the data lines in serial poll mode can be either open collector or tristate driven.

The transfer of data or commands on the interface is controlled using the three handshake lines.

DAV – DATA VALID
> Indicates that the data lines are carrying valid information

NRFD – NOT READY FOR DATA
> High when all listeners are ready to receive data. The first drive to be 'not ready' asserts this line, and when low prevents the talker from sending a new byte. The slowest active listener on the system will release the line.

NDAC– NOT DATA ACCEPTED
> Indicates that all listeners have received the information sent by the talker. While NDAC is low, at least one has not accepted data. The slowest acceptor on the bus will release the line.

The handshake sequence is shown in Figure 3.7. The sequence is:

1   The slowest acceptor is ready for data and causes NRFD to be released.
2   The data source sees NRFD high and activates DAV having placed data on the bus.
3   The acceptors see DAV low and activate NRFD, the fastest device to activate this bringing the link low.
4   NDAC is released as data is accepted by the listeners. The data

source sees NDAC released only when slowest acceptor has released it.

5   Source sees NDAC inactive and releases DAV.

6   NDAC is asserted by acceptors indicating that data byte has been saved. The next data transfer can now take place.

Five control lines define and govern the nature of the information on the eight data lines, e.g. defining whether they carry data or address information.

ATN – ATTENTION
This line is driven by the active controller and is used to define the nature of the information on the data lines. ATN LOW implies the data lines carry address or control information; ATN HIGH implies that they carry data.

IFC – INTERFACE CLEAR
The system controller uses this line to initialize or regain control of the bus (active low).

SRQ – SERVICE REQUEST
Any device wanting attention by the controller pulls this line low.

EOI – END OR IDENTIFY
When driven low it indicates the end of a block of information transmitted on the data lines.

REN – REMOTE ENABLE
This line is driven by the system controller and monitored by instruments capable of remote operation.

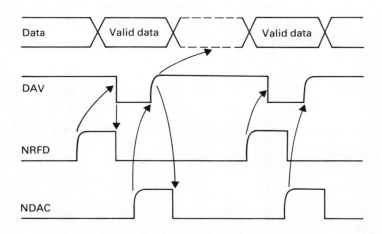

Fig. 3.7 DAV, NRFD, NDAC timing diagram

A Controller — The HP85 Microcomputer

The HP85 Personal Computer, like the Pet, Apple and many other popular microcomputers can be easily interfaced to the IEEE 488 bus. Hewlett–Packard market an 'add on box' containing the interface together with a set of ROMs providing the necessary software to operate the bus. This section illustrates how the HP85 can be used as a system controller driving the bus from a BASIC program.

The REM control line is used by the system controller to inform an instrument that it is being placed under remote control. In BASIC, this is achieved using the REMOTE statement, e.g.

10 REMOTE 716

which places the device at address 16 under remote control. It is usual to place the HPIB interface in slot 7, hence the 7 in this and other instructions.

If desired the remote device can have its own operator controls disabled using the LOCAL LOCKOUT statement thus preventing any interference during remote operation, e.g.

10 REMOTE 716
20 LOCAL LOCKOUT 7

Command Code	Function
F00	return to READY state
F01	event count
F02	transition count
F03	period/width
F04	delay
F05	frequency
F06	signatures
F07	line signatures
F08	line data
F10	volts d.c.
F11	current d.c.
F12	resistance
F13	temperature
F14	self-test
F15	logic level
F16	volts a.c.
F17	current a.c.
F18	option select

Fig. 3.8 Solartron Locator command set

Having gained control of the instrument the controller then transmits data to select the mode of operation (e.g. with a multimeter to select VOLTS and range). These codes will obviously depend on the instrument but they usually take the form of ASCII strings. A selection for a typical instrument, the Solartron Locator, is shown in Fig. 3.8. In BASIC the OUTPUT statement transmits the data to the selected device, e.g.

    30 OUTPUT 716;"O1F5"

transmits the ASCII string O1F5 to the device at address 16. Although this statement appears simple it initiates the following sequence on the bus:

1   Unlistens all devices (makes sure no eavesdroppers).
2   Designates the talker (HP85).
3   Designates the listener (the instrument).
4   Transfers the data.

In a similar manner the BASIC statement ENTER allows the controller to take on the role of a listener and accept data, e.g.

    50 ENTER 716;A$

enables the controller to accept data from address 16 and assign it to the string variable A$. The following operations are performed on the bus:

1   Unlisten all devices.
2   Designate the listener (HP85).
3   Designate the talker (the instrument).
4   Transfer data.

The simple operations described represent only a small part of the capabilities of the IEEE 488 bus. However, as we will see later they provide enough power to drive a test instrument remotely, enabling computer controlled testing.

A Listener/Talker — The Solartron Locator

The 7201A Locator connects to the IEEE 488 bus through an external interface adapter. Small switches on the interface allow the operator to select its bus address as well as configure it as either a listener only, a talker only or as a listener/talker.

The wide range of functions available on the Locator, ranging from the conventional multimeter role to signature analysis, can all be selected and operated remotely over the bus. To select any function and initiate a measurement the system controller transmits an ASCII string made up of a series of codes.

The short BASIC program shown below illustrates how the HP85 and the Locator could be used to continuously monitor frequency:

```
10 REMOTE 716
20 OUTPUT 716; "T1 O1 F5"
30 ENTER 716;A$
40 PRINT A$
50 GOTO 30
```

The command string is made up of three codes:

T1 – selects continuous tracking with the locator taking readings continuously
O1 – enables output from locator
F5 – selects frequency measurement

These codes are specific to the instrument, not to the bus. Any other instrument could be controlled by a similar sequence but might need totally different control codes.

Executing this sample program would produce the following output on the controller's display:

```
FREQUENCY     5000000  HZ
FREQUENCY     5000000  HZ
       .                .
       .                .
       .                .
```

If, instead of continuous readings, measurements are required only when the operator presses the small HOLD button on the logic probe the following program could be used:

```
10 REMOTE 716
20 OUTPUT 716;"T1O1R2F6"
30 GOSUB 100
40 PRINT B$
50 GOTO 30
60 END

100 REM WAIT FOR HOLD BUTTON ROUTINE
110 ENTER 716;A$
120 IF POS (A$, "TIMOUT") THEN 150
130 B$=A$
140 GOTO 110
150 RETURN
```

Here the R command has been used in the command string to induce a TIME OUT message to the system controller if the HOLD button is depressed for 2 seconds. Line 120 in the subroutine monitors the character string returned from the Locator and only returns to the main program, with the last measurement of frequency stored in B$, after the TIMOUT message is received.

The IEEE 488 bus is installed in a growing range of instruments. Some microcomputers such as the OSBORNE included it as standard, others, including the IBM PC and the APPLE II, can be fitted with an IEEE 488 card. It is the most important bus system for the interconnection of instruments on a measurement system.

SERIAL INTERFACING

Transfer of data between two points in parallel using a system such as the IEEE interface is only cost effective over short distances. Cabling costs and the need to buffer the lines make the link cost too much in proportion to the system cost for long lines.

Consider, for example, a parallel printer interface using three control lines. This requires at least a 12-core cable, ribbon cable being commonly used when the printer is close to the data source. If the printer is, however, to be located some distance from the source, e.g. 200 meters away, then the cable will have to be more substantial and will usually consist of twisted pairs with an overall screen, and if the route is in a harsh environment the cable will also have to be armoured. Line drivers and receivers will have to be used at each end of the cable to produce a matched transmission line, and to reject common mode interference. This makes the whole arrangement more complex, but it is sometimes used.

Serial interfaces overcome the disadvantage of having to use one line for each bit of data by using a single line to carry the data, and sending the data one bit at a time down this line (a common or return line will also be used for each data line). To introduce the ideas behind this method of data transmission, it will be developed in stages starting with the system shown schematically in Fig. 3.9.

The data source loads its data to a parallel load shift register, then initializes the clock circuitry and a counter when the data is to be transmitted. Each clock edge will shift the data one place to the right so that it appears on the data line. The receiver consists of another shift register, a counter and logic driven from the same clock. When the correct number of clock pulses has been counted, the receiver counter can initiate the parallel transfer from the shift register to the receiver. This method of sending data serially is a form of synchronous serial transmission, and requires the clock signal to be transmitted along with the data. A timing diagram for the above system would be as shown in Fig. 3.10.

Having thus reduced the number of lines and increased circuit

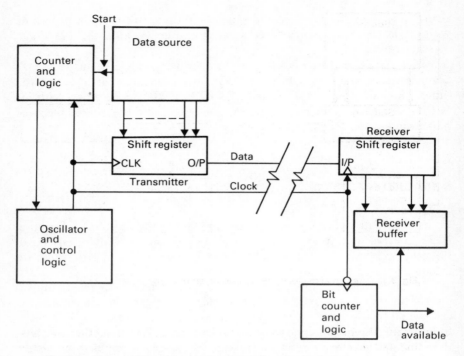

Fig. 3.9   Using shift registers to send data down a single line

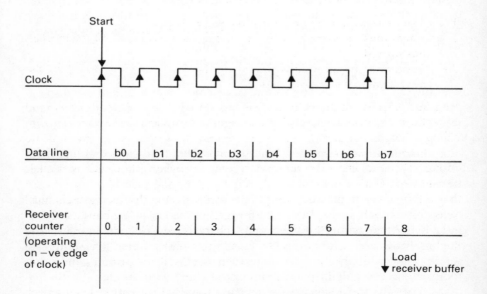

Fig. 3.10   Timing diagram for simple shift register serial system

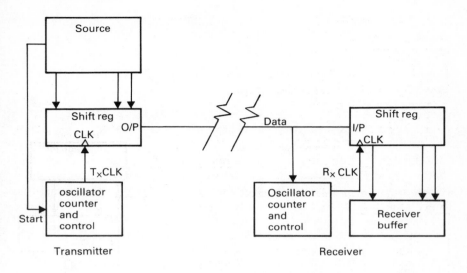

Fig. 3.11 Removal of clock line to make system asynchronous

complexity, the next step is to remove the clock signal from the transmission line and produce a modified version of the above, which is no longer synchronous. A diagram for such a system is shown in Fig. 3.11. This system will only work if it has the following design features:

1   The two oscillators must run at the same frequency.
2   There must be some way to indicate to the receiver that transmission has started.
3   Time must be allowed for resetting the receiver circuitry before the next data item is transmitted.

The first of these features gives rise to a set of standard frequencies, and asynchronous serial transmission is normally restricted to frequencies from this set. These standard frequencies are known as baud rates and indicate the number of bits transmitted per second when the line is carrying data. Table 3.2 shows the most commonly used data rates, and indicates their application areas.

The lower baud rates up to 110 were used with electromechanical teleprinters such as the Teletype 33 which operated at 110 baud, the data rate being limited by the mechanical characteristics of the devices. The higher rates are used for VDUs and data links based on solid-state technology, while the intermediate rates are used for printers and other peripherals with moving parts and relatively simple electronics.

The next two features give rise to a standard way of packaging each block of data (7 or 8 bits usually), with start and stop bits at the beginning and end of transmission of each data item. This will be described in detail in the next section.

Asynchronous Serial Transmission

Various standards have been developed for the signal levels and circuits used when data is transmitted in asynchronous serial form. The situation is not, however, static since old standards are being replaced by newer and better ones. It is more useful, therefore, to discuss asynchronous serial transmission in a way which is independent of the different standards. Since binary data is being transmitted, a definition is required of the logic levels used on the data line in relation to the 1s and 0s in the data.

It is useful to adopt the convention that data is transmitted in 'true' form, that is, that when a data bit is a '1' and that bit is being transmitted then the line is also at the '1' level. The line may not have a signal level equivalent to the 1s and 0s of the logic family being used to perform the parallel–serial conversion, since some form of level conversion interface is generally used between the logic circuits and the transmission line. Using this convention the idle state of the line, when no data is being transmitted is caused to be '1'.

The start of each transmission of a data item (usually 7 or 8 bits) is a 1-bit period during which the line changes state to the '0' level, to indicate to the receiver that transmission has started. Immediately after this start bit, the data bits will appear one at a time, least significant bit first. If a parity check bit is to be sent (to keep the total number of 1s in the data plus parity either even or odd) this is included after the most significant data bit.

The data line must now be held at the idle level for a minimum time known as the stop period. This is to allow for resynchronization of the receiver logic before a new data item is transmitted. This stop period usually lasts 1, 1.5 or 2 bit periods., depending on the system. If a new data item is not sent immediately then the line remains at the idle state for longer than the stop period. The sequence described above is thus:

1   idle state '1'
2   1 start bit '0'
3   7 or 8 data bits, LSB first
4   1 parity bit
5   1, 1.5 or 2 stop bits at least at idle state '1'
6   next start bit '0'

This data package is shown in Fig. 3.12, as it would appear on an oscilloscope. The 7-bit data is 0110001 which with even parity makes the 8 bits (data + parity) equal to 10110001. This is drawn assuming 2 stop bits and that the next data is transmitted immediately after the stop period ends.

The most commonly used number of bits for the stop period is 1 (2 bits were used in electromechanical teletypes because it was not possible to resynchronize in a one bit period). The total number of bits per data package for 8 bits of data or 7 data bits plus parity is thus 10, and the maximum transmission rate for the system is one-tenth of the baud rate, e.g. at 1200 baud the maximum data rate is 120 items/s.

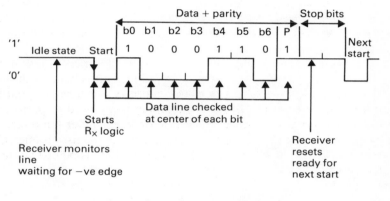

Data   0110001   (ASCII 1)

Fig. 3.12   Serial data format for asynchronous transmission

Serial-Parallel and Parallel-Serial Data Conversion

Serial data streams such as that shown above have to be derived from system data which is in parallel form. The receiver of serial data has, also, to be able to reconstruct the parallel data.

The ideas used to introduce the concepts of serial data transfer, using shift registers, counters and logic can be implemented using SSI and MSI logic. This was, in fact, done in the past and some currently used computer systems still have serial transmit and receive circuits which consist of a card of discrete logic circuits. The advances in LSI technology, however, have given rise to complete circuits for serial data conversion on a single integrated circuit. These are the devices sometimes known as UARTs (universal asynchronous receiver transmitters).

In a microcomputer system a software solution is possible. Programs can be be written which manipulate data in a register so that it appears at one pin of an output port in serial form with the added start and stop bits. The reverse process can also be carried out using a program which monitors an input pin, and detects the changes which occur in the logic level, as the data is received.

It is useful at this point to look at the flowcharts to perform the conversions, since they can be used to describe the operation of both the hardware devices and the software routines. They are given in Figs. 3.13 and 3.14, with Programs 3.1 – 3.3 as practical implementations.

```
                          HEWLETT–PACKARD: 8085 Assembler

LOCATION OBJECT CODE LINE       SOURCE LINE

                     1  "8085"
         <0000>      2  OBTIM          EQU   0000
         <0000>      3  STPTIM         EQU   0000          ;VALUES REQUIRED HERE TO SUIT
                     4                                     ;CLOCK FREQ AND BAUD–RATE
                     5  ;NAME:          SEROP
                     6  ;INPUTS:        C–REG, A CHARACTER FOR SERIAL O/P
                     7  ;OUTPUTS:       CHARACTER TO SOD PIN IN SERIAL FORM
                     8  ;CALLS:         DELAY
                     9  ;ALTERS:        A,FLAGS
                    10  ;DESCRIPTION:   SENDS CHARACTER TO SOD ONE BIT AT A TIME
                    11  ;               PRECEDED BY A START BIT AND FOLLOWED BY ONE
                    12  ;               STOP BIT.
                    13  ;
0000                14  SEROP:
0000 F3             15                 DI                  ;INTERRUPTS DISABLED
0001 C5             16                 PUSH B
0002 D5             17                 PUSH D              ;B,C,D,E SAVED
0003 0608           18                 MVI B,08            ;BIT COUNTER
0005 3E40           19                 MVI A,01000000B     ;A–REG SET TO O/P START BIT
0007                20  LOOP:
0007 30             21                 SIM                 ;OUTPUT BIT
0008 110000         22                 LXI D,OBTIM         ;O/P BIT DELAY IN DE
000B CD0025         23                 CALL DELAY          ;WAIT BIT TIME
                    24  ;
000E 79             25                 MOV A,C             ;INTO A WITH CHARACTER
000F 1F             26                 RAR                 ;LSB INTO CARRY
0010 4F             27                 MOV C,A             ;SAVE SHIFTED RESULT IN C
                    28  ;
0011 3E80           29                 MVI A,10000000B
0013 1F             30                 RAR                 ;A–REG IS NOW C1000000B
0014 05             31                 DCR B
0015 F20007         32                 JP LOOP
                    33  ;
0018 3EC0           34                 MVI A,11000000B     ;A–REG SET FOR STOP BIT
001A 30             35                 SIM                 ;OUTPUT TO SOD
001B 110000         36                 LXI D,STPTIM        ;STOP DELAY VALUE
001E CD0025         37                 CALL DELAY          ;WAIT THIS TIME
                    38  ;
0021 D1             39                 POP D
0022 C1             40                 POP B               ;B,C,D,E RESTORED
0023 FB             41                 EI                  ;INTERRUPTS RE–ENABLED
0024 C9             42                 RET
                    43  ;
                    44  ;NAME:          DELAY
                    45  ;INPUTS:        DELAY VALUE IN DE
                    46  ;OUTPUTS:       NOTHING
                    47  ;CALLS:         NOTHING
                    48  ;ALTERS:        A,FLAGS,D,E
                    49  ;DESCRIPTION:   DECREMENTS DE RETURNING TO CALLER WHEN DE=0
                    50  ;
0025                51  DELAY:
0025 1B             52                 DCX D               ;DECREMENT DE
0026 7A             53                 MOV A,D             ;D–REG IS IN A FOR COMPARISON WITH E
0027 B3             54                 ORA E               ;THIS GIVES ZERO IF A=E=0
0028 C20025         55                 JNZ DELAY           ;BACK IF NOT ZERO
002B C9             56                 RET
```

Program 3.1   8085 serial output routine with 16-bit delay

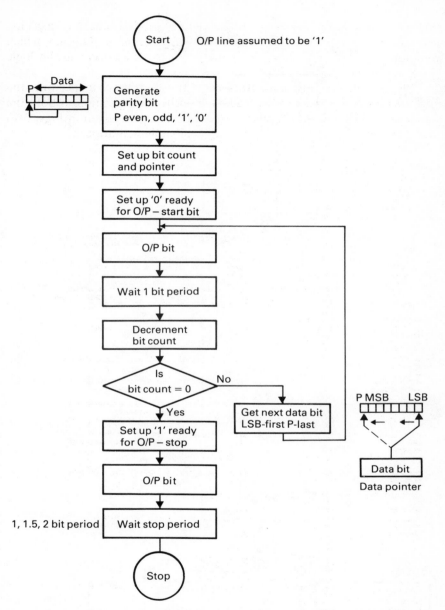

Fig. 3.13 Flowchart for serial transmit

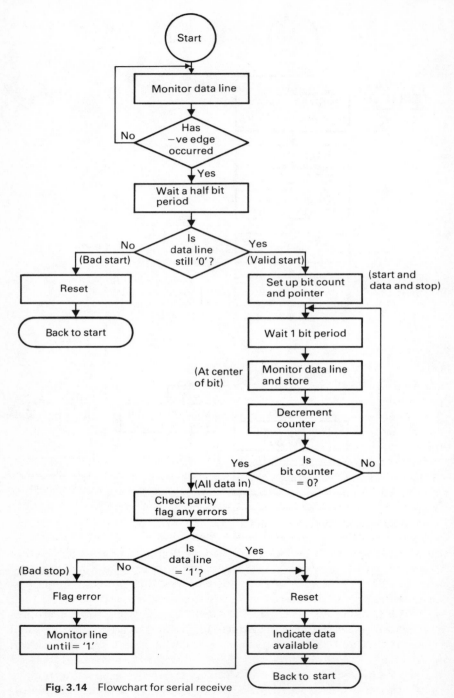

Fig. 3.14 Flowchart for serial receive

HEWLETT—PACKARD: 8085 Assembler

LOCATION OBJECT CODE LINE   SOURCE LINE

```
                         1  "8085"
                         2                      EXT              HBIT,BTIM,STPTIM,DELAY
                         3  ;NAME               SERIN
                         4  ;INPUTS             DATA FROM SID ON 8085
                         5  ;OUTPUTS            CONVERTED DATA TO A-REG
                         6  ;CALLS              DELAY
                         7  ;ALTERS             A,FLAGS
                         8  ;DESCRIPTION
                         9  ;                   THIS ROUTINE MONITORS THE SID PIN AND ON
                        10  ;                   DETECTION OF A VALID START BIT SHIFTS THE SID
                        11  ;                   DATA ONE BIT AT A TIME INTO A
                        12  ;                   THE PARALLEL VERSION OF THE CHARACTER IS LEFT IN A-REG
                        13  ;
0000                    14  SERIN:
0000 F3                 15                      DI                ;INTERRUPTS MUST BE DISABLED
0001 D5                 16                      PUSH D            ;SAVE DE
0002 C5                 17                      PUSH B            ;SAVE BC
0003 0600               18                      MVI B,00          ;B WILL BE USED FOR PARTIAL RESULT
0005 0E08               19                      MVI C,08          ;NO OF BITS
0007                    20  RDIP:
0007 20                 21                      RIM               ;READ INT MASK
0008 17                 22                      RAL               ;INTO CARRY WITH I/P DATA
0009 DA0007             23                      JC RDIP           ;BACK IF NO START BIT
000C 110000             24                      LXI D,HBIT        ;OTHERWISE WAIT HALF A BIT
000F CD0000             25                      CALL DELAY
0012 20                 26                      RIM               ;CHECK FOR VALID START
0013 17                 27                      RAL               ;INTO CARRY WITH SID DATA
0014 DA0007             28                      JC  RDIP          ;BACK IF INVALID START
0017                    29  LOOP:
0017 110000             30                      LXI D,BTIM        ;ONE BIT DELAY
001A CD0000             31                      CALL DELAY        ;WAIT TILL MIDDLE OF NEXT BIT
001D 20                 32                      RIM               ;GET BIT
001E 17                 33                      RAL               ;INTO CARRY WITH IT
001F 78                 34                      MOV A,B           ;PARTIAL RESULT TO A
0020 1F                 35                      RAR               ;CARRY TO MSB
0021 47                 36                      MOV B,A           ;BACK INTO B
0022 0D                 37                      DCR C             ;DECREMENT COUNTER
0023 C20017             38                      JNZ LOOP
0026 110000             39                      LXI D,STPTIM      ;DELAY VALUE FOR STOP BIT
0029 CD0000             40                      CALL DELAY
002C 78                 41                      MOV A,B           ;DATA IN A
002D C1                 42                      POP B
002E D1                 43                      POP D
002F FB                 44                      EI                ;RE-ENABLE INTERRUPTS
0030 C9                 45                      RET
```

Program 3.2   8085 serial input routine

HEWLETT—PACKARD: Z80 Assembler

LOCATION OBJECT CODE LINE   SOURCE LINE

```
                        1 "Z80"
          <0000>        2 PORTA          EQU   0        ;A VALUE IS REQUIRED HERE
          <000C>        3 OBTIM          EQU   12       ;A VALUE IS REQUIRED TO GIVE CORRECT
          <0018>        4 STPTIM         EQU   24       ;STOP BIT DELAY VALUE
                        5                               ;DELAY FOR APPROPRIATE BAUD RATE
                        6 ;NAME          SEROP
                        7 ;INPUTS        CHARACTER TO BE O/P IN C—REG
                        8 ;OUTPUTS       CHARACTER TO B0 OF PORTA
                        9 ;CALLS         NOTHING
                       10 ;ALTERS        A,FLAGS
                       11 ;DESCRIPTIONB
                       12 ;
                       13 ;Z80 SERIAL O/P PROGRAM
                       14 ;USES BIT 0 OF PORT 0
                       15 ;IDLE STATE =1
                       16 ;CHARACTER TO BE PLACED IN C BY CALLER
                       17 ;LINE MUST BE SET TO 1 WHEN THIS IS CALLED
                       18 ;CHARACTER IS PLACED IN C—REG BY CALLER
                       19 ;
0000                   20 SEROP:
0000 F3                21              DI
0001 C5                22              PUSH BC
0002 D5                23              PUSH DE
                       24 ;
0003 0608              25              LD B,08
0005 DB00              26              IN A,[PORTA]       ;READ PORT TO PRESERVE IT
0007 E6FE              27              AND 11111110B      ;SET BIT 0 TO START BIT
0009                   28 LOOP:
0009 D300              29              OUT [PORTA],A      ;OUTPUT BIT
000B 11000C            30              LD DE,OBTIM        ;BIT DELAY IN DE
000E CD0036            31              CALL DELAY         ;WAIT THIS TIME
                       32 ;
0011 79                33              LD A,C             ;GET CHARACTER FROM C
0012 0F                34              RRCA               ;LSB INTO CARRY
0013 4F                35              LD C,A             ;SAVE ROTATED CHAR IN C
0014 3807              36              JR C,SET1
0016                   37 SET0:
0016 DB00              38              IN A,[PORTA]
0018 E6FE              39              AND 11111110B      ;SET B0 TO 0
001A C30022            40              JP CONT
001D                   41 SET1:
001D 00                42              NOP                ;TO EQUALIZE TIME IN THE TWO PATHS
001E DB00              43              IN A,[PORTA]
0020 F601              44              OR  00000001B      ;SET B0 TO 1
0022                   45 CONT:
0022 05                46              DEC B
0023 F20009            47              JP P,LOOP
                       48 ;
0026 DB00              49              IN A,[PORTA]
0028 F601              50              OR 00000001B       ;STOP BIT SET
002A D300              51              OUT [PORTA],A      ;OUTPUT BIT
002C 110018            52              LD DE,STPTIM
002F CD0036            53              CALL DELAY         ;WAIT
                       54 ;
0032 D1                55              POP DE
0033 C1                56              POP BC
0034 FB                57              EI
0035 C9                58              RET
                       59 ;
                       60 ;NAME          DELAY
                       61 ;INPUTS        DELAY VALUE IN DE
                       62 ;OUTPUTS       NOTHING
                       63 ;CALLS         NOTHING
                       64 ;ALTERS        A,D,E,FLAGS
                       65 ;DESCRIPTION   DECREMENTS DE RETURNING TO CALLER WHEN DE=0
                       66 ;
0036                   67 DELAY:
0036 1B                68              DEC DE             ;DECREMENT COUNTER
0037 7A                69              LD A,D             ;INTO A WITH D FOR COMPARING WITH E
0038 B3                70              OR E               ;THIS GIVES ZERO ONLY WHEN D=E=0
0039 C20036            71              JP NZ,DELAY        ;GO BACK AND DECREMENT IF NOT FINISHED
003C C9                72              RET
```

Program 3.3 Z80 serial output routine with 16-bit delay

The use of software techniques to perform parallel–serial and serial–parallel data conversion does not make efficient use of processor time and is only used in small systems. In such situations the delays required in the conversion process, to operate at a given baud rate, will depend on the processor clock frequency, so care must be taken to ensure that this frequency is not changed by a fault in the system (or by replacing the crystal with one of a different frequency).

In systems with a number of serial channels the integrated circuit devices mentioned above are more likely to be used than software routines. A block diagram of a typical circuit is shown in Fig. 3.15.

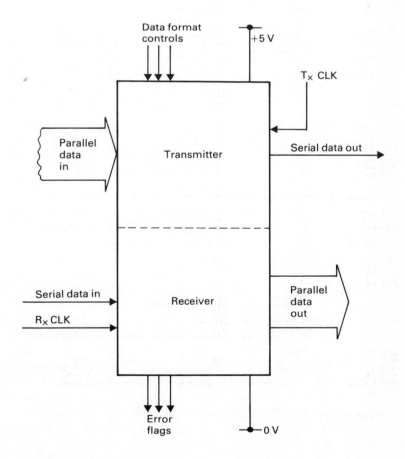

Fig. 3.15 Block diagram of a simple UART

Serial Communications Standards

A number of standards have been and are being introduced to define the
way serial transmission of data is to be achieved in terms of the signal levels
on the lines and the performance of the circuits used to generate these
signals (Table 3.2).

Data rates (bits/s)	Applications
50	Electromechanical printers and readers
75	
110	
150	
300	Medium speed printers and data loaders
600	
1200	
1800	High speed printers, VDUs, and data links
2400	
3600	
4800	
9600	
19200	

Table 3.2   Data rates and typical applications

(a) Single-Ended Voltage Interfaces – RS232, V24, RS423

This is the most commonly used family of interface standards and uses a
single-ended voltage source at the transmitter. The logic levels are:

−ve voltage – '1'
+ve voltage – '0'

The RS232 standard not only defines the signal levels but also the
connector to be used and the pins which are to be used for the various
handshaking signals required when this interface is used with a modem,
(modulator–demodulator) for transmission of data over telephone lines.

The V24 interface is the CCITT (Committee Consultatif International de Télégraphie et Téléphonie) equivalent of the American RS232
standard, and thus appears on equipment of European origin.

Although the RS232 standard defines the function of each pin of the
connector, some manufacturers of devices using this interface do not use
the pins as they are defined, thus giving rise to problems of compatibility.
The RS232 signal levels and pin functions are described below.

Logic '1' is defined as a voltage between −3 V and −25 V
Logic '0' is defined as a voltage between +3 V and +25 V

RS232 makes use of a 25-way connector which should always be connected in the manner indicated. There are, however, minor variations which depend on the application and are referred to in makers' handbooks. The following is a list of the circuit functions of each pin.

Pin Nos.	Description
1	Protective ground
2	Tx Data
3	Rx Data
4	Request to send (RTS)
5	Clear to send (CTS)
6	Data set ready (DSR)
7	Signal ground (OV)
8	Rx line signal detector
9 10	Test pins
11	Secondary Rx line
12	Signal detector
13	Secondary CTS
14	Transmission signal
15	Element timing (DCE source)
16	Secondary Rx Data
17	Receiver signal element
18	–
19	
20	Data terminal ready (DTR)
21	Signal quality detector
22	Ring indicator
23	Data signal rate selector
24	Transmit signal element
25	–

RS232 is not intended for long distance use. The maximum length is usually quoted as 65 ft. In fact it is designed for use with modems (modulator/demodulator) which then permit the data to be transmitted over long distances using either the public network or private lines (usually at 300 or 1200 baud) (Table 3.3).

Integrated circuit manufacturers making interface circuits, produce devices to convert to and from standard logic levels to RS232 levels. The transmitters on these devices require a $\pm$ 12 V supply for the output stage but can accept standard logic level inputs. The receivers accept RS232 level inputs and produce logic level outputs. This means that the logic devices which perform the serial–parallel and parallel–serial conversion can be easily interfaced to an RS232 system. The arrangement of the RS232 signal converters is shown in Fig. 3.16 for a two wire system.

System	Description	Circuit configuration			Data rate (Kb/s)	Max line length (m)
		Logic	Line	Logic		
RS232C (U24)	Single ended 1 driver – 1 receiver	+12 V '1' '0'	−12 V +12 V −12 V 0 V	+5 V '1' '0'	20 (max)	16 Can be increased with reduced data rate. Not intended for long distances
RS423	Single ended 1 driver – up to 10 receivers	+5 V '1' '0'	−5 V +5 V −5 V 0	+5 V '1' '0'	100 (max) 10 1	10 100 1300
RS422	Differential 1 driver – up to 10 receivers	+5 V '1' '0' 0 V	'1'↓'0'↑	+5 V '1' '0' 0 V	10 000 (max) 1000 100	13 130 1300
20 mA loop	Current loop can be multidrop but usually 1 driver – 1 receiver	Source 15 – 22 mA '1' '0' 0 – 2 mA Switch Active transmitter		Detector '1' '0' Passive receiver	10 1	300 2000 In multidrop situations length of line must be reduced for each additional receiver

Table 3.3   Comparison of serial communications interface standards

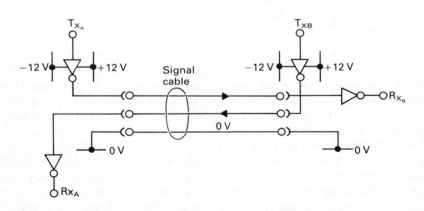

Fig. 3.16   The interface for a two wire RS232C circuit

The RS423 standard uses lower voltages usually ± 5 V on the transmission line and is suitable for higher data rates (100 Kbit/s over 100 m) and longer distances (1300 m at 1 Kbit/s). One other advantage over RS232 systems is that a number of receivers (up to 10) can be used on the same transmission line.

Signal converters are available for interfacing the line signals to TTL level signals in the same way as for RS232 systems. The first-line test of one of these systems is to check the voltage of the two data lines, which should be negative in each case when the lines are inactive. Any other voltage indicates a fault, which must be cleared before any action is taken to check the serial-parallel or parallel–serial circuits.

(b) Current Loop Systems

In this mode of transmission the line consists of a pair of wires which form a circuit with a switchable current source and a receiver as shown schematically in Fig. 3.17.

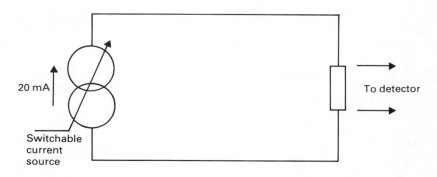

Fig. 3.17 Schematic arrangement of a current loop interface

The convention in this case is that a current of greater than 17 mA constitutes the logic '1' state, and a current of less than 2 mA constitutes the logic '0'. This type of interface is less standardized than the RS232 interface, but is used in many industrial systems because it can be used over longer distances without a modem.

Current loop systems can be designed to have an isolated transmission line using isolated supplies and opto-isolators at both transmitter and receiver. The transmitters and receivers can usually be configured to be active or passive, thus giving rise to many different data link configurations, some examples of which are shown in Fig. 3.18. Some recently produced transmit and receive devices simplify current loop interfacing still further (HCPL-4100 and HCPL-4200).

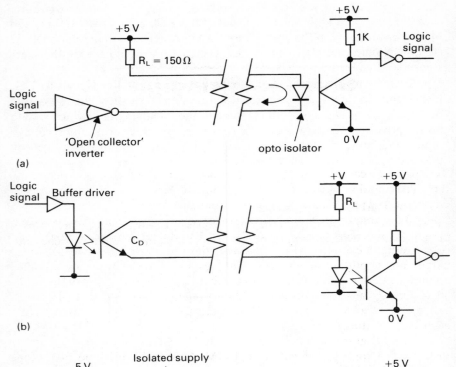

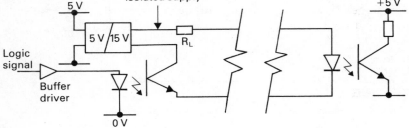

Fig. 3.18 Some practical current-loop circuits
(a) Current source at transmitter
(b) Current source at receiver
(c) Isolated transmission line

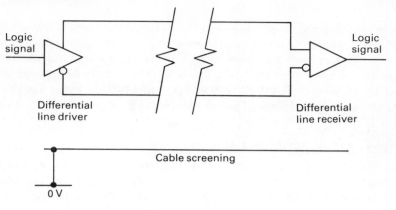

Fig. 3.19 Differential mode serial interface

(c) Differential Mode Systems, e.g. RS422 and RS485

A third type of interface standard is used for serial interfacing. This uses differential line drivers and receivers for the transmission line interface. The common-mode noise immunity of the transmission system is improved when using such a system, and as a result the length of line and baud rate can both be substantially increased compared with the other two systems 1300 m at 100 Kbits/s, 10 Mbits/s over 13 m (Fig. 3.19).

The RS422 standard permits, in addition, the use of more than one receiver on the line, and a newer standard RS485, is designed for use with multiple sources and receivers. The RS232 standard is intended for use as a single source–single receiver system, so cannot be used in this way. Current loop systems can be designed to have more than one receiver in the loop but with a reduction in transmission distance for each additional device.

REPRESENTATION OF PRINTABLE CHARACTERS

In any computer system the binary numbers stored in the memory devices are normally used to represent numerical values. It is, however, necessary to have some way of representing printable characters using some binary code.

The American Standard Code for Information Interchange (ASCII) has been developed and is the standard for all applications where printable characters have to be used in a computer system. The ASCII character set covers 128 different symbols and control codes. All devices which are used to display information are designed to interpret this particular code. The code uses 7 bits so that in an 8-bit computer there is a spare bit which need not be used as part of the code. It is, however, usual to make use of this spare bit for error detection. The 7 bits of ASCII code are placed in the least significant 7 bits of the 8-bit word and the MSB is used as a parity bit. Parity bits can be determined in one of two ways:

1   To ensure that the total number of 1s in a word is always even.
2   To ensure that the total number of 1s is odd.

The first is known as even parity, the second as odd parity. Thus eight lines are used to carry the 7 data bits and parity between a microcomputer and a printer, for example, or 8 bits are used for data and parity in serial transmission. In the case of serial transmission the data is always transmitted least significant bit first, following the start bit, and parity will be the bit before the stop period. Any single corrupted bit will change the total number of logic 1s and hence the parity which can be checked for each received character. More than one bit could be corrupted giving an apparently correct parity: more complex checking methods are used on other communications and networking systems to cope with this problem.

        Sometimes there is doubt as to which pin (2 or 3) is used to transmit, and whether a one-to-one connector pair is correct for linking two systems. Again a check on which of the two is negative at each end should clarify the position. For example if pin 2 is negative at one device while pin 2 is negative at the other a direct 2–2, 3–3 link would short together the two outputs (pin 2 in this case). The correct method for such a system is to use a connector pair with a twist in the connections to pins 2 and 3.

SUMMARY

The transmission of data within microprocessor systems and between them and peripheral devices can be in parallel or serial form. Three standards are discussed – Centronics, IEEE 488 and RS232/V24. By giving specification details on these standards, the resulting servicing problems can be pinpointed.

PART II

Servicing Techniques

4

Fault-Finding Techniques

Despite recent trends towards automation, fault-finding in microprocessor based equipment employs the same basic philosophy used in more conventional electronic circuits. The serviceman still must become familiar with the circuit and have a basic understanding of how it works. Circuit diagrams together with additional documentation in the form of memory maps and even program listings can all help towards this end.

Many of the problems encountered in microprocessor systems and microcomputers are common to those found in all electric circuits, e.g.

- faulty power supplies
- poor connections
- dirty switches
- faulty capacitors and resistors, etc.

However, added to this list are a whole range of new problems unique to microprocessor based equipment, e.g.

- The signals inside microcomputers travel in buses typically made up of 8, 16 or 32 tracks.
- The information on these buses is changing rapidly and depends on the particular function the micro is performing, i.e. the signals are not necessarily repeatable.
- Many of the system components are connected in parallel on the system buses. Even when a fault is discovered on a bus line or node there still remains the problem of identifying which component is generating the fault.
- The buses do not always contain meaningful information. At times they may be undergoing switching transients or be inactive if driven by tristate outputs.

The list of problems is formidable and a solution looks imposible with conventional test instruments. However, this section will outline some of the new fault-finding techniques that have been developed to deal with these problems – logic analysis, signature analysis and in-circuit emulation.

No single technique solves all the problems but each supplies clues to the source of the fault.

In addition, many problems can be traced to parts of the system outside the microprocessor section, e.g. in the power supplies or interface circuitry. There is no need to abandon common sense, and the insights gained from more conventional digital and analog circuits can play a big part in solving these problems. Rather than attempt an all-embracing fault chart which might become just as confusing, a selection of suggestions is presented. They represent the kind of tests that have been carried out by electronics technicians and service engineers for years; they are relatively quick and cheap and should catch many problems that might otherwise be wrongly attributed to the microprocessor hardware.

For each new range of equipment the experienced service engineer will be able to produce a corresponding set of hints and tips – incorporating such general points and adding those specific to the new equipment.

BASIC SYSTEM TESTS

To start with, consider some of the tests that can be carried out on microprocessor systems with very little equipment. Their simplicity makes it worthwhile to include them in this introductory chapter.

System Clock

Poor clock signals can lead to many problems ranging from no activity, with the system completely dead, to an apparantly erratic behavior. Many microprocessors including the 6502 are sensitive to clock speed and will not operate when the clock frequency falls outside the tolerance limits. Similarly dynamic memory devices rely on refresh activity to keep their memory cells topped up. If the refresh rate falls too low the memory will begin to present problems. Clock frequencies and the distribution of the clock throughout the system can be checked using frequency meters or oscilloscopes.

Reset

Most microprocessors begin operation from a specific address whenever the reset pin undergoes a transition from logic 0 to logic 1. Normally, on-board circuitry delays this transition until all the circuits in the system have been powered up and undergone any internal reset that they might require.

Problems can arise, however, if the reset to the processor appears too quickly or contains noise spikes that lead to it attempting multiple starts. A reset line stuck low would obviously prevent the system from running. Again the reset pin can be checked to some extent with a conventional oscilloscope although the one-shot nature of the signal can be best observed using a storage oscilloscope.

Other Control Lines

Noise or a faulty circuit connected to processor inputs such as interrupt, wait or bus request pins can also cause erratic behavior or complete failure of the system. An oscilloscope or even a logic probe can be used to monitor these inputs. If one is suspected of presenting a problem it may be possible to disable it temporarily during testing.

STIMULUS TESTING

The basic strategy involved in testing any device, electrical or mechanical, involves stimulation in conjunction with observation to assess whether it is functioning correctly. For example, if a motorist suspects a brake light is not functioning he presses the brake pedal while a colleague inspects the rear brake lights. The same philosophy holds when investigating a micro-computer system. If the operator suspects a printer interface problem then the interface should be exercised by a stimulus program designed to 'put it through its paces' sending all possible ASCII characters to the printer while observations are made either visually or using test equipment.

Program 4.1 gives an example stimulus routine designed to exercise the chip select outputs from a suspect address decoder chip. The example is based on the SDK-85 single board computer (Appendix 2) but can be applied in a similar way to most systems. The routine toggles each of the decoder's outputs allowing the operator to check their performance using an oscilloscope.

```
2020      LDA 0000 ; In first ROM

          LDA 0800 ; In second ROM

          LDA 2000 ; In first RAM

          LDA 2800 ; In second RAM

          JMP 2020 ; back to start
```

Program 4.1   Stimulus program for address decoder on SDK85

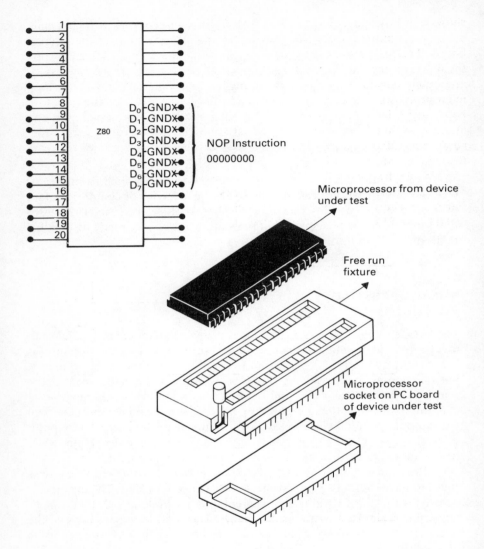

Fig. 4.1   Free-run fixture is placed between the microprocessor and the unit
under test

FREE RUNNING THE MICROPROCESSOR

A simple yet powerful technique that can be used to exercise a large part of
a microcomputer system involves free running the microprocessor. Fig. 4.1

shows how it is achieved. The processor is first removed from its socket and a free-run fixture is inserted between the microprocessor and the circuit board. The fixture hardwires the code for NOP (00 on the Z80, EAH on the 6502) on the data bus pins. All the other connections to the processor are left connected to their corresponding bus lines on the board. When the microprocessor is reset it goes to its first location where it finds the code for NOP. After incrementing the address bus it reads the next location in an attempt to find a more meaningful instruction. However, its search is in vain; the NOP code appears at every location forcing the processor to cycle through its entire address range.

While free running, the microprocessor's address bus acts like a binary counter, each pin generating a characteristic frequency (Fig. 4.2). Further, since the processor is producing all possible addresses between 0000H and FFFFH any address decode logic on the board is also fully exercised.

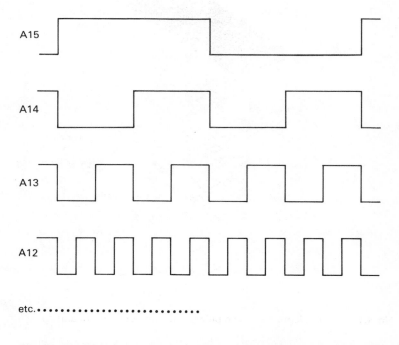

Fig. 4.2   Free running the microprocessor – the address bus acts like a binary counter

The multiplexed bus on the 8085 and some of the new 16-bit processors such as the 8086 leads to a slightly more complicated design for the free-run fixture (Fig. 4.3). A bidirectional buffer ensures that the

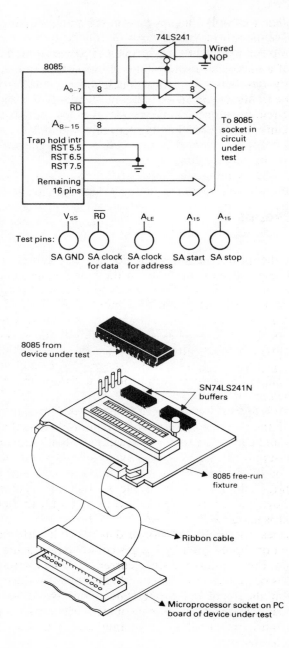

Fig. 4.3   Free running the 8085 (similar circuits can be used with other multiplexed bus processors, including the 16-bit 8086)

hardwired code for NOP only appears on the address/data pins during the time they have the role of data bus.

The free-run fixture offers a simple yet powerful method of testing a large part of a microprocessor system. Each address line can be checked for continuity as well as for shorts with neighboring lines by observing their characteristic frequency on an oscilloscope. Similarly the outputs from any chip select circuitry can be observed and tested for continuity between the decoder circuits and the individual system components.

POWER SUPPLIES

Checks on the power supplies should not be restricted to voltmeter readings. These will show up faults in the new voltage, but not ripple or spikes. Even an oscilloscope check needs to be carried out carefully. Any mains ripple is easily detected, and more than a few millivolts on a nominally regulated line is highly significant. At the reservoir capacitor the ripple may be 1 or 2 volts peak–peak. A well-designed regulator should reduce that by a factor of a thousand – until a critical level is reached at which the regulator saturates. At this stage even a small increase in load current (or fall in line voltage) will produce a disproportionate increase in ripple on the regulated output.

If there is a suspicion of such a fault the following quick test is worth trying. Find the normal current drain (check the manual, estimate or measure it) and choose a resistor that will pull an additional 10 percent or so from the supply. Double check to avoid mistakes and then connect this additional load for a few seconds. The extra load should be well within normal ratings and the output ripple should not change significantly. Anything more than an extra few millivolts might mean that the regulator performance is marginal.

This does not imply any risk of damage, but rather that any other small current or supply voltage changes could be producing sharp changes in the output. For example the spike currents caused by transitions in TTL output stages or switch on of external loads might produce corresponding transients on the regulated supply lines. This could be the source of apparently random errors in internal counters or jumps in a program. Such occasional transients though not truly random (there is an internal cause) are difficult to observe.

Similarly any suspicion of high-frequency oscillation should be investigated – it may seem too small to worry about at the point it is detected but may be caused by a more serious level elsewhere in the system.

TEMPERATURE EFFECTS

Associated with these problems are the effects of high temperature. It is not uncommon for systems to acquire extra functions, boards, memory circuits, as users find new roles for them. In some cases, like the classic Apple microcomputer, expansion was planned for, but even in the best of circumstances overeager expansion can cause problems. Firstly the original power supply may be taken close to its limit of good regulation as above. Secondly the resulting rise in temperature can bring reliability problems – intermittent contacts in a variety of devices for example. It is a good idea to look for obvious hot-spots: even the old-fashioned 'finger-on-the-chip' test gives a warning of unusually high temperatures though the more complex devices inevitably draw high currents and can be hot to the touch. This is a subjective test, but experience with other samples of a product is a guide to unexpected temperatures.

If a particular device is suspected to be the source of a problem then a quick squirt with one of the commercial 'freezing' aerosols is worth trying. The rapid fall in temperature may remove or modify the fault symptoms temporarily if the fault location has been pinpointed. This can also apply to dry joints expanding and contracting under the influence of localized heat sources.

Where a heating problem is more generalized, the opening of a cabinet, or otherwise improving the air flow, can verify a diagnosis. Here it will need a longer time to show up, and such faults are more likely to be associated with a pattern of occurrence later in the working day. It may take several hours after switch-on before a fault occurs allowing for the rise in laboratory or workshop temperature as midday approaches.

NOISE

This leads to other thoughts on time-of-day problems in the context of intermittent faults. Look for patterns in the appearance of faults. What at first seems to be random, with no connection to any local activities, may in fact by synchronized with events outside the room where the unit is being checked. This is particularly true of mains-borne interference when high-power loads are activated somewhere else in the plant. These faults are hard to trace, but with a particularly stubborn fault it may be necessary to move the unit to a different room, or at least feed it from a different power outlet. As an extension, a filter in the supply lines could prove the simplest solution, both confirming the source of the problem and removing its effects.

None of this is a substitute for a well-designed power supply with good transient suppression, and there is certainly the risk that additional suppression that (just) works on test, may not cope in the electrically noisy 'home' environment of the equipment.

INTERFACE FAULTS

As a first step against these, the hardware and software should be checked against the specifications to spot any discrepancies. The printed circuit boards may have hand-wired patches or the software manual may have additional routines. On the interface side, bus systems are notorious for the ambiguities of their documentation. Some pins on a connector have precisely defined characteristics, others are at the whim of the manufacturer. The length of interconnection cable that can be supported is related to the signal rate being transmitted. It is worth checking that the baud rates at the send and receive ends are set to the same value and that the cable length is not introducing unexpected delays. There should be no problems in most systems for rates from 25 to 1200 baud but at the higher rates operation may become unreliable.

The interface between the microprocessor system and the outside world is a fertile breeding ground for problems: to the electronic problems of the board are added the contact problems of the connectors and the compatibility difficulties of the interconnected systems. The peripherals themselves may introduce faults that then appear to indict the microprocessor system. A typical example is the printer with a limited buffer memory. For small amounts of text and at low baud rates the printer behaves impeccably. If either is increased substantially the buffer may fill before the printer can print the text and characters are lost or misprinted. A short test sequence would have revealed no fault and at a later stage a full run would show up such faults which could be attributed to problems elsewhere in the system – 'the printer was fine before, so it must be the fault of the electronics'.

PERIPHERALS

Disk drives can suffer from alignment problems or disk imperfections. The user may simply have inserted the disks carelessly. Disk faults should show up with a clear and unambiguous error message. There should always be a backup disk and it would be wise not to use the original master while there is still doubt as to the drive itself. Disk heads can be cleaned easily enough, but disk alignment, and disk drive electronics repairs are not to be undertaken so lightly.

–   The monitors and VDUs represent a different level of problem. Though complex internally, the technology is well established, with much of the design amenable to the skills of radio and TV servicemen given the appropriate training. Keyboard decoding may be unfamiliar but the faults can be relatively straightforward mechanically, while the displays are of higher resolution but broadly similar in principle to the video and tube sections of a television receiver.

TYPES OF FAULTS

We can distinguish different categories of faults, e.g. those which develop as the result of some breakdown or loss of performance of a component; interference from some outside source; design faults; user errors. The first two have been discussed, while design faults should only occur at the research and development stage.

The exceptions are in prototypes and small runs where the same rigor of checking and cross-checking may not have occurred. Typical examples are in educational and research laboratories where novel designs are produced under time pressure, and where the designer may be a scientist or engineer without much experience of microprocessors. The resulting prototype may then work under the favorable circumstances of the laboratory only to fail on site. Marginal design of clock circuits, reset lines with edges either too slow or with multiple transitions, inadequately buffered or improperly terminated interfaces, are some of the things to look out for. These can also go wrong in systems from experienced designers but will normally be caught and rectified well before the production stage.

'User errors' is shorthand for a multiplicity of faults that cannot be blamed on design, manufacturer or components, though they are sometimes made more likely by inadequate documentation. They can include:

–   Interface faults where the user has not allowed for loading effects, has selected an incompatible peripheral or misunderstood the connector arrangement.
–   Software faults in not allowing for some aspect of an operating system, using program 'tricks' that improve efficiency but make future errors more likely when changes are needed.
–   Hardware faults where the user has modified a board to add some special function and caused additional loading or time delays.

FAULT LOGGING

These thoughts all point to the importance of patterns and of cause–effect relationships. We may not be able to identify the latter but the former represent the best clue available. If a fault frequently occurs at the same time of day, when the equipment is in the same place or after a particular series of actions, it is no longer a random fault. We may not yet be sure of the cause, but the despair induced by the truly random intermittent fault is no longer justified. All faults should be carefully logged, preferably in a form that allows for the associated operating conditions to be noted. This helps in several ways:

–   It can help in feeding back information to the designers or suppliers of the equipment so that design weaknesses can be eliminated.
–   It provides an early warning system for other units of the same kind.
–   It identifies external sources of error that might affect totally different pieces of equipment.
–   It builds into a library a databank of faults and their cures invaluable to all future service engineers.
–   In the process it identifies weaknesses in particular types of equipment or of specific manufacturers: microcomputers may always be plagued by one particular fault because of marginal design in a critical area.

CHECKLISTS AND FLOWCHARTS

The experienced individual tackling a servicing problem often appears to go intuitively to the heart of the problem. This is misleading: he (or she in these enlightened days) will have subconsciously rejected some approaches, made a number of surface observations and relied on prior experience to get close to that heart. For the trainee or the less gifted individual a more rigorous approach is advised. A checklist of actions should be prepared and adhered to. The servicing experts in the organization should draw up such a list taking great care to spell out all the functions that they normally deal with automatically. Such a list will include many obvious items:

–   is the system connected to the supply
–   is the power on
–   note the contents of any displays
–   note the status of any indicators
–   check the regulated voltage

At each stage of the check list a go/no go action may be appropriate. If the list is to proceed on to cover the more subtle faults then yes/no answers and the actions based on them become inadequate. A proper flowchart may be needed with branching to subsidiary tests depending on whether particular faults have been identified or eliminated. It may be possible to construct a universal flowchart or at least one to cover a wide range of devices, but the resulting complexity can make it preferable to provide a simpler version for each particular item of equipment.

The experienced user will still be inclined to skip sections of such a chart and rely on experience or intuition, but if it is well constructed it is a time saver. The early tests are kept straightforward and quick, but can eliminate whole areas rapidly. As an example, if the power supply is faulty but is not checked, then apparent faults elsewhere in the system may simply be reflections of the power supply imperfections. A moment or two with a voltmeter and a scan around key points with an oscilloscope and this risk is removed.

SUMMARY

Microprocessor systems are bus oriented and have faults which are difficult to detect without bus-oriented test equipment. Test with oscilloscopes and logic probes can detect straightforward faults by forcing the system to go through a defined sequence. System faults may be traceable to power supply imperfections, internal or external temperature rise or interfering signals. They may also be caused by designer or user errors as well as by component faults. In all cases faults should be logged to detect patterns and aid in tracing causes. This can be achieved by simple checklists or by flowcharts to guide the less experienced user.

5

Self-Test Principles

Test routines can be built into microprocessor systems and microcomputers. They feed and detect standard patterns to memory and input/output circuits. Examples from working systems are included.

Many microprocessor based systems use the integral processor for system testing. Test programs resident in ROM and initiated at power up or on request can check ROM, RAM, the processor itself and to some extent any input/output devices. The results of these tests are usually communicated to the operator through the systems display or using a special indicator that confirms satisfactory completion of the tests. However, some test software is designed to operate with an external instrument, such as a signature analyzer.

Test programs need not reside in ROM. Many can be loaded from disk or tape for final execution in RAM. Obviously this type of testing assumes a larger part of the system is working satisfactorily or at least well enough to load and run the test routines.

RAM TESTING

The normal technique for testing RAM involves writing a pattern into the memory, reading it back and then verifying that both operations were successful. Several strategies can be employed to detect possible sources of failure with the RAM. These include the following.

(A) CHECKERBOARD TESTING – Alternative bits are set to 1 and 0 and checked. The pattern is then reversed and again checked, thus ensuring that each bit of the RAM can store both a logic 1 and a logic 0 (Fig. 5.1). Using the checkerboard pattern as opposed to flooding the whole memory with logic 0s and then logic 1s makes the test sensitive to possible corruption between neighboring bit positions.

	00	01	10	11
00	0	1	0	1
01	1	0	1	0
10	X	X	X	X
11	X	X	X	X

1 Alternate bits are set to 1 and 0
   and checked.

2 The pattern is then reversed and checked
   before moving off to the next row of
   cells.

Fig. 5.1   Checkerboard testing RAM

(B) MARCHING 1S AND 0S – With this test, the memory is initialized by writing 0s and 1s into all locations. The first cell is read and a 1 written in its place. This procedure of reading 0s and replacing with 1s is continued on all the remaining cells until the memory contains only 1s. The process is then repeated starting at the last cell and working backwards until the memory contains only 0s again. The pattern is then repeated starting with a background of only 1s (Fig. 5.2).

(C) COMPLEMENTARY ADDRESS SEQUENCE – This third test pattern can be used to reveal faulty operation of a RAM chip's internal address decoder. The test begins by writing a pattern of alternating 0s and 1s into the memory. The first cell is then read, followed by a read of the cell with the complementary address, followed by a second read of the original cell. The test then continues in a similar manner for the next cell until all cells have been read. The background pattern of 1s and 0s is then reversed and the test repeated (Fig. 5.3).

Repeatedly complementing the memory address supplied to the chip will impose a severe test on its internal memory decoder highlighting any delays.

Some memory tests are extremely time consuming and can take up to several hours to complete. Hence, normally only simple algorithms, such as the checkerboard test, are used for self-checking, reserving the more

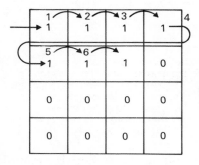

First the memory is filled with 0s

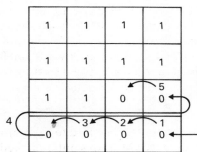

The 0 in the first cell is read, checked and replaced with a 1. The procedure continues until the memory fills with 1s.

Starting at the last cell a similar procedure fills the memory with 0s.

The whole of the above procedure is then repeated starting with 1s and replacing with 0s.

Fig. 5.2   Marching 1s and 0s test pattern for RAM

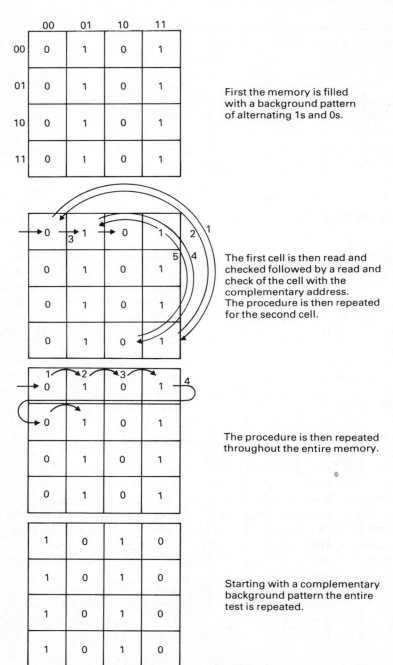

First the memory is filled
with a background pattern
of alternating 1s and 0s.

The first cell is then read and
checked followed by a read and
check of the cell with the
complementary address.
The procedure is then repeated
for the second cell.

The procedure is then repeated
throughout the entire memory.

Starting with a complementary
background pattern the entire
test is repeated.

Fig. 5.3   Complementary address sequence RAM test pattern

detailed pattern sensitivity tests for when a definite RAM fault is suspected. No memory test can guarantee the memory is completely fault free. If RAM passes a test it is more than likely good, if it fails there is definitely something wrong.

Program 5.1 illustrates a typical routine to 'checkerboard test' RAM. The program is typical of most quick test routines, writing and reading AA H and 55 H to each memory location. If an error is detected control can return to the monitor program or the user's own error handling routine with the contents of the Z80's HL register pair pointing to the address where the error was detected.

ROM TESTING

The simplest method of testing ROM involves forming a checksum. The contents of each memory location within the ROM are added together and then truncated to form a checksum byte. A program initiated during the self-check sequence computes the checksum and compares it with the stored value. If they do not match, a ROM failure has been detected. If they do match, the ROM is probably functional but there still remains a possibility that several errors have cancelled each other out.

A more sensitive technique, less likely to mask errors, involves forming a cyclic redundancy check (CRC). The method originated as a means of error checking data transfers between computers and their peripherals, e.g. disks or tapes. To understand how the technique is applied to ROM testing, imagine the entire contents of a ROM chip laid out end to end to form one large linear bit stream. The bit stream is then fed into a shift register with feedback paths that effectively perform an addition to the base 2 between the feedback data and the new data from the bit stream. The remainder left in the register, after all the data bits forming the ROM have been entered, is the cyclic redundancy check (Fig. 5.4). (The technique forms the basis of signature analysis which is described in Chapter 9.) As with most tasks in computing the procedure can also be implemented in software. Program 11.3 shows a routine, written in assembly language, to evaluate a cyclic redundancy check of a 2K byte block of data.

The sensitivity of the technique follows from the feedback paths that ensure that every single bit fed into the register contributes towards the final signature. If even one bit is missing the probability is high that the final CRC will differ greatly from the original.

Program 5.1 QUIKTST – checkerboard test for RAM (reprinted by permission of Comart Ltd.)

```
0001 ;
0002 ;
0003 ;       COMART LTD.
0004 ;       8 LITTLE END ROAD
0005 ;       EATON SOCON
0006 ;       ST. NEOTS
0007 ;       CAMBRIDGESHIRE
0008 ;
0009 ;       SEPTEMBER 1980
0010 ;
0011 ;       THIS IS A QUICK TEST FOR COMART MEMORY BOARDS. IT IS DESIGNED
0012 ;       FOR THE OPERATOR TO TYPE IN THE OBJECT CODE, SET UP THE START
0013 ;       AND END ADDRESS, AND RUN UNDER CONTROL OF A MONITOR, SUCH AS
0014 ;       THE NORTH STAR MONITOR OR THE CROMEMCO DEBUGGER.
0015 ;
0016 ;       THE PROGRAM IS ORIGINED AT 100HEX BUT OTHER ORIGINS MAY BE
0017 ;       USED EITHER BY RELOCATION BY THE OPERATOR OR BY REQUESTING A
0018 ;       LISTING FROM COMART AT THE SPECIFIED ORIGIN
0019 ;       THE PROGRAM EXPECTS TO FIND THE START AND END ADDRESS AT LOCATIONS
0020 ;       ORIGIN AND ORIGIN+2 RESPECTIVELY.(THESE ADDRESSES MUST BE STORED
0021 ;       IN THE INTEL REVERSE FORMAT). NO CHECK IS MADE ON THE VALIDITY OF
0022 ;       THESE ADDRESSES.  THE REQUIRED CONDITIONS ARE :-
0023 ;               START+1<END
0024 ;       ENSURE THAT THE PROGRAM AREA IS NOT INSIDE THE TEST AREA!!!
0025 ;
0026 ;       A SUCCESSFUL TEST WILL TERMINATE AT TESTEND AND A JUMP MAY BE PUT
0027 ;       HERE TO YOUR MONITOR (OR A BREAKPOINT IF YOU HAVE THIS FACILITY)
0028 ;
0029 ;       AN ERROR CONDITION WILL TRANSFER CONTROL TO ERROR AND ONCE AGAIN
0030 ;       A JUMP TO YOUR MONITOR OR A BREAKPOINT MAY BE PLACED HERE. AT THE
0031 ;       ERROR ADDRESS THE REGISTERS MAY BE INTERPRETED AS FOLLOWS:-
0032 ;               A=ACTUAL DATA
0033 ;               B=EXPECTED DATA
0034 ;               HL=ERROR ADDRESS
0035 ;
0036 ;       IF A JUMP TO YOUR MONITOR IS USED AT THE ERROR LOCATION IT IS RECOMMENDED
0037 ;       THAT THE REGISTERS ARE SAVED FIRST TO AVOID CORRUPTION BY THE MONITOR
```

```
                           0038  ;         TO FACILITATE THIS THE ERROR ADDRESS IS THE LAST LOCATION IN THE PROGRAM
                           0039  ;         ALLOWING FOR EXPANSION
                           0040  ;
                           0041  ;         THE PROGRAM REQUIRES AT LEAST 10 BYTES OF STACK. THE STACK POINTER
                           0042  ;         MUST BE SET UP PRIOR TO PROGRAM EXECUTION.NOTE THAT THE ERROR EXIT DOES
                           0043  ;         NOT RECOVER THE STACK
                           0044  ;
                           0045  ;         THE TEST WILL FIND ANY STUCK BITS AND SOME ADDRESSING FAULTS
                           0046  ;
                           0047  ;
0000'  (0002)              0048  START    DS    2                ;START ADDRESS
0002'  (0002)              0049  END      DS    2                ;END ADDRESS
0004'  06AA                0050  QUIKTST  LD    B,0AAH           ;FIRST WRITE AA TO EVERY MEMORY LOCATION
0006'  CD1100'             0051           CALL  TEST             ;THEN READ IT BACK AND VERIFY
0009'  0655                0052           LD    B,055H           ;THEN WRITE AND VERIFY 55'S
000B'  CD1100'             0053           CALL  TEST             ;NOTE THAT THIS TESTS EVERY BIT AT 1 AND 0
000E'  C30E00'   R         0054  TESTEND  JP    $                ;END OF TEST
                           0055  ;
                           0056  ; TEST FILL MEMORY AND READ BACK FROM B
                           0057  ;
0011'  CD2500'             0058  TEST     CALL  GETEND           ;GET END ADDRESS IN DE
0014'  CD2B00'             0059           CALL  FILL             ;FILL MEMORY FROM B
0017'  2A0000'             0060           LD    HL,(START)       ;GET START ADDRESS FROM LOC 100
001A'  7E                  0061  TEST100  LD    A,(HL)           ;GET BACK NEXT BYTE
001B'  B8                  0062           CP    A,B              ;SAME AS WRITTEN?
001C'  2048                0063           JR    NZ,ERROR         ;NO SO FAIL!
001E'  CD3600'             0064           CALL  CHLDE            ;SEE IF WEVE REACHED THE END YET
0021'  C8                  0065           RET   Z                ;YEP SO GO HOME
0022'  23                  0066           INC   HL               ;INC POINTER FOR NEXT BYTE
0023'  18F5                0067           JR    TEST100          ;LOOP FOR ALL MEMORY UNDER TEST
0025'  2A0200'             0068  GETEND   LD    HL,(END)         ;GET END ADDRESS FROM LOC 102
0028'  E5                  0069           PUSH  HL
0029'  D1                  0070           POP   DE
002A'  C9                  0071           RET                    ;TRANSFER TO DE AND RETURN
002B'  2A0000'             0072  FILL     LD    HL,(START)       ;GET START ADDRESS IN HL
002E'  70                  0073  FILL100  LD    (HL),B           ;WRITE B INTO MEMORY UNDER TEST
002F'  CD3600'             0074           CALL  CHLDE            ;FINISHED YET?
```

```
0075   0032'  C8        RET Z       ;INC POINTER AND LOOP FOR ALL MEMORY
0076   0033'  23        INC HL
0077   0034'  18F8      JR FILL100
0078                  ;
0079                  ; CHLDE COMPARE HL AND DE FOR EQUALITY
0080                  ;
0081   0036'  7C      CHLDE   LD A,H          ;GET H
0082   0037'  BA              CP A,D          ;COMPARE WITH D
0083   0038'  C0              RET NZ          ;NOT EQUAL
0084   0039'  7D              LD A,L
0085   003A'  BB              CP A,E
0086   003B'  C9              RET             ;COMPARE AN L.S.BYTE
0087                  ;
0088                  ;ADTEST ADDRESS TEST WRITE AND VERIFY ADDRESS TO EACH LOC
0089                  ;
0090   003C'  CD2500'  ADTEST  CALL GETEND     ;GET END ADDRESS TO DE
0091   003F'  2A0000'          LD HL,(START)   ;START ADDRESS TO HL
0092   0042'  74       ADT100  LD (HL),H       ;WRITE MSB OF ADDRESS
0093   0043'  CD3600'          CALL CHLDE      ;CHECK FOR END
0094   0046'  2808             JR Z,ADT200     ;END FOUND
0095   0048'  23               INC HL          ;INC POINTER
0096   0049'  75               LD (HL),L       ;AND WRITE LSB OF ADDRESS
0097   004A'  CD3600'          CALL CHLDE      ;CHECK FOR END
0098   004D'  23               INC HL
0099   004E'  20F2             JR NZ,ADT100    ;NOT END SO LOOP
0100   0050'  2A0000'  ADT200  LD HL,(START)   ;GET START ADDRESS BACK AGAIN
0101   0053'  7E       ADT300  LD A,(HL)       ;GET NEXT BYTE
0102   0054'  BC               CP A,H          ;VERIFY HIGH ADDRESS BYTE
0103   0055'  200F             JR NZ,ERROR     ;WRONG!!!!
0104   0057'  CD3600'          CALL CHLDE      ;CHECK FOR END
0105   005A'  C8               RET Z
0106   005B'  23               INC HL          ;INC POINTER
0107   005C'  7E               LD A,(HL)       ;GET NEXT BYTE
0108   005D'  BD               CP A,L          ;VERIFY LOW ADDRESS BYTE
0109   005E'  2006             JR NZ,ERROR
0110   0060'  CD3600'          CALL CHLDE      ;CHECK FOR END
0111   0063'  C8               RET Z
0112   0064'  18ED             JR ADT300       ;LOOP FOR ALL MEMORY
0113   0066'  C36600'  ERROR   JP $
0114 R 0069'  (0000)           END
```

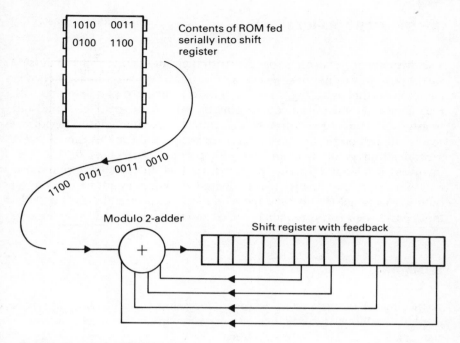

Fig. 5.4 Forming a ROM signature

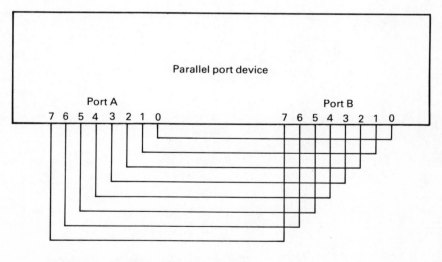

A simple test fixture linkes PA0 to PB0,
PA1 to PB1, etc.

Fig. 5.5 Test fixture for checking ports

INPUT/OUTPUT DEVICES

The diversity of I/O devices together with their interaction with the outside world pose problems for effective self-testing. Typically, devices encompass several functions, e.g. the 6522 VIA contains two parallel ports with four handshake lines, two counter/timers and a serial–parallel–serial shift register. One limited test strategy that can be implemented is to perform a read-write test on those registers that are known to have this capability. A second strategy, often employed with parallel port chips or UARTs, involves installing a special port fixture that links neighboring ports together (Fig. 5.5). One port is configured as an input and the other as an output. A test pattern is then fed to the output port and checked at the input port. Their roles are then reversed and the test repeated.

SUMMARY

If the kernel of the system is functioning and particularly if it retains display capability, it can be made to generate and monitor test patterns in the memory and input/output sections.

6
Logic Analysis

One approach to fault finding in a programmed device is to monitor the system buses while executing a known, documented program. At each step the bus activity is compared with the program listing and checks made to ensure the system is indeed following the intended program. This procedure is known as a program trace.

Although a number of devices can be employed to monitor bus activity, the logic analyzer provides the most convenient method. Typically, analyzers provide 8, 16 or 32 input channels which can be used to record the time behavior of any of the signals found in a microcomputer system, e.g.

– data bus
– address bus
– control bus
– input/output ports

Unlike the cathode ray oscilloscope, the analyzer does not coninuously monitor its inputs but instead samples them when it receives an active clock edge (Fig. 6.1). Captured data is not placed immediately on display but instead stored in the analyzer's own digital memory, from which it can be recalled and analyzed at leisure.

Most analyzers give a choice of display mode for the captured data. Fig. 6.2 shows three of the most common formats. In Fig. 6.2 (a) the display is similar to a multichannel oscilloscope trace, whereas in Fig. 6.2 (b) it takes the form of a state table with the data given in either hexadecimal, octal or binary. Some analyzers contain a disassembler program for one or more microprocessor families. With this option, information captured from a microcomputer's address and data buses can be presented in the easily interpreted mnemonic form shown in Fig. 6.2 (c).

Commercial analyzers fall into two categories:

– Timing analyzers,
– Data domain or state analyzers.

117

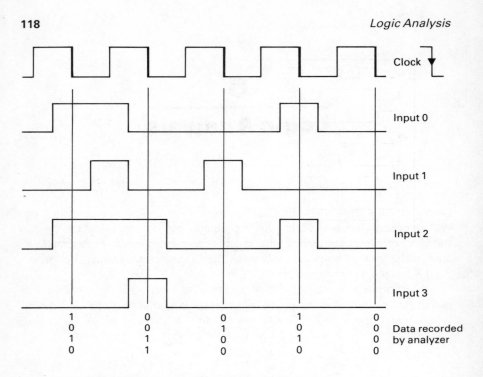

Fig. 6.1 A logic analyzer sample on active clock edges

A timing analyzer generates its own sampling clock using an internal oscillator operating at a higher frequency than the system signals. Since the analyzer only records data on an active clock edge, any changes between clock edges are not detected until the second edge. Therefore, the maximum time an input can go unnoticed is one clock cycle, known as the sampling ambiguity. To reduce this ambiguity, the sample rate should be several times the maximum frequency being observed. This is achieved in timing analysis by using clock oscillators operating at frequencies up to the order of 200 MHz.

State analyzers employ a different approach when capturing data. Instead of using an internal clock, they sample data on clock edges derived from the system under observation. The example shown in Fig. 6.3 should help illustrate the principle. A state analyzer is attached to the address bus of a Z80 system and used to monitor address bus activity. The clock input to the analyzer is attached to the $\overline{\text{MREQ}}$ strobe from the processor and the analyzer is configured to accept a falling edge as a valid clock signal. Z80 timing diagrams illustrate that choosing this point in the cycle to capture address bus information will ensure that the analyzer will capture each address (including refresh address) when it is stable.

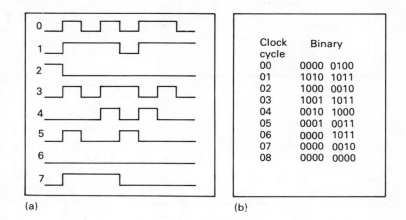

Clock cycle	Binary
00	0000 0100
01	1010 1011
02	1000 0010
03	1001 1011
04	0010 1000
05	0001 0011
06	0000 1011
07	0000 0010
08	0000 0000

(a)   (b)

ADDRESS, DATA

AFTER	0006H	INC	HL
+001	0007H	CP	L
+002	0008H	JP	NZ, ****
+003	0005H	LD	[HL], B
+004	0006H	INC	HL
+005	0007H	CP	L
+006	0008H	JP	NZ, ****
+007	0005H	LD	[HL], B
+008	0006H	INC	HL
+009	0007H	CP	L
+010	0008H	JP	NZ, ****
+011	0005H	LD	[HL], B
+012	0006H	INC	HL
+013	0007H	CP	L
+014	0008H	JP	NZ, ****
+015	0005H	LD	[HL], B

(c)

Fig. 6.2 Different display formats offered on logic analyzers
(a) Data displayed in timing mode
(b) Data displayed in binary
(c) Data displayed in mnemonics

LOGIC ANALYZERS – BASIC OPERATION

The range of features available on logic analyzers, as with all processor based products, continues to grow. This section restricts itself to describing those features common to a wide range of instruments.

Fig. 6.4 illustrates a typical 16-channel state analyzer. Connection to

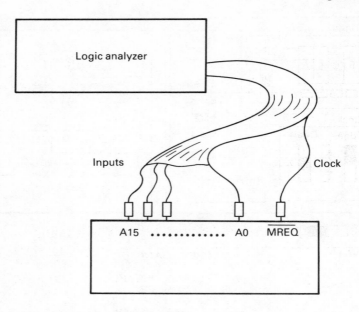

Fig. 6.3 Capturing address bus signals on the Z80

the system under test is made through a ribbon cable terminated in either individual probes or an IC test clip. Along with the 16 data inputs, connections are provided for clock, common and other control signals called qualifiers (described later). At the heart of the analyzer, high speed RAM provides the recording medium. In a 16-channel device, the memory would be organized as 16 bits wide by typically 128 words deep, allowing the analyzer to record for 128 clock cycles (Fig. 6.5). The memory serves two functions: firstly to record data when the instrument is armed, and secondly to replay the captured data to the instrument's display.

To give the analyzer flexibility and enable users to monitor particular areas in a program or data sequence, all analyzers provide trigger or event selection circuitry. When armed, the analyzer continuously monitors its input channels and triggers when a previously defined trigger word occurs. Depending on the sophistication of the analyzer, various extra conditions can be placed on the trigger word, e.g.

–   Trigger after N occurrences of the trigger word,
–   Trigger N clock cycles after the trigger word.

Like oscilloscopes, logic analyzers can display the data that occurs after the trigger event. Unlike most scopes, they can also display information prior to the trigger event. This capability is called negative time recording, and can be used for troubleshooting by choosing a faulty system operation as

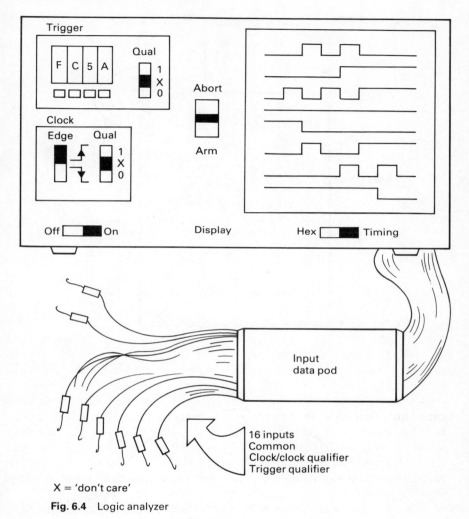

X = 'don't care'

Fig. 6.4 Logic analyzer

the trigger event and then observing the events that led up to it. The concept of negative time recording can be understood by considering the analyzer's 128 memory locations to lie in a circle as shown in Fig. 6.6. Once armed the analyzer records data as well as 'keeping a lookout' for the trigger event. At each clock edge, data is placed in the next available memory location. Once the trigger event is observed, the analyzer marks the position of the current memory location and continues recording for another 63 clock edges before returning to the display mode. The data displayed will then be made up of 64 states before the trigger event and 63 states after the event.

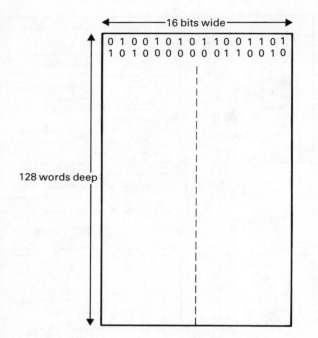

Fig. 6.5   Analyzer's memory layout

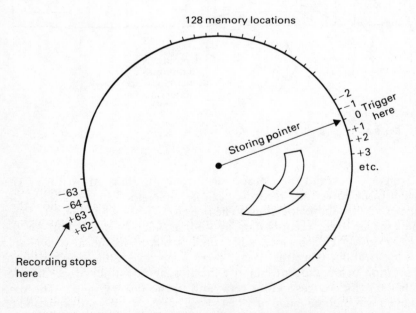

Fig. 6.6   Simple model to explain 'negative time recording'

The controls on the front panel of the analyzer can be divided into three groups:

- Arm/abort control,
- Clock/clock qualifier controls,
- Trigger/trigger qualifier controls.

Arm/Abort Control

When the arm control is activated, the analyzer enters the data gathering mode. On each clock edge a data word corresponding to the logic states of the 16 inputs is placed in the memory. This procedure continues until the trigger event is identified after which recording will continue for a further 63 clock cycles before the analyzer returns to the display mode. If a trigger event is not detected, the abort control also returns the analyzer to the display mode.

Clock and Clock Qualifier Controls

The clock edge control allows the operator to select the active edge, i.e. either rising or falling, of the external signal that is used to strobe data into the analyzer's memory. With a state analyzer, the user has to choose a suitable signal to act as a clock for the data under observation. When making this decision, two important analyzer parameters must be taken into account – the data set-up time and the data hold time. The former defines the time the data must be stable prior to the clock edge (typically 35 ns), whereas the latter defines the minimum time for which the data must remain stable after the clock edge; in many applications this may be zero.

With some applications not all the clock edges are required to store data. An extra input called a clock qualifier can be used to select only those edges where data is required. This input operates in conjunction with a front panel switch that allows the operator to define the state of the qualifier input for acceptance of data (Fig. 6.7). In the above example where the analyzer is used to capture address bus information in a basic Z80 system, the falling edge of $\overline{\text{MREQ}}$ is used as a clock signal. All addresses, memory addresses and refresh addresses established by the Z80 are recorded in the analyzer's memory. If only memory addresses were required, refresh addresses could be rejected by attaching the clock qualifier input to the $\overline{\text{RFSH}}$ output from the processor and setting the clock qualifier control to logic 1. This would ensure that only the first falling edge of $\overline{\text{MREQ}}$ (corresponding to a memory address) is used to strobe data into

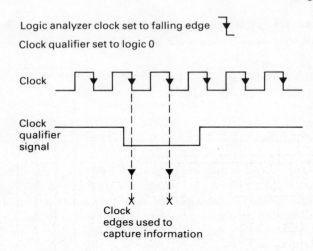

Fig. 6.7 Effect of clock qualifier

the analyzer. If the clock qualifier is left in the 'don't care' position, all clock edges are used to store data.

Trigger and Trigger Qualifier Controls

The trigger controls allow the operator to define the pattern of 1s and 0s that must be found on the inputs before triggering occurs. An extra input called trigger qualifier can be used as a 17th bit extension on the trigger word. The trigger qualifier control on the front panel allows the operator to select the condition of this extra input for triggering to occur.

TESTING A MATRIX KEYBOARD

Application of the logic analyzer need not be confined to following the behavior of computer bus signals. This example illustrates how the analyzer can be used to monitor some of the signals that pass between the computer and one of its major peripherals, namely the keyboard.

Most keyboards are made up of a number of switches arranged in the form of a matrix (Fig. 6.8). Two techniques are commonly used to interface the switch matrix to the computer.

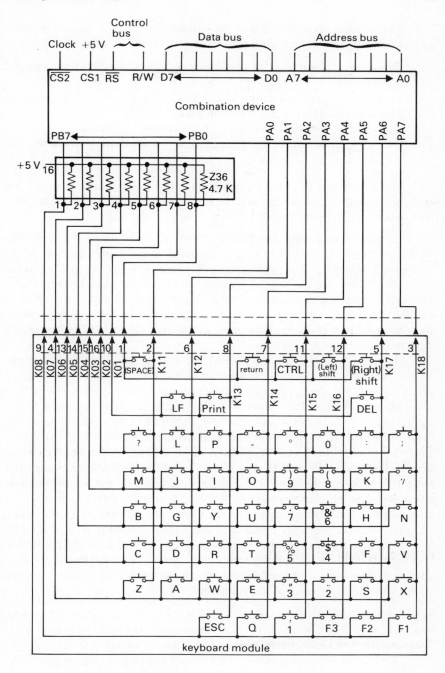

Fig. 6.8 Key matrix and interface

(A) HARDWARE ENCODED – This approach uses a special purpose keyboard encoder integrated circuit which performs the following tasks:

–   detecting a depressed key and generating a strobe signal for the computer;
–   encoding the key presenting the ASCII code for the selected character, in parallel format, to the computer;
–   debouncing the switch contacts 'on make' and 'on break';
–   providing other features often found on modern keyboards, e.g. rollover and auto-repeat.

(B) SOFTWARE ENCODED – A second approach found in many low cost microcomputers uses the system's own microprocessor, together with software routines to perform the tasks of the encoder chip.

An example of a software encoded keyboard is shown in Fig. 6.8. The switch matrix is interfaced to the processor through a combination device containing RAM, two input/output ports and a timer, as well as other functions, all housed in a 40-pin package. Both ports are used to service the keyboard; port A is configured as an output port connected to the columns of the switch matrix, and port B as an input port monitors the rows of the matrix. A set of pull-up resistors ensure that port B reads FFH if no key is depressed.

To detect and decode the position of a depressed key, the microprocessor performs a software routine that scans the key matrix. The scan is made up of two parts. Firstly the processor latches out a bit pattern through port A onto the columns of the matrix. It then performs a read operation on port B, comparing the result with FFH, to detect a depressed key. For example, if the processor were to latch out 00H on port A, i.e. pull all the column sides of the switches to logic 0, any depressed key would result in the input to port B changing. The pattern established on port B would depend on the row of the depressed key but not its column. To overcome this the microprocesor does not output 00H on port A but instead performs a scanning operation where one column at a time is held at logic 0. Hence from the position of the logic 0 in the input of port B, the processor determines the row of the depressed key and from the position of the logic 0 in the scan it determines the column. The keyboard software also contains routines to debounce switch contacts and provide rollover along with shift and control key functions.

Connecting the Logic Analyzer

To monitor the keyboard scan, eight of the analyzer's inputs are connected to port B. The analyzer inputs and controls are configured as follows.

	Binary Key	
7F	0111 1111	
7F	0111 1111	
BF	1011 1111	Port A activity
BF	1011 1111	captured by logic analyzer
DF	1101 1111	
DF	1101 1111	
⋮	⋮	
FE	1111 1110	
FE	1111 1110	

Zero migrates across port A as micro
searches for a depressed key

Fig. 6.9 Using the logic analyzer to capture scan of matrix keyboard

1   The clock input is connected to $\overline{CS2}$ (chip select) on the device and set to operate on falling edges. Hence each time the processor communicates with the RIOT, the analyzer receivers a clock signal.

2   The clock qualifier is attached to $\overline{RS}$ (RAM select) on the device and set for logic 1. Since it is a combination device, not all accesses are directed to the ports. The $\overline{RS}$ signal is low when RAM is selected and high when the ports are selected. Setting the clock qualifier high ensures that only those accesses directed at the ports result in data being recorded by the analyzer.

3   The trigger word is set at 7FH to catch the beginning of the 'working zero' scan. The most significant 8 bits together with the trigger qualifier are set 'don't care'.

After arming, the analyzer triggers and displays the trace shown in Fig. 6.9. The logic zero signal can be seen to migrate across each of the eight columns as the microprocessor completes one scan of the keyboard. Each voltage pattern is recorded twice: once as the pattern is latched out by the processor and again when the processor performs a read operation on port B (Fig. 6.9).

SUMMARY

Logic analyzers sample the logic states on groups of bus lines. There are two main categories: state and timing. The former provides the engineer with a tool capable of monitoring bus or port activity at time intervals defined by any system signal. The latter allows the engineer to examine critical timing relationships between bus signals, and is used primarily as a hardware debugging tool.

7

Serial Interface Fault Finding

The location of faults in serial communication systems is complicated by the multiplexed nature of the data and the nonstandard logic levels produced by the interface circuitry. A fault detected at the receiver can originate at the parallel–serial or serial–parallel conversion circuitry. Noise picked up by the transmission line or on the power supplies of the interface conversion circuitry can also produce data errors. The range of faults which can occur has given rise to a number of techniques for serial interface testing which help to isolate faults to a particular part of the circuit.

GENERAL TECHNIQUES

Since serial interfaces have many user selectable features, apparent faults can occur when the settings at each end of the transmission line are incompatible. This makes it even more important to perform some preliminary checks on a system, before assuming that a circuit malfunction has occurred and attempting to find it using one of the techniques to be described below.

It is not unknown for a system which has been working satisfactorily to fail to work for no apparent reason, and after many fruitless hours of fault diagnosis, to discover that someone has inadvertently altered a baud-rate select switch. In addition to baud rate the character format will be switch or program selectable. In small systems where UARTs are not used to perform the serial–parallel, parallel–serial conversions the data rate is determined by the processor clock frequency, so changing this, perhaps as part of some other fault-finding procedure, will cause failure of the serial link.

A useful checklist for serial interfaces which can avoid wasting time and effort looking for nonexistent faults is given below:

1   Baud rate
2   Number of data bits
3   Parity select features
4   Number of stop bits

These four features should generally be set to be the same at each end of the line, although it is possible to have minor differences in data format without causing data transmission failure. For example, a transmitter which sends two stop bits for each character will work with a receiver which only requires one; a transmitter which generates parity will function with a receiver which does not check parity, as long as the receiver word length is correctly set to take account of the parity bit used in the transmitted data.

The above checks should be made in switch-selectable systems even before power is applied. In programmable systems the features have to be checked with the systems energized at each end of the line and, if changes are made, it is essential to ensure that they are memorized when power is removed and reapplied (by writing the new data to disk for example). When the systems are energized, some additional checks can be performed with simple test equipment. In single-ended voltage source transmission systems such as RS232, V24 or RS423 the transmission line should be at a negative voltage with respect to ground when no data is being transmitted. This can be checked with a voltmeter or an oscilloscope, and if a fault is discovered this points to earth faults, transmitter interface faults or, quite commonly, transmitter interface power failure. In RS232 type systems the −12 V supply is sometimes only used for the serial interface and a malfunction will not exhibit itself until an attempt is made to transmit data. In current loop systems a milliammeter inserted in the loop will indicate whether a fault exists (idle line should have 20 mA flowing). A quick check for a system of this type is to remove and replace the link connector a few times to create random make and break sequences in the current thus generating spurious characters (useful for a visual display unit).

Having completed these basic checks on the integrity of the cabling and connector system it is then necessary to proceed with more specialized techniques if no fault has been found.

SPECIALIZED SERIAL INTERFACE TESTING

When the preliminary checks mentioned above fail to get a serial data link to work, it is necessary to use one or more of the following techniques:

1   Serial data analyzers
2   Special purpose data generators
3   Back-to-back test software

Serial Data Analyzers

These are instruments which have facilities similar to those on a logic analyzer (some logic analyzers incorporate serial analysis as a feature or as an option). Since the data to be analyzed can be a logic signal or an interface level signal the analyzer requires a probe with suitable circuitry to interface to a wide range of signal levels, and the facility to select positive or negative logic. The serial data is usually converted to parallel data and then stored in memory, using the end of conversion for each data unit received as a clock to the logic analyzer part of the circuitry. This is shown schematically in Fig. 7.1. It is, of course, necessary to select the correct baud rate and data format if the serial to parallel conversion is to be done correctly and the data stored is to be meaningful. Data will normally be stored continuously, until a defined trigger word occurs, when a fixed amount of additional data is stored and recording stops.

Serial analyzers with CRT displays usually have options which permit the data to be displayed in binary, hexadecimal or ASCII form. Fig. 7.2 shows how a serial analyzer can be used to trace a fault.

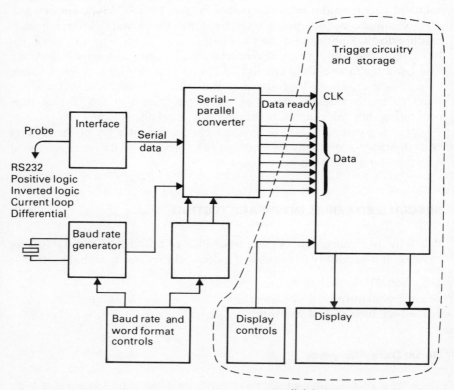

Fig. 7.1   A serial data analyzer   parallel data logic analyzer

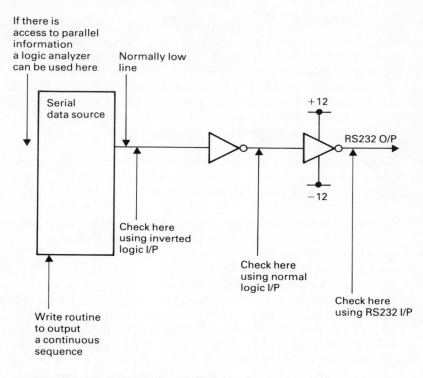

Fig. 7.2 Tracing serial data in a system

Special Purpose Data Generators

To reduce the number of unknowns when testing a faulty serial transmission system, it is useful to have a stand-alone device which can generate known streams of data with selectable baud rates and character formats. Such character generators are useful for checking links to peripherals since they can indicate whether the fault lies in the link and peripheral or in the microprocessor system. They can also be used to inject data into an input to check system response to known data streams. When a purpose built data generator is not available a VDU with keyboard can be used. Character generators usually have a number of user selectable tests in addition to the baud rate, parity and character format functions. Typical tests include:

1   The printable characters of the ASCII set usually in 80 column format with the option of using 132 column format. Printable characters are used so that the results can be read if used to test a display device such as a printer.

2   U*U* tests – These two ASCII characters have complementary
     binary patterns and adjacent bits are different. An alternating
     sequence of these two characters produces a serial pattern with a
     greater number of bit changes than any other using printable charac-
     ters and will be a good way of exercising input hardware or software,
     which may have a synchronizing fault since this is a worst-case pattern
     for this problem. The alternative when binary information is trans-
     mitted is to send AAH alternatively with 55H.

3   Single selected character or binary pattern. The facility to transmit a
     given data byte either singly or continuously can be used if a
     particular pattern is known to cause problems.

4   In systems with input buffers and handshaking lines which indicate
     when the buffer is full, it is useful to have some kind of test which
     quickly fills this buffer. Since a printer for example usually takes
     longer to line feed than to print a character, the buffer will fill more
     quickly when the number of line feeds is a high proportion of the total
     characters transmitted (this also happens during CR in unidirectional
     printers). A test pattern of two printable characters followed by CR
     LF and repeated will ensure that the buffer does fill, and if the printer
     is faulty the printout will exhibit random missing characters. This test
     helps to isolate a fault which could be in the computer output or in
     the printer. (It is also a good way to test the line feed mechanism.)
     The character source must, of course, be designed to stop transmit-
     ting when the buffer full signal is generated and should indicate by
     flashing a lamp when this occurs. The complete character set can be
     used to test an input port which has a small buffer. Fig. 7.3 is a block
     diagram of a typical serial generator.

Back-to-Back Test Software

In this approach the serial input/output facilities of a microcomputer are
exercised using a self-test program to output data in various patterns and to
receive and check the data using an output port on the same system. The
technique can only be used with systems which can transmit and receive
simultaneously, so is not suitable for systems where serial conversion is
done using software routines. The main aim of this kind of test is to
transmit data in sequence which are likely to cause transmission or
reception errors or which can help to isolate a fault to a particular area of
the input/output system. Since serial input/output is usually performed
using some kind of UART, a back-to-back test can also be a UART self-
test. In systems with many input/output lines one UART can be used to
output to any other in the system.

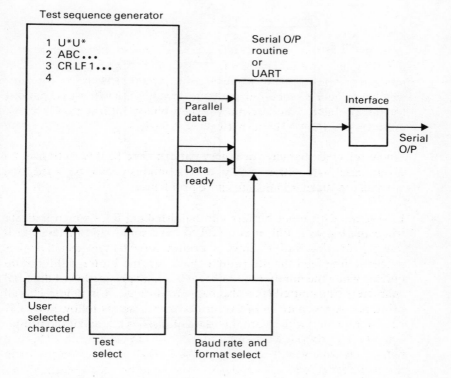

Fig. 7.3 A serial character generator

This kind of test can also be used in conjunction with a serial analyzer, to help locate the fault – for example if the back-to-back test fails because the transmitter is not functioning. Connecting an analyzer to the output can indicate if this is the case. Fig. 7.4 shows such an arrangement.

SUMMARY

Faults in serial communications systems include those introduced by users in changing some feature of the hardware or software. Checks on the cabling and connectors should precede more detailed testing with data generators and analyzers. The patterns generated will include printable characters of the ASCII set to check display devices and printers, and timing tests to identify synchronization problems.

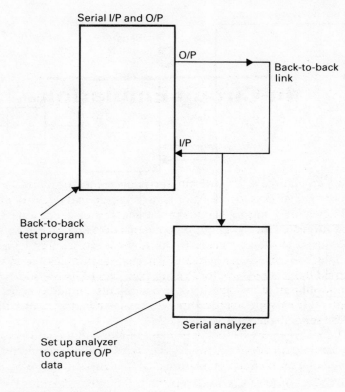

Fig. 7.4   A back-to-back test

8
In-Circuit Emulation

In-circuit emulation is a powerful servicing technique allowing the test engineer to gain access to a microprocessor system that does not respond to normal keyboard control. The technique finds its origin as a development tool and forms one of the major components on Microprocessor Development Systems. However, recent trends have led to several devices aimed primarily at the servicing engineer. This chapter outlines the basic principles behind the technique before giving examples of its use and capabilities in both development and servicing environments. In addition, as outlined in Chapter 11, existing microcomputers can be adapted to provide such a tool in the servicing laboratory.

The microprocessor socket usually provides all the address, data and control bus lines needed to gain access to most of a microcomputer system. The technique of in-circuit emulation (ICE) makes use of this by removing the processor from the unit under test and imitating or emulating its functions using another computer. Fig. 8.1 illustrates the principle. The

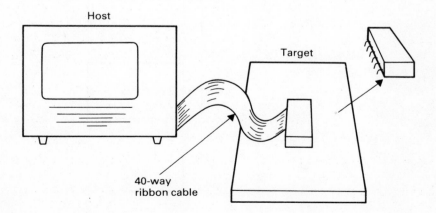

Fig. 8.1 In-circuit emulation

host system is connected to the unit under test (target) through a dual in-line plug and ribbon cable. Normally the host computer uses a similar microprocessor to that removed from the target to provide all the signals that are required by the target system. At first glance it might seem pointless to remove the original microprocessor only to replace it by another in the host. However, the technique allows the host to get between the target system and its microprocessor enabling it to monitor bus activity or to inject signals into the target system.

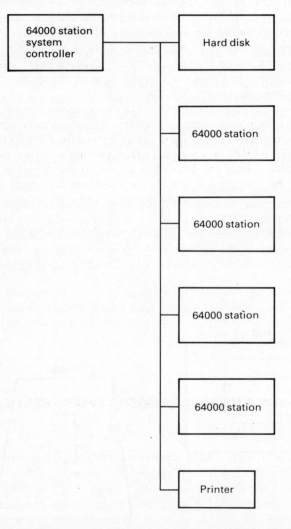

Fig. 8.2   HP 64000 Multiuser Development System (hard disk/hardware and software stations interconnected on HPIB interface bus)

ICE AS A DEVELOPMENT TOOL

The technique was first introduced by INTEL on their microprocessor development system (MDS) to help debug hardware and software problems encountered during the development phase of a project. Early development systems were software oriented, providing editors, assemblers, linkers and to a limited extent some facility to execute and debug the final machine code. However, to test hardware and software effectively it was necessary to commit the final code to EPROM before transferring it to the unit under development. Any further debugging that was required was now carried out using a logic analyzer. If faults were discovered the engineer returned to the development system to update the software before programming a new EPROM.

The introduction of ICE into microprocessor development systems shortened this time-consuming procedure, allowing the design engineer to run the system under development directly from the MDS, eliminating the need to use EPROMs as a means of transporting software into the target system. Further, since the MDS has access to the target system's buses during program execution it can also be used as a debugging tool. To help with this task most microprocessor development systems provide on-board logic analyzer functions.

To describe a 'typical' microprocessor development system is almost a contradiction in terms. The range of options is wide and the terminology of particular manufacturers may differ substantially. Instead this section picks a specific system and uses it to illustrate the kind of functions and characteristics available for in-circuit emulation. The example chosen is the Hewlett–Packard 64000 which can deal with the majority of standard 8-bit and 16-bit microprocessors. Other systems are available from the major microprocessor manufacturers.

EMULATION ON A MICROPROCESSOR DEVELOPMENT SYSTEM

The Hewlett–Packard 64000 development system provides the design engineer with a multiuser, hard disk based system capable of supporting a wide range of microprocessor families (Fig. 8.2). Multiuser capability greatly eases the problem of integrating the software produced by a team of development engineers, allowing different parts of a project to be developed independently and yet allowing them to be shared between members of the team.

In common with most microprocessor development systems it provides software aids including the following:

Editor   – to write source programs either in assembly language or
high level languages.
Assemblers – to generate code from assembly language.
Compilers   – to generate code from a high level language, in this case
Pascal.
Linker   – to link program modules.

Hardware options include:

In-circuit emulators.
Eprom programmers.
Logic analyzers – both state and timing.

Fig. 8.3 shows the configuration of a typical hardware station equipped to
perform in-circuit emulation and trace or logic analysis on a target system.

The emulation capability is powerful, allowing it not only to take the
role of the microprocessor but also to:

– produce a system clock for the target system;
– take the place of all or some of the ROM and RAM on the target
   board;
– simulate input or output devices.

Fig. 8.4 gives examples of possible emulation configurations between the
two systems. In Fig. 8.4 (a) the host system takes on the job of imitating

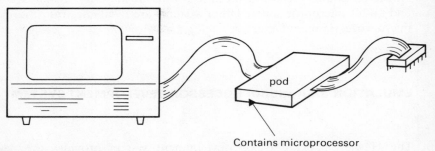

Contains microprocessor

Hardware station may contain
● Emulation control board
● Analysis board
● Emulation memory control board
● Emulation memory

Fig. 8.3   Typical hardware station

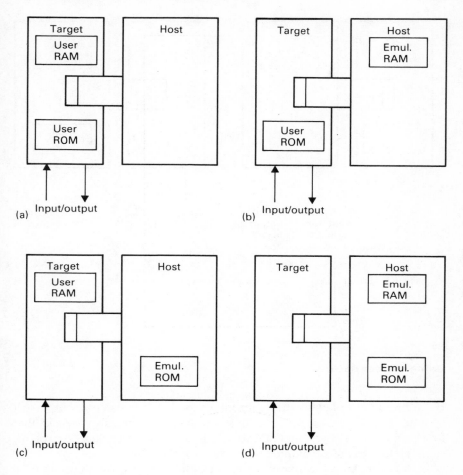

Fig. 8.4 Possible emulation configurations

the microprocessor only. All the memory used by the target system lies on the target board (termed user memory). Fig. 8.4 (c) illustrates how the memory map of the target system can be made up of its own hardware, user RAM, and memory from the host system, emulation ROM.

Finally, Fig. 8.5 shows how the peripheral devices to the 64000, namely disk, keyboard, printer, etc., can be used to simulate input and output signals to the target system.

This flexibility has led to the description 'soft machine', since it can be easily configured to imitate part or all of a target microcomputer system.

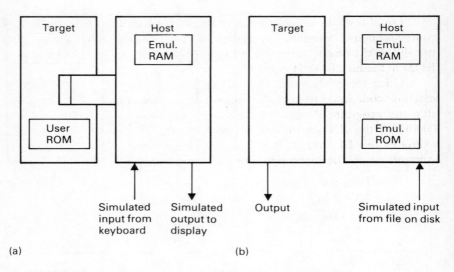

Fig. 8.5   Emulation configurations using simulated input/output

Using the emulator

Before emulation begins, the appropriate pod is connected to the target system. The emulation probe in this case has an identical pinout to that found on the Z80 processor and carries all the address/data and control bus signals between the development and the target system.

After making the hardware connection the operator then enters a configuration phase in which the host asks a series of questions about the target micro to determine how much of the system has to be emulated, e.g.

– Do you wish to use the processor clock on the target board or do you wish me to supply one?
– Do you wish to run at full speed always or can I slow down to do clever things? e.g. examine registers or examine user memory during a run.
– Do you wish me to flag an error if I meet an illegal op-code?
– Tell me the range of emulation ROM and emulation RAM you require.
– Tell me the range of user ROM and user RAM that will be used in the target system.
– Do you wish to simulate I/O? If so what type of simulation do you want?

Fig. 8.6 shows an example configuration for emulation with the Z80 controller board described in Appendix 2. The emulator has been set up to use the RAM on the target board (8000H–83FFH) and to use emulation ROM in the host (0000H–0FFFH).

Once the configuration is complete the operator can then load the machine code into either the emulation or user memory and run or single step the program. Program 8.1 gives an example routine with origin at 0000H in the Z80 board's memory map. When running, the program exercises the 1K byte of RAM on the board, sequentially changing the contents of all the memory locations from 00 to 01 to 02 . . . FFH, etc.

```
        Emulation and User Memory Assignment
        −000 −400 −800 −C00        −000 −400 −800 −C00

0 − − −  EROM EROM         8 − − −  URAM
1 − − −                    9 − − −
2 − − −                    A − − −
3 − − −                    B − − −
4 − − −                    C − − −
5 − − −                    D − − −
6 − − −                    E − − −
7 − − −                    F − − −
```

Record # 2   size = 128
Configuring Z80 processor in slot # 9. Memory slot # 7. Analysis slot # 8.
Processor clock: external
Clock speed greater than wait threshold: no
Restrict processor to real time runs: no
Stop processor in illegal opcodes: no
Simulate I/O: no

Fig. 8.6 Example emulation configuration for Z80 controller board

```
>FILE: CHANGE:HONEY        HEWLETT−PACKARD: Z80 Assembler

LOCATION OBJECT CODE LINE    SOURCE LINE

                           1  "Z80"
                           2  ****************************************
                           3  * CHANGE   SAMPLE PROGRAM FOR EMULATION
                           4  *
                           5  *         PROGRAM WRITES 00,01,02 ....FF
                           6  *         INTO ALL LOCATIONS  BETWEEN
                           7  *         8000H AND 83FFH
                           8  ****************************************
                           9  *
                           10              ORG        000H
0000 0600                  11              LD         B,00H       ;B REG CONTAINS NUMBER
0002 218000                12 NEXT         LD         HL,8000H    ;USE HL AS POINTER TO LOCATION
0005 70                    13 AGAIN        LD         [HL],B      ;WRITE CONTENTS OF B INTO LOCATION.
0006 3EFF                  14              LD         A,0FFH      ;A MARKS THE LAST VALUE OF L
0008 23                    15              INC        HL          ;NEXT LOCATION
0009 BD                    16              CP         L           ;HAS L REACHED FFH
000A C20005                17              JP         NZ,AGAIN    ;IF NOT NEXT LOCATION
000D 3E83                  18              LD         A,83H       ;A MARKS LAST VALUE OF H
000F BC                    19              CP         H           ;HAS H REACHED 83
0010 C20005                20              JP         NZ,AGAIN    ;IF NOT NEXT LOCATION
0013 70                    21              LD         [HL],B      ;LAST LOCATION
0014 04                    22              INC        B           ;NEXT VALUE FOR STORING
0015 C30002                23              JP         NEXT        ;REPEAT FOR NEW VALUE
```

Program 8.1 Example program CHANGE exercises all RAM locations between 8000H and 83FFH

During program execution the operator can examine either the contents of memory or the internal registers of the Z80. For example the command

'display memory 8000H'

would give a 'snapshot' picture of the RAM being exercised (Fig. 8.7). If the command were altered to

'display memory 8000H dynamic'

the display would give a 'movie picture' of the memory, presenting a dynamic display of the memory contents (Fig. 8.8). However, during this

```
MEMORY
Adr      – – – – Data (hex) – – – – –        –(ASCII)–
8000   6B   6B   6B   6B     6B   6B   6B   6B     kkkk    kkkk
8008   6B   6B   6B   6B     6B   6B   6B   6B     kkkk    kkkk
8010   6B   6B   6B   6B     6B   6B   6B   6B     kkkk    kkkk
8018   6B   6B   6B   6B     6B   6B   6B   6B     kkkk    kkkk
8020   6B   6B   6B   6B     6B   6B   6B   6B     kkkk    kkkk
8028   6B   6B   6B   6B     6B   6B   6B   6B     kkkk    kkkk
8030   6B   6B   6B   6B     6B   6B   6B   6B     kkkk    kkkk
8038   6B   6B   6B   6B     6B   6B   6B   6B     kkkk    kkkk
8040   6B   6B   6B   6B     6B   6B   6B   6B     kkkk    kkkk
8048   6B   6B   6B   6B     6B   6B   6B   6B     kkkk    kkkk
8050   6B   6B   6B   6B     6B   6B   6B   6B     kkkk    kkkk
8058   6B   6B   6B   6B     6B   6B   6B   6B     kkkk    kkkk
8060   6B   6B   6B   6B     6B   6B   6B   6B     kkkk    kkkk
8068   6B   6B   6B   6B     6B   6B   6B   6B     kkkk    kkkk
8070   6B   6B   6B   6B     6B   6B   6B   6B     kkkk    kkkk
8078   6B   6B   6B   6B     6B   6B   6B   6B     kkkk    kkkk
```

Fig. 8.7   Example memory display
('display memory 8000H')

display the host system would default from a full speed run to a pseudo run, stopping the processor periodically to enter and examine the user memory. Finally Fig. 8.9 shows how the display command can be used to present memory contents in a disassembled or mnemonic format.

The power of the display command when debugging a program can be seen in Fig. 8.10 where the entire contents of the processor's internal registers are displayed at each program step.

Trace analysis

The development system offers many analysis options ranging from a purely software logic analyzer that monitors the emulator's address, data and control buses through to plug-in cards supporting real-time state and timing analysis.

MEMORY— –DYNAMIC

Adr	— — — — Data (hex) — — — —								–(ASCII)–
8000	00	00	00	00	00	00	00	00	
8008	00	00	00	00	00	00	00	00	
8010	00	00	00	00	00	00	00	00	
8018	00	00	00	00	00	00	00	00	
8020	00	00	00	00	00	00	00	FF	
8028	FF	FF	FF	FF	FF	FF	FF	FF	# # # # # # # #
8030	FF	FF	FF	FF	FF	FF	FF	FF	# # # # # # # #
8038	FF	FF	FF	FF	FF	FF	FF	FF	# # # # # # # #
8040	FF	FF	FF	FF	FF	FF	FF	FF	# # # # # # # #
8048	FF	FF	FF	FF	FF	FF	FF	FF	# # # # # # # #
8050	FF	FF	FF	FF	FF	FF	FF	FF	# # # # # # # #
8058	FF	FF	FF	FF	FF	FF	FF	FF	# # # # # # # #
8060	FF	FF	FF	FF	FF	FF	FF	FF	# # # # # # # #
8068	FF	FF	FF	FF	FF	FF	FF	FF	# # # # # # # #
8070	FF	FF	FF	FF	FF	FF	FF	FF	# # # # # # # #
8078	FF	FF	FF	FF	FF	FF	FF	FF	# # # # # # # #

Fig. 8.8 Example memory display
('display memory 8000H dynamic')

```
MEMORY
0000H    LD    B, 00H
0002H    LD    HL, 8000H
0005H    LD    [HL], B
0006H    LD    A, FFH
0008H    INC   HL
0009H    CP    L
000AH    JP    NZ, 0005H
000DH    LD    A, 83H
000FH    CP    H
0010H    JP    NZ, 0005H
0013H    LD    [HL], B
0014H    INC   B
0015H    JP    0002H
0018H    LD    E, [HL]
0019H    LD    A, L
001AH    LD    B, C
```

Fig. 8.9 Display in mnemonics
('display memory 0006H mnemonic')

The analysis board gives a hardware station a real-time state analyzer capable of recording:

8 data bus lines
16 data bus lines
8 status or control lines (Fig. 8.11)

for 256 states. Basically three strategies can be used to fill the trace buffer (Fig. 8.12).

REGISTER (Hex)

pc	opcode		a	b c	d e	h l	i	ix	iy	sp	szxhxpnc	nxt-pc
0000	06	LD B, 00H	FF	00FF	FFFF	82C7	00	FFFF	7FFF	00FF	00000010	0002
0002	21	LD HL, 8000H	FF	00FF	FFFF	8000	00	FFFF	7FFF	00FF	00000010	0005
0005	70	LD [HL], B	FF	00FF	FFFF	8000	00	FFFF	7FFF	00FF	00000010	0006
0006	3E	LD A, FFH	FF	00FF	FFFF	8000	00	FFFF	7FFF	00FF	00000010	0008
0008	23	INC HL	FF	00FF	FFFF	8001	00	FFFF	7FFF	00FF	00000010	0009
0009	BD	CP L	FF	00FF	FFFF	8001	00	FFFF	7FFF	00FF	10000010	000A
000A	C2	JP NZ, 0005H	FF	00FF	FFFF	8001	00	FFFF	7FFF	00FF	10000010	0005
0005	70	LD [HL], B	FF	00FF	FFFF	8001	00	FFFF	7FFF	00FF	10000010	0006
0006	3E	LD A, FFH	FF	00FF	FFFF	8001	00	FFFF	7FFF	00FF	10000010	0008
0008	23	INC HL	FF	00FF	FFFF	8002	00	FFFF	7FFF	00FF	10000010	0009
0009	BD	CP L	FF	00FF	FFFF	8002	00	FFFF	7FFF	00FF	10000010	000A
000A	C2	JP NZ, 0005H	FF	00FF	FFFF	8002	00	FFFF	7FFF	00FF	10000010	0005
0005	70	LD [HL], B	FF	00FF	FFFF	8002	00	FFFF	7FFF	00FF	10000010	0006
0006	3E	LD A, FFH	FF	00FF	FFFF	8002	00	FFFF	7FFF	00FF	10000010	0008
0008	23	INC HL	FF	00FF	FFFF	8003	00	FFFF	7FFF	00FF	10000010	0009
0009	BD	CP L	FF	00FF	FFFF	8003	00	FFFF	7FFF	00FF	10000010	000A

Fig. 8.10   Displaying the processor's registers

1   'Trace about' a trigger event where the buffer records 128 events before the trigger and 128 events after the trigger.
2   'Trace before' the trigger event.
3   'Trace after' the trigger event.

A fourth option, 'trace only' for a particular event, will enter only those events meeting the trigger condition into the trace buffer. With this option the trigger position defaults to a 'trace after' strategy to fill the buffer.

The definition of a trigger event or more completely the 'trace specification' gives the operator the ability to record the particular sequence of events where trouble is suspected. Figs. 8.13–8.15 show a variety of trace specifications ranging from the simple 'trace after address = 8000H' to the complex 'trace in sequence data = 0AAH trigger after address = 8000H'.

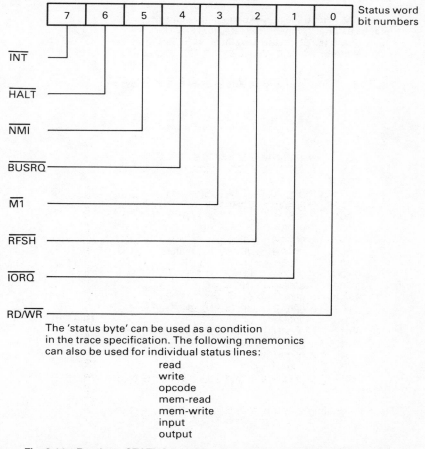

The 'status byte' can be used as a condition in the trace specification. The following mnemonics can also be used for individual status lines:

read
write
opcode
mem-read
mem-write
input
output

Fig. 8.11   Emulator STATUS byte (the state of some of the Z80 control lines is reported as a status byte by the analyzer)

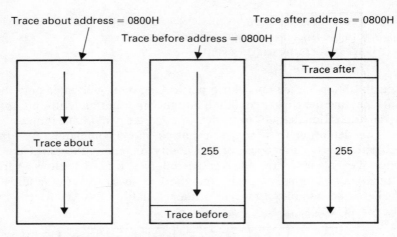

Trace only: With trace only the trigger position
defaults to 'after'. Only those states that
satisfy the stated condition are placed in
the trace buffer.

Fig. 8.12   Different trigger positions used by the analyzer

trace after address = 8000H

```
TRACE
        ADDRESS, DATA, STATUS
AFTER   8000H   E2H   3FH
+001    0006H   LD    A, FFH
+002    0008H   INC   HL
+003    0009H   CP    L
+004    000AH   JP    NZ, 0005H
+005    0005H   LD    [HL], B         [HL] E2H
+006    0006H   LD    A, FFH
+007    0008H   INC   HL
+008    0009H   CP    L
+009    000AH   JP    NZ, 0005H
+010    0005H   LD    [HL], B         [HL] E2H
+011    0006H   LD    A, FFH
+012    0008H   INC   HL
+013    0009H   CP    L
+014    000AH   JP    NZ, 0005H
+015    0005H   LD    [HL], B         [HL] E2H
```

Fig. 8.13   Example trace

trace only address = 8000H or address = 8100H

```
TRACE
     ADDRESS, DATA, STATUS
AFTER    0007H    FFH    3EH
+001     8000H    42H    3FH
+002     8100H    42H    3FH
+003     8000H    43H    3FH
+004     8100H    43H    3FH
+005     8000H    44H    3FH
+006     8100H    44H    3FH
+007     8000H    45H    3FH
+008     8100H    45H    3FH
+009     8000H    46H    3FH
+010     8100H    46H    3FH
+011     8000H    47H    3FH
+012     8100H    47H    3FH
+013     8000H    48H    3FH
+014     8100H    48H    3FH
+015     8000H    49H    3FH
```

Fig. 8.14   Example trace

trace in—sequence data = 0AAH trigger after address = 8000H

```
TRACE
     ADDRESS, DATA, STATUS
SEQN     8000H    AAH    3FH
AFTER    8000H    ABH    3FH
+001     0006H    LD     A, FFH
+002     0008H    INC    HL
+003     0009H    CP     L
+004     000AH    JP     NZ, 0005H
+005     0005H    LD     [HL], B          [HL] ABH
+006     0006H    LD     A, FFH
+007     0008H    INC    HL
+008     0009H    CP     L
+009     000AH    JP     NZ, 0005H
+010     0005H    LD     [HL], B          [HL] ABH
+011     0006H    LD     A, FFH
+012     0008H    INC    HL
+013     0009H    CP     L
+014     000AH    JP     NZ, 0005H
```

Fig. 8.15   Example trace

ICE AS A FAULT FINDING TOOL

A microprocessor development system offers an extremely powerful fault-finding tool, but the number of service personnel with access to this type of equipment is limited. Other factors, including physical size and the need for skilled operators as well as price, rule out the MDS as a routine service tool. However, several manufacturers, including Applied Microsystems, Fluke, Hewlett–Packard, Millenium and Solartron, have marketed stand-alone emulators, some of which are more appropriate to the serviceman's needs.

To the service engineer, in-circuit emulation provides a method of gaining control of the unit under test, and injecting test or stimulus programs onto its buses. This is important if the unit under test does not respond to normal keyboard operation or perhaps does not contain a keyboard. Once in control the emulator can run routines to check the operation of the target system's functional components using routines similar to those employed in self-testing. If faults are discovered, the emulator's display reports its location giving the serviceman clues to the possible source of trouble. The Fluke troubleshooter, described in Chapter 10, is an example of this type of emulator. However, not all emulators contain a keyboard and a display. For example the Solartron Micropod is designed to be used with test software developed on another machine and loaded into the emulator in EPROM. The test routines exercise the target system, generating data streams that are monitored using a signature analyzer.

Recent market developments have seen the appearance of stand-alone emulators that provide many of the functions found on an MDS at a fraction of the cost. An example of these is Microtek's 'Micro-In-Circuit Emulator' (MICE). A range of personality cards allow it to emulate most industry standard microprocessors, both 8- and 16-bit. Models differ in the size of the emulation RAM and the trace facilities, with real-time trace as an advanced option. They are controlled via an RS232 interface, using either a display terminal or a computer system with a compatible port.

Driving a stand-alone emulator from VDU would only be satisfactory for short test routines (e.g. the check RAM or form signatures of ROM using its on-board test programs). The functions include a line assembler, useful for small routines or when patching a larger piece of software, and a two-pass disassembler that generates labels for all subroutine and jump instructions – a nice touch not found even in expensive systems.

Serious applications, however, would utilize a host computer system allowing test programs generated by assemblers or compilers to be down-loaded, in either Intel or Tektronix format, to the emulation memory. When a host system is used it requires a driver program to communicate with the emulator. A range of routines is provided by the manufacturer for some popular systems, including CP/M and Apple microcomputers and DEC minicomputers.

Trace facilities are good, allowing the operator to perform a real-time forward or backward trace capturing address, data and processor status information in a massive 2048 word buffer. However, the triggering is less sophisticated in that it is restricted primarily to address and status trigger events.

These examples illustrate two different approaches – the development system that includes in-circuit emulation as one of its functions, and the stand-alone emulator driven by a microcomputer for lower cost. In fact the stand-alone units can be more useful in some applications because they contain test routines in the firmware, i.e. stored in ROM.

SUMMARY

Systems can be forced to execute a program under the control of an external host system that takes over the CPU functions of the target. The bus, memory and I/O behavior can all be monitored by the host even if the target has no input device or one that is faulty. In-circuit emulation is available on microprocessor development systems and on stand-alone units, with real-time tracing as an option on many systems.

9
Signature Analysis

The traditional approach to fault finding in an analog system is to produce an annotated schematic that clearly shows the voltage levels and waveforms expected at different points within the circuit (Fig. 9.1). By comparing voltmeter readings and oscilloscope traces with those given on the diagram, a serviceman can detect faults and make repairs without a detailed knowledge of the circuit. Adopting the same approach with digital circuits meets with several problems. Neither voltmeters nor oscilloscopes yield such useful information: voltage levels lie at either 0 V or +5 V, waveforms are long, complex and have a random appearance that makes all data streams look much alike.

Clearly what is required is an instrument capable of recording these complex data streams and yet able to present them to the serviceman in a

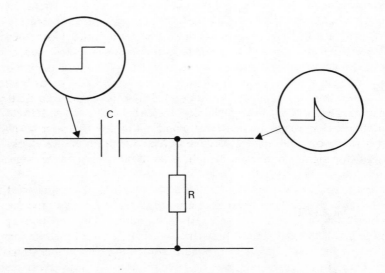

Fig. 9.1 Conventional annotated schematic showing expected waveforms at circuit nodes

compact form. The signature analyzer fills this role ideally. Like the oscilloscope, it monitors the logic activity at a circuit node, but instead of replaying a picture of this activity it produces a four digit code or signature to represent the data stream. The signature itself has no meaning and serves only as a token representing the pattern of logic 1s and 0s forming the data stream. If the pattern changes, by even one bit, the signature changes.

Using signature analysis, an annotated schematic for a digital circuit might look like Fig. 9.2. Instead of voltages and sample waveforms, each circuit node is labelled with a signature that characterizes the data stream at that point.

In microprocessor based systems the activity at a circuit node, and hence the signature, will depend on the program being executed. An integral part of signature analysis is the stimulus or test program that exercises circuit components and nodes generating data streams. Only limited information can be obtained from a circuit node that remains in one state. The stimulus program should ensure that circuit nodes are switched between logic 0 and logic 1 creating meaningful data streams that reflect the system's performance.

THE SIGNATURE ANALYZER

The function of the signature analyzer is to monitor the logic levels at some point in a circuit and produce a code or signature that characterizes the activity at that point. Fig. 9.3 shows the layout of a typical instrument. In operation five connections are made to the circuit under test. Data from the selected node enters the analyzer directly through the data probe; the other connections start, stop, clock and ground are made via an external pod. As with the logic analyzer a clock signal is used to strobe data into the signature analyzer. Typically clock frequencies between dc and 10 MHz are acceptable and switches on the front panel allow the operator to choose either a rising or a falling edge as the active transition of the clock. The start and stop signals define the length of the data stream or the 'signature window'.

At the heart of the instrument lies a 16-bit shift register with feedback (Fig. 9.4). On receipt of a valid start signal the register is reset to zero and data is shifted in using the selected clock edge. The feedback paths scramble the data entering the register and ensure that all the bits forming the data stream, not just the last sixteen, contribute to the final signature. On receipt of a stop signal the 16 bits remaining in the register are displayed in a hexadecimal format to give the signature of the observed data stream.

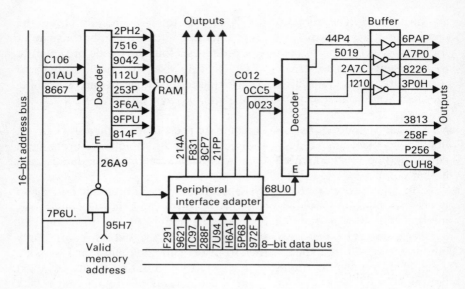

Fig. 9.2 Signatures displayed on digital annotated schematic

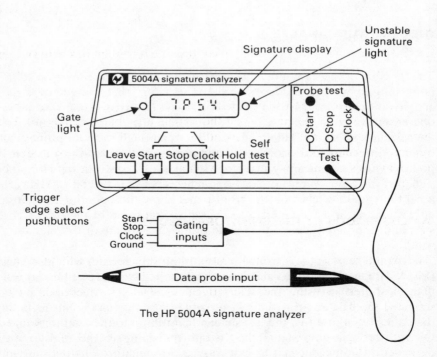

The HP 5004 A signature analyzer

Fig. 9.3 Signature analyzer with connections for unit under test

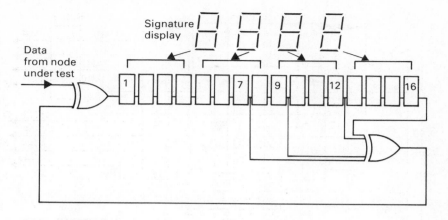

Fig. 9.4   16-bit feedback register used in signature analyzer

A nonstandard hexadecimal character set, 0 1 2 3 4 5 6 7 8 9 A C F H P U, is used to display the signature code. This set has two advantages over the standard code:

1   Each character can easily be reproduced on a seven-segment LED display with none of the confusion between 6 and small b or 8 and capital B found in the standard set.

2   The operator is not tempted to confuse the four-digit hex with system addresses or to work backwards from the signature in search of further information.

In the instrument as illustrated, indicators labelled 'gate' and 'unstable signature' give information on the signals used by the analyzer. The gate indicator shows when the window opens and closes, flashing for repeated opening and closing. The unstable signature indicator flashes if the signatures obtained in successive windows differ.

A CLOSER LOOK AT THE SIGNATURE WINDOW

The signature window is controlled by the three inputs 'start', 'stop' and 'clock'. In operation these signals can be provided by the circuit under test. To allow flexibility the active or trigger edges for each signal can be selected by the controls on the front panel of the analyzer. Normally the clock edge is chosen to define a time when data is stable on the selected node. The logic state of the node is sampled only at the clock edge and ignored at all other times. The clock is also used together with the start and stop signals to define the signature window or gate. Fig. 9.5 shows that a

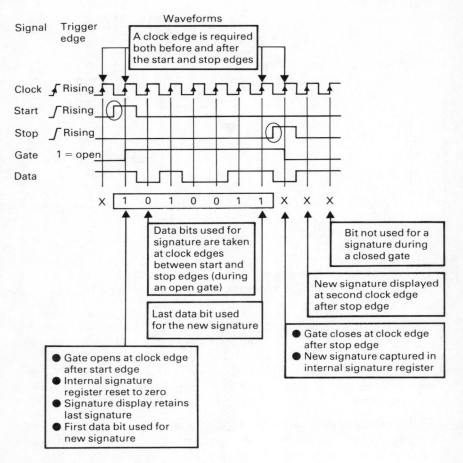

Fig. 9.5 Forming the signature window

clock edge is required both before and after the start and stop edges for the instrument to detect the change in state of these inputs.

Notice the window opens not at the start edge but at the clock edge following the start edge. In the same manner the window closes at the clock edge following the stop edge. The first piece of data to enter the shift register occurs at the first clock edge following the start edge. The final data bit is clocked into the analyzer by the clock edge prior to the stop edge.

Gating signals must be chosen with care to ensure proper opening and closing of the signature window. The diagrams given in Figs. 9.6 and 9.7 illustrate the problems that can arise from a bad choice. One improvement is to provide two triggering modes to ease the problem of forming the signature window. The normal mode requires a clock edge before and after the change in state of the start and stop signal. However, if suitable long-duration start and stop signals are not available an alternative mode allows triggering with signals less than one-half cycle of the clock. Although this situation is less satisfactory (random pulses could cause spurious gating leading to unstable signatures) it may be the only method by which signatures can be obtained from the system under test.

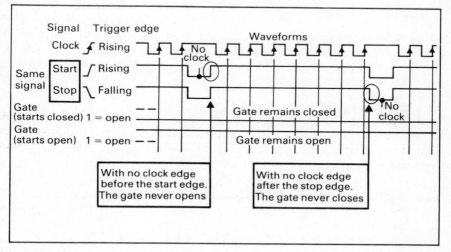

(a)

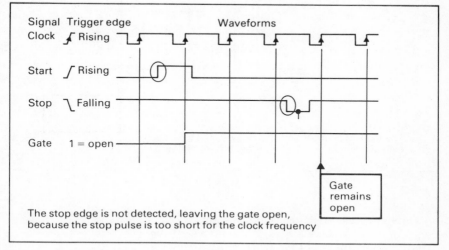

(b)

Fig. 9.6 Problems that can arise with a bad choice of signature windows
  (a) No clock before or after the START or STOP edge
  (b) The START or STOP pulse is too short for the CLOCK frequency

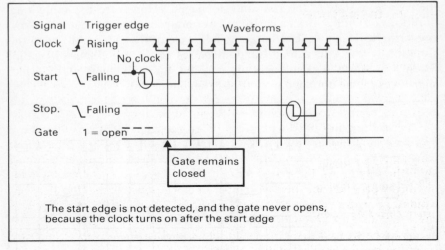

(a)

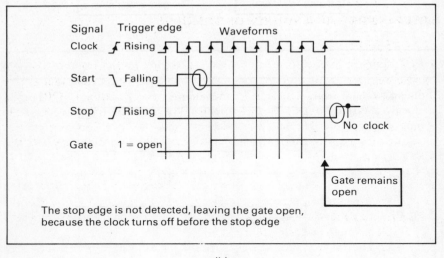

(b)

Fig. 9.7   Problems with signature windows
        (a) The CLOCK turns on after the START edge
        (b) The CLOCK turns off before the STOP edge

Vcc, Vss SIGNATURES

A look in some detail at how the analyzer deals with two simple data streams should help to illustrate the function of the feedback shift register. Consider first a 'data stream' constantly at ground potential. At each clock edge a logic 0 enters the analyzer. As the feedback mechanism is also delivering logic 0s to the exclusive OR gate at the input of the shift register the register remains filled with zeros. Therefore the signature of a node at ground potential is always 0000. If, however, the probe monitors a point constantly at logic 1 the contents of the register will change as the feedback algorithm alters the bit stream entering the register. The final signature obviously depends only on the number of clock pulses within the signature window. For this reason the Vcc signature is often used as a preliminary check on the gate to ensure that the correct number of clock edges are occurring between the start and stop signals before proceeding to measurements on more complicated data streams.

FREE RUNNING AS A SOURCE OF STIMULUS

Free running a microprocessor provides a simple method of exercising a microcomputer circuit (see Chapter 4). In the following example a Z80 is induced to free run by 'hardwiring' the code for no operation (NOP) on its data bus pins. Fig. 4.2 shows how this is achieved. The microprocessor is removed from its socket and a test module, with the NOP code hardwired, is placed between the Z80 and the main board. The module provides the following functions.

1   Disconnects the microprocessor from the system data bus, preventing it from executing the system program.
2   Provides the NOP code at every address, forcing the processor to cycle through its entire address range.
3   The address and control pins remain connected, to exercise the address bus and any address decode circuitry on the board.

After reset, the processor reads the NOP code, upon which it increments ·the program counter and the address bus to attempt a read operation at the next location. As NOP appears at each address, the microprocessor cycles through its entire address range, exercises the address decode circuitry and draws data from the ROM and RAM chips onto the data bus. The resulting data streams are suitable for testing by signature analysis.

AN EXAMPLE – Z80 CONTROLLER BOARD

This example illustrates the use of a free-run test module with the Z80
controller board (as outlined in Appendix 2) to implement signature
analysis, describing the signals used by the analyzer. It covers the prepara-
tion of the documentation that forms the basis of future testing.

Address Bus – Decode Logic Signatures

Address bus line A15 provides the start and stop signals for the signature
window. Fig. 9.8 shows its behavior as the processor increments through its
address range (the effect of refresh has been omitted). On reading address
8000H, A15 toggles high and remains high until FFFFH after which it falls
low at the start of a new scan. Choosing falling edges for the start and stop
signals defines a signature window in which the processor places all
possible addresses on the bus.

With the Z80, the falling edge of the $\overline{RD}$ strobe defines a time at
which the address is established and stable. Using it as the clock input for
the analyzer ensures that only valid addresses are seen by the analyzer. (It
is worth noting that the $\overline{RD}$ line is not activated during a refresh operation,
and signatures produced using this clock will exclude any bus activity due
to refresh.)

The address bus and decode logic signatures obtained are shown in
Fig. 9.9. This style of signature documentation offers an alternative to the
annotated schematic. It includes details of the stimulus exercising the
circuit, the signals used for clock, start and stop and the configuration of
the analyzer. The Vcc signature is given at the start of the table: the ground
signature is always 0000. Next to each circuit node are listed the component pins connected to that node and their characteristic signature.

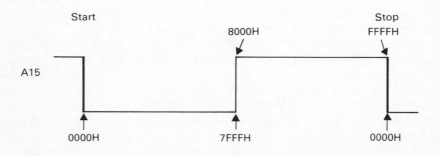

Fig. 9.8 Address line A15 provides the signature window for the free-run
address bus signatures

MEDC Signature Report Form　　　　　　　　Title: Free run – Z80 Board

Function	Start	Stop	Clock	Mode	Vcc sign	Start ID	Stop ID	Clock ID
				1	0001	Z80 P (A15)	Z80 P (A15)	Z80 P ($\overline{RD}$)

Clock qualifier : N/A

Node	Circuit ID	Circuit ID	Circuit ID	Circuit ID	Circuit ID	Signature
•	•	•			•	2H70
	•	•	•	•	•	HPPO
•	•	Z2–18				1293
A12	Z1–2					HAP7
A13	Z1–3					3C96
A14	Z1–4					3827
A15	Z1–5	Z9–13				755U

Fig. 9.9　Z80 board free-run signatures

ROM Signatures

In the free-run mode, the microprocessor attempts to read every possible address, drawing information from the system memory on to the data bus and generating data streams that characterize memory contents. The break in the data bus formed by the free-run module prevents any of this information reaching the processor and also separates the NOP code at the processor from the system bus. However, before taking signatures on the data bus two changes are required. Firstly, to observe data as opposed to address, the clock used by the analyzer has to be moved to a point later in the Z80 timing cycle, namely to the rising edge of the $\overline{RD}$ strobe. Secondly, allowing the signature window to encompass the processor's reading of the entire 64K would yield signatures formed by ROM and RAM. As there is no simple method of ensuring the system always powers up with the same RAM contents, these signatures would be unrepeatable and therefore useless. However, meaningful signatures can be obtained if the signature window is redefined to enclose only data streams from the system ROM; Fig. 9.10 shows how this is achieved by connecting the start and stop inputs to the chip select signal for the ROM (IC2). A point worth attention is that changing the signature window from the previous test will result in a new value for the Vcc signature.

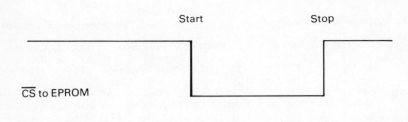

Fig. 9.10   Eprom CS signal forms the signature window for the free-run ROM
signatures

STIMULUS SOFTWARE

Components such as RAM or input/output devices can only be effectively
tested when driven by a stimulus program. Software driven analysis uses
such a program, stored in read-only memory, to write repeatable data
streams onto the data bus and to generate the start/stop signals defining the
signature window.

EXERCISERS AND EMULATORS

The ideal time to implement signature analysis is at the product design
stage. At this point, thought can be given by the engineer to the design of
stimulus software and to the inclusion of any extra hardware that may be
required, e.g. an extra ROM socket, latches to provide start and stop
signals, switches or jumpers to enable ROMS or break feedback paths.
Some systems, notably those from manufacturers of signature analyzers,
do come with signature analysis built in. Unfortunately the majority do
not. This reluctance to implement the technique at the design stage could
stem from many sources such as:

- extra development time required;
- extra hardware cost;
- unfamiliarity with the technique.

Whatever the reasons, failure to include the necessary hardware and
software does not close the door. Existing products can be retrofitted with
the technique. To help with this task, several manufacturers have developed exercisers or emulators that 'inject' stimulus software into the system
under test. A typical example, the Solartron Micropod, is shown in Fig.
9.11.

With both devices the microprocessor is removed from the unit under test (UUT) and connection is made through the processor socket. The processor is then inserted into a zero force insertion socket on the emulator where it can be tested and then used to run stimulus software in the UUT.

Along with their emulation capability, both the exerciser and the Micropod provide other useful test functions, e.g. free-run test fixture, microprocessor test, etc. The following section outlines the principles and operation of the Micropod.

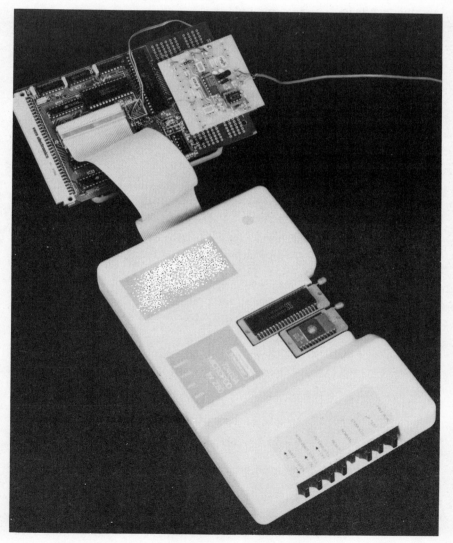

Fig. 9.11 Typical emulator pod

Micropod

A different Micropod is needed for each microprocessor type. A row of pushbuttons on the side of each pod allows the operator to select any of the following functions.

  (A) FREE RUN – The pod contains the necessary hardware to induce the microprocessor to free run, providing stimulus for the data bus, address bus and decode logic on the unit under test.

  (B) MICROPROCESSOR TEST – A stimulus program supplied in ROM inside the Micropod exercises the microprocessor itself. The program uses most of the instruction set and generates characteristic signatures on each pin.

  (C) NORMAL – Selecting this function will allow the unit under test to run its own monitor program after reset.

  (D) STIMULUS – This button selects the emulation function. A second zero force insertion socket is provided to hold an EPROM containing test software.

To ease the problem of finding suitable control signals to define the signature window, a start/stop output is provided under software control. This together with clock and common pins appear at the edge of the pod. To toggle the stop/start output high or low the stimulus program merely has to write to a control address in the pod (F000 in the 6502 and 0000 in the Z80). The least significant bit written to the control address is latched out at the stop/start pin. Hence

        LDA   # XXXX XXX0
        STA   F000H

would toggle the output low, and

        LDA   # XXXX XXX1
        STA   F000H

would set it high.
  When stimulus is selected, the pod overwrites a 4K byte block of memory on the unit under test. With the Z80 version of the pod, any memory addresses between 0000H and 0FFFH set up by the processor do not reach the target system and are instead directed to the stimulus EPROM. In the 6502 pod the stimulus EPROM sits in the top 4K bytes between F000H and FFFFH.

A Stimulus Program for a Single Board Computer

The flowchart of Fig. 9.12 is for the stimulus program (Program 9.1) designed to test the random access memory and user ports on a single board microcomputer (Fig. A2.1, Appendix 2). It was chosen because its straightforward design and range of RAM, ROM and I/O make it convenient for demonstrating this test technique. The program is located in EPROM and designed for operation with the 6502 micropod.

After ensuring the reset vectors FFFCH and FFFDH are set up to point to the start address of the stimulus program, namely F800H, the

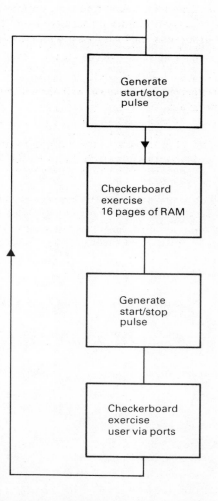

Fig. 9.12 Stimulus flowchart for memory and ports

```
FILE: AIMSIG:AIM            HEWLETT-PACKARD: 6500 FAMILY ASSEMBLER

LOCATION OBJECT CODE LINE      SOURCE LINE
                            1 "650X"
                            2 ****************************************************
                            3 *AIM65 STIMULUS PROGRAM FOR SIGNATURE ANALYSIS.
                            4 *THIS PROGRAM IS DESIGNED TO TEST THE 4K RAM IN
                            5 *THE AIM IN REPETITIVE 255 BYTE BLOCKS.
                            6 *THE VIA I/O PORTS ARE ALSO TESTED.
                            7 ****************************************************
                            8 *
                            9 *FOR COMMENCEMENT OF PROGRAM RESET VECTOR MUST
                           10 *CONTAIN START ADDRESS.
                           11
                           12            ORG      0FFFCH
FFFC 00F8                  13            HEX      00,F8       ;START ADDRESS LOADED
                           14
                           15 ;TEST PATTERN IS 55H THEN AAH WRITTEN TO AND READ
                           16 ;FROM RAM.THIS IS CALLED A CHECKERBOARD PATTERN.
                           17
                           18 ;EQUATE ALL RAM BLOCKS
          (0000)          19 RAMST0     EQU      00000H
          (0100)          20 RAMST1     EQU      00100H
          (0200)          21 RAMST2     EQU      00200H
          (0300)          22 RAMST3     EQU      00300H
          (0400)          23 RAMST4     EQU      00400H
          (0500)          24 RAMST5     EQU      00500H
          (0600)          25 RAMST6     EQU      00600H
          (0700)          26 RAMST7     EQU      00700H
          (0800)          27 RAMST8     EQU      00800H
          (0900)          28 RAMST9     EQU      00900H
          (0A00)          29 RAMSTA     EQU      00A00H
          (0B00)          30 RAMSTB     EQU      00B00H
          (0C00)          31 RAMSTC     EQU      00C00H
          (0D00)          32 RAMSTD     EQU      00D00H
          (0E00)          33 RAMSTE     EQU      00E00H
          (0F00)          34 RAMSTF     EQU      00F00H
                           35            ORG      0F800H
                           36            EXTEND
                           37 ;LOAD ACCUMULATOR WITH 55 TEST DATA
F800 A955                  38            LDA      #055H
                           39 ;CLEAR X REGISTER
F802 A200                  40            LDX      #000H
                           41
                           42 ;START PULSE FOR RAM,STOP FOR VIA
F804 8DF000                43 START      STA      0F000H
                           44
                           45 ;NOW TO TEST RAM 256 BYTES AT A TIME
                           46 ; COMMENCING ON PAGE 0
                           47
F807 9D0000                48 LOOP0      STA      >RAMST0,X ;STORE 01010101B
F80A DD0000                49            CMP      >RAMST0,X ;READ LOCATION
F80D 0A                    50            ASL      A         ;SHIFT LEFT ALL BITS
F80E 9D0000                51            STA      >RAMST0,X ;STORE 10101010B
F811 DD0000                52            CMP      >RAMST0,X ;READ LOCATION
F814 4A                    53            LSR      A         ;SHIFT RIGHT ALL BITS
F815 E8                    54            INX                ;NEXT LOCATION
F816 D0EF                  55            BNE      LOOP0     ;DO FOR 256 BYTES
                           56
                           57 ;DO PAGE 1 NEXT 256 BYTES AS PAGE 0
```

Program 9.1 Stimulus program for RAM and I/O testing   1.

```
LOCATION OBJECT CODE LINE       SOURCE LINE
                       58
       F818 9D0100     59 LOOP1     STA      RAMST1,X
       F81B DD0100     60           CMP      RAMST1,X
       F81E 0A         61           ASL      A
       F81F 9D0100     62           STA      RAMST1,X
       F822 DD0100     63           CMP      RAMST1,X
       F825 4A         64           LSR      A
       F826 E8         65           INX
       F827 D0EF       66           BNE      LOOP1
```

REPEAT FOR PAGES 2-15

```
                      216 ;DO PAGE 15 NEXT 256 BYTES AS PAGE 0
                      217
       F906 9D0F00    218 LOOPF     STA      RAMSTF,X
       F909 DD0F00    219           CMP      RAMSTF,X
       F90C 0A        220           ASL      A
       F90D 9D0F00    221           STA      RAMSTF,X
       F910 DD0F00    222           CMP      RAMSTF,X
       F913 4A        223           LSR      A
       F914 E8        224           INX
       F915 D0EF      225           BNE      LOOPF
                      226 ;THAT IS THE END OF TESTING RAM
                      227 ;NOW GENERATE THE STOP PULSE FOR
                      228 ;RAM WHICH IS START PULES FOR VIA
                      229
       F917 8EF000    230           STX      0F000H
                      231
                      232 ;PORTS CHECK STARTS HERE
                      233
       F91A A9FF      234           LDA      #0FFH
       F91C 8DA003    235           STA      0A003H    ;PORT A AS O/P
       F91F 8DA002    236           STA      0A002H    ;PORT B AS O/P
       F922 A9AA      237           LDA      #0AAH     ;LOAD CHECKERBOARD
       F924 8DA000    238 PORTL1    STA      0A000H    ;STORE 10101010B IN B
       F927 8DA001    239           STA      0A001H    ;STORE 10101010B IN A
       F92A CDA000    240           CMP      0A000H    ;READ PORT B
       F92D CDA001    241           CMP      0A001H    ;READ PORT A
       F930 E8        242           INX                ;DO AGAIN
       F931 D0F1      243           BNE      PORTL1    ;DONE 256 TIMES
       F933 4A        244           LSR      A         ;SHIFT RIGHT 8 BITS
       F934 8DA001    245 PORTL2    STA      0A001H    ;STORE 01010101B IN A
       F937 8DA000    246           STA      0A000H    ;STORE 01010101B IN B
       F93A CDA001    247           CMP      0A001H    ;READ PORT A
       F93D CDA000    248           CMP      0A000H    ;READ PORT B
       F940 E8        249           INX                ;DO AGAIN
       F941 D0F1      250           BNE      PORTL2    ;DONE 256 TIMES
       F943 4CF804    251           JMP      START     ;BEGIN CYCLE AGAIN
```

2.

program begins by driving the start/stop pin low with a dummy write to the control address F000H. Each of the board's RAM locations is then exercised using a checkerboard pattern, writing and reading 55H and AAH. The program may appear clumsy since it utilizes neither subroutine calls nor indirect addressing. This avoidance if intentional as these operations rely on the correct functioning of both page 0 and page 1, i.e. including areas of memory the test itself is meant to validate. On completing RAM stimulus, the program toggles the start/stop pin high and then performs a similar checkerboard test of the two user ports before returning to the start to repeat the whole procedure.

The start/stop signal effectively defines two signature windows: the first encompassing the RAM test and the second the port test. The eight data bus signatures obtained from the RAM test are shown in Fig. 9.13. To capture data, the clock input to the analyzer is connected to the processor's ϕ_2 clock. A clock qualifier attached to the RAM $\overline{CS}$ signal ensures that only data in transit to or from the RAM contributes to the final signatures, i.e. the data that appears on the bus due to the program itself is not clocked into the analyzer. Hence, as Fig. 9.13 shows, alternate data lines have identical signatures.

Finally, Fig. 9.14 lists the signatures obtained from the port test in a similar manner to the RAM test. The $\overline{CS}$ signal to the user port chip is used as a clock qualifier, restricting the data bus activity clocked by the analyzer to those read or write operations directed at the user ports.

MEDC Signature Report Form   Title: AIM SIG 9:ROM   Stimulus: RAM

Function	: Start	: Stop	: Clock	: Mode	: Vcc	: Start	: Stop	: Clock
	: ⌐	: ⌐	: ⌐	: 2	: Sign	: ID	: ID	ID
					: P254	: M/P	: M/P	M/P
Clock qualifier : ⌐ On CS	: On RAM	: Selected	:	N/A	:	N/A	N/A	
Node	: Circuit ID	: Circuit ID	: Circuit ID	: Circuit ID	: Circuit ID	: Signature
D0	: Z2–14	: Z6–14	: Z11–14	: Z17–14	:	: 958F
D1	: Z2–13	: Z6–13	: Z11–13	: Z17–13	:	: 9CU7
D2	: Z2–12	: Z6–12	: Z11–12	: Z17–12	:	: 958F
D3	: Z2–11	: Z6–11	: Z11–11	: Z17–11	:	:
D4	: Z3–14	:				

Fig. 9.13 RAM test signatures

MEDC Signature Report Form   Title: AIM SIG 10: ROM   Stimulus: VIA

Function :	Start :	Stop :	Clock :	Mode :	Vcc :	Start :	Stop :	Clock
:	:	:	:	:	Sign :	ID :	ID :	ID
:	L :	_⌐_ :	⌐ :	2 :	P254 :	M/P :	M/P :	M/P

Clock qualifier : L Z1–23 :   N/A   :   N/A   :   N/A   :   N/A   :   N/A

Node :	Circuit ID :	Circuit ID :	Circuit ID :	Circuit ID :	Circuit ID :	Signature
D0 :	Z1–33 :	:	:	:	:	1HP7
PA0 :	Z1–2 :	:	:	:	:	U075
PB0 :	Z1–10 :	:	:	:	:	776P
:	:	:	:	:	:	:
D1 :	Z1–32 :	:	:	:	:	6797
PA1 :	Z1–3 :	:	:	:	:	19C6
:	:	:	:	:	:	
D2 :	Z1–31 :	:	:			
PA2 :	Z1–4 :	:				

Fig. 9.14   Port test signatures

SUMMARY

Free running the microprocessor provides a relatively simple method of stimulating a large part of a microcomputer system, thereby enabling testing by signature analysis. Signatures taken on the address bus and the decode logic serve as a means of verifying their operation. Data bus signatures not only provide a check on the operation and contents of ROM but also on possible defects on the bus, e.g. lines stuck or shorted, solder bridges or devices with outputs permanently enabled, etc.

A software stimulus program is required for efficient testing of RAM or input/output devices by signature analysis. The program should ensure that the data streams generated are repeatable and depend on satisfactory performance of the components under test.

Emulators or exercisers provide an efficient method of retrofitting signature analysis to an existing product, allowing the test engineer to inject suitable stimulus software into the unit under test.

10

Computer-Aided Testing

The history of testing in each area of technology is the progression from individual to mass testing, from manual to automatic. In the early stages of this transition the automatic test systems are designed by individual users for their own organizations: the hardware costs can be low and the design costs ignored. As techniques become established and interest in them grows, specialist manufacturers appear who in turn generate new automatic test methods. Their market is still limited and the tendency is towards large, expensive systems for high volume manufacturers. The experience gained makes it possible to design simplified versions within the cost range of smaller customers. In time some of the ideas appear in test equipment for the individual engineer or technician. The problems are different: testing or servicing small numbers of items, perhaps of a wide variety of types, rather than quality control of large numbers of identical items. The test equipment thus looks different and techniques important for one area may be of only marginal interest in the other.

We can see one further stage in this development. The test equipment can still seem expensive – it is likely to cost a significant fraction of the user's salary! This should be no barrier where the test equipment is used regularly since it will pay for itself in time saved. We are left with the problems of the smaller departments, R & D laboratories, training departments and educational institutions. They will either use the equipment infrequently or may need large numbers of them for training students. If we can harness the power of the microcomputers already present in most organizations, then the cost of test equipment can be cut. Let the micro take over the jobs of control, computing and display. In this chapter we look at all three aspects:

–   automatic test equipment (ATE);
–   semi-automatic test equipment for bench use;
–   microcomputer-controlled test equipment.

AUTOMATIC TEST EQUIPMENT

We can deal with this without attempting a detailed study. The subject is large, the products expensive and the number of people directly involved relatively small. As a result, automatic test equipment tends to be used mainly by large manufacturers in the production process. It has to deal rapidly with many products. For example a semiconductor manufacturer would need to test integrated circuits after assembly, but also to test the chips at many previous stages in the process. It is a waste of money to bond wires to a chip that has already failed during a diffusion stage. It is a waste of money to continue diffusion if there has been a failure in the purity of a prior cleaning process and so on.

Some of these tests might be identical for many different devices – those for the quality of metallization or diffusion depth, for example. Others are device specific: an offset-voltage test on an operational amplifier needs a totally different approach to checking the propagation delay for a logic gate. What the tests have in common is the ability to make contact with at least the critical points on the device and to impose a series of voltages or currents, monitoring the resulting signals at other points on the circuit. The tests are often static, checking in quick succession the output voltage corresponding to a series of input voltages, but holding each just long enough for a stable output reading. Tests of this kind can equally well be applied to complete printed circuit boards. Signals can be applied to selected points, usually at an edge connector, and the board response compared with the predicted values.

In this case the test would be called a 'functional' test in that the board is being forced to perform some of its usual functions in a way gauged most likely to show up faults. How does it differ from the device tests already described? In principle it does not. A logic gate has a series of logic signals applied and the output is checked against its expected values. The range of signals applied may be restricted to speed up the testing, in the knowledge that they will still show up the vast majority of faulty chips at the lowest possible cost. This is a functional test of the device, i.e. the gate.

When the gate forms part of a board then to probe the gate could properly be called a device test, though it is more usually referred to as 'in-circuit testing'. So we already have a hierarchy of tests:

– device;
– in-circuit;
– functional.

These can be extended by looking at the board as part of some instrument or piece of equipment which in turn is a component of a system. For the assembled system we could either try an overall functional test or devise a means of probing the individual pieces of equipment. Given a faulty instrument we could either try a functional test or probe to board level.

This kind of pattern, in which 'one man's unit is another man's system', is behind the coming together of in-circuit and functional testing in recent years. The simple logic tests described in Chapter 1 perform in-circuit testing, forcing specific test patterns on to digital devices without disconnecting them from the boards. The overall function of the system is not tested. Faults are traceable to a single chip but timing difficulties cannot be spotted. Logic analysis is a functional test because the signals are 'real', i.e. operating at full speed and showing up timing errors.

The general principle of automatic test equipment is shown in Fig. 10.1. Let us take each block in turn.

UNIT UNDER TEST – This could be the material of which a component is made, the circuit in which the component occurs, or the assembly of circuits, the instrument using that assembly, or the system of which that instrument is part.

ADAPTOR – this is used to connect the unit being tested into the system. It could be a test board, a socket, cables, anything that allows two-way communication between the unit and the system.

INPUT – We may need to connect many units in turn to the same test system and the input equipment might include the component feeders, robot arms, conveyor belts.

CONDITION – The unit under test will need to operate under suitable conditions to make the test a sensible one. Such conditions might include the power supply, operating temperature or mechanical orientation of the device.

SWITCHING – The unit or device being tested may have many pin connections and the switching section of the system can use multiplexers or reed relays to select which of the pins is to be connected at any one time.

STIMULUS – A variety of signals may be needed ranging from sine waves to high frequency pulses or controlled waveforms. In an automatic test system these signals may need to be controllable over a wide operating range.

MEASURE – A corresponding range of measuring equipment would be needed ranging from digital voltmeters, frequency/phase measurement, and so on. These also might need to be controllable to match the range of stimulus values being supplied.

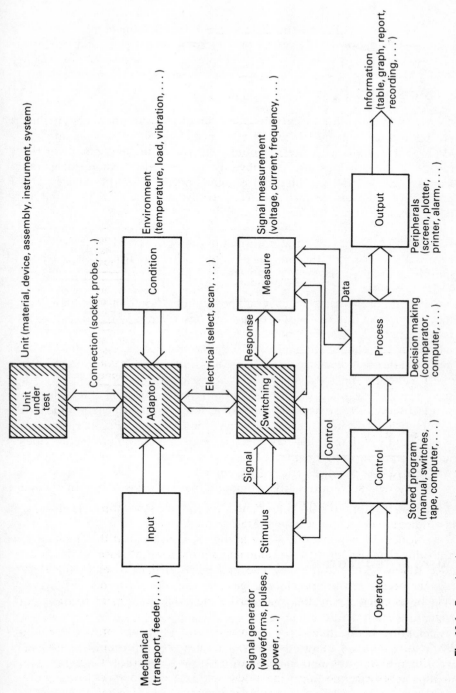

Fig. 10.1 Functional representation of measurement system

CONTROL – This could be as simple as direct manual control from an operator. In an automatic system the operator would start and stop the process but there would also be some preprogrammed sequence which might be as simple as an electrical patch board or as complex as a minicomputer.

DATA – The information obtained from the measurement system may not be in a form useful to the observer, nor to the control program. It is likely that a sequence of tests would be carried out, dependent on the results of the previous test. An obvious case would be where measured values exceeded the maxima and minima specified for the device. The process block also includes any conversions needed such as serial to parallel conversion.

OUTPUT – Finally, the information is transferred to display or recording devices for the human observer. This could include the final loop-back to the operator.

No diagram of this kind can cover all possibilities. Some of these functions may be merged into one block, others not described may be difficult to fit into the pattern. Two final points can be made. For it to be called a truly automatic test equipment it must be optimized for testing and fault location and must be able to make choices as the test is running.

Although the fully automatic systems for testing of semiconductor devices on a large scale, or for in-circuit or functional testing of boards on a production basis are extremely expensive, some of the principles appear in relatively low cost items designed initially for servicing. Their performance is sufficiently high that they have been pressed into use on production lines and for servicing departments and they are only now beginning to find their way into field servicing as originally intended.

The next section describes some alternative forms of automatic and computer-aided testing equipment for the servicing engineer.

AUTOMATED TESTING

The new digital test techniques of logic analysis, in-circuit emulation and signature analysis are effective means of fault finding in microprocessor systems. However, they have their weaknesses, being either difficult to use without a detailed knowledge of the system, or difficult to implement, requiring the design and installation of stimulus software together with extensive documentation.

Several manufacturers have realized the need for a fault-finding tool that provides the power of these techniques but in a form usable by the semiskilled technician. For example IBM developed an in-house product, the 'maintenance device'. This is a portable microcomputer based tool for use by their own field personnel. The unit uses a hand-held keyboard display and downloads maintenance software from an integral floppy disk. Interfacing to the unit to be tested is provided by a series of special adaptors.

On the other hand, the Fluke 9010A Troubleshooter is directed at a wider market, providing a comprehensive test instrument usable with a wide range of microprocessor based equipment. The following section outlines some of its features and follows its application to a typical small microcomputer system with a variety of memory circuits and I/O devices.

The procedures would be similar for any microcomputer with differences of detail, for example in the I/O tests.

Fluke 9010A Troubleshooter

The 9010A Troubleshooter is designed around a microprocessor-based computer called the Mainframe. Connection to the unit under test is made through an interface pod that plugs into the target system's processor socket. A flexible logic probe can read logic state information or provide stimulus at any point in the UUT (Fig. 10.2). Each interface pod is tailored to a particular microprocessor family. It contains a microprocessor of the same type it replaces, and forms the basis of the 9010A's emulation capability. The Mainframe contains a miniature tape cassette system on which programs and UUT details can be stored and retrieved. The operator communicates with the instrument through a keyboard and 32 character LED display. An input/output RS232 serial option is also available.

Operational Functions

The 9010A acts as an in-circuit emulator gaining control of the UUT's address, data and control buses through its processor socket. It has a range of special functions that simplifies and speeds up the generation of test procedures. These functions range from a 'learn' mode where the memory map of the UUT is logged (i.e. address range of ROM, RAM and I/O) to the 'test' mode that uses 'canned' test routines in firmware or 'tailor-made' test programs downloaded from cassette tape.

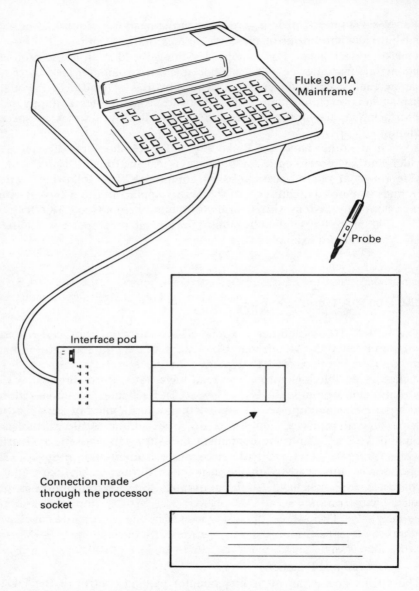

Fig. 10.2 Connecting the Fluke 9010A to a target system

Example – Implementing a Test Program for a Single Board Microcomputer

This single board unit (AIM 65 by Rockwell International) contains elements typical of popular microcomputers. It is 6502 based with 4K bytes of static RAM and up to 20K bytes of resident ROM, depending on the software options selected (Appendix 2). A wide range of interfaces are provided for the following devices:

- qwerty matrix keyboard (6532 RIOT);
- printer (part of 6522 VIA);
- 20 character LED display (6520 PIA);
- serial interface – tape/current loop (part of 6522 VIA);
- user parallel port (6522 VIA).

The first step in generating a test program involves some investigations on a known working system. This procedure begins by removing the micro-processor from the board and inserting the 9010A interface pod in its place. Power is then applied to the board and the operator commences investigation of the system memory map.

Memory Mapping

A unique feature of the Fluke is its learn mode. A learn algorithm explores the system's address space, writing and reading data to each location. Depending on the data read back, the algorithm dimensions and classifies the regions of the map occupied by ROM, RAM and I/O devices. For each block of ROM detected, a signature is generated based on a cyclic redundancy check (CRC) of its contents.

If desired, the learn phase can be edited or bypassed by entering address information directly at the keyboard. Fig. 10.3 shows the resulting memory map. The address details generated by the learn mode have been edited in order to obtain separate signatures for each 4K byte ROM chip rather than a single signature for the 20K byte block of ROM.

Built-in Test Functions

After the memory map of a good working system has been defined, the Fluke can then test identical boards using its built-in test programs. Routines are provided in the mainframe's firmware to exercise and test the system's buses, ROM, RAM and, to a limited extent, I/O devices.

```
ADDRESS SPACE INFORMATION
RAM      @     0000–0FFF
RAM      @     A400–A47F

ROM      @     B000–BFFF    SIG   EA7C
ROM      @     C000–CFFF    SIG   E7E4
ROM      @     D000–DFFF    SIG   7915
ROM      @     E000–EFFF    SIG   6E7E
ROM      @     F000–FFFF    SIG   BD87

I/O      @     A002–A003    BITS   FF
I/O      @     A00A–A00C    BITS   FF
I/O      @     A481         BITS   FF
I/O      @     A483         BITS   FF
I/O      @     A802–A805    BITS   86
I/O      @     A80A         BITS   FF
I/O      @     AC00–AC03    BITS   3F
```

Fig. 10.3   AIM 65 address information produced by the LEARN function

- The bus test checks the electrical integrity of the address, data and control buses by trying to establish test patterns and then reporting on its success.
- The ROM test performs the same CRC carried out during the learn mode. Any departures from the original signature are reported on the display.
- Two tests are provided for RAM; RAM short and RAM long. The former tests the read/write capability of each data bit and proper functioning of the RAM's address decoder. RAM long goes a stage further, including a pattern sensitivity test.
- Input/output testing is similar to the RAM short test with a check on the bits declared capable of read/write activity in the learn mode.

Programmed Testing

Any of the built-in tests described above can be initiated directly from the keyboard or called from within a program. The 9010A uses a programming language, similar to BASIC, that allows the programmer to combine tests to form a complete test sequence involving messages to guide the operator, specifying what action he has to perform next. The programming facility is not restricted to sequencing on-board tests. It also provides a simple method of designing routines to perform more efficient testing of I/O devices. The following examples illustrate possible routines for three of the multifunction interface chips found on the board.

6522 (VIA) Test

The VIA dedicated to user applications provides two input/output ports on the application connector at the rear of the machine. During testing, a pre-wired plug is attached, shorting each pin of port A to the corresponding pin of port B (PA0 to PB0, PA1 to PB1, . . ., etc.). A test pattern is written to port B and then read at port A and checked. The procedure continues using a 'ramping test pattern', transmitting data between 00 and FF. On completion, the role of each port is reversed and the procedure repeated. Any failures are reported to the operator, with the message 'VIA ERROR', together with an audible bleep, and the test stops (Program 10.1).

The 9010A contains sixteen 32-bit registers, REG0 to REGF, that can be used as variables along with arithmetic and logical operations. Some

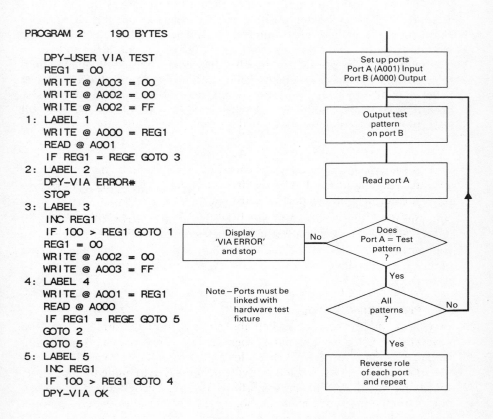

```
PROGRAM 2      190 BYTES

      DPY–USER VIA TEST
      REG1 = 00
      WRITE @ A003 = 00
      WRITE @ A002 = 00
      WRITE @ A002 = FF
1:    LABEL 1
      WRITE @ A000 = REG1
      READ @ A001
      IF REG1 = REGE GOTO 3
2:    LABEL 2
      DPY–VIA ERROR#
      STOP
3:    LABEL 3
      INC REG1
      IF 100 > REG1 GOTO 1
      REG1 = 00
      WRITE @ A002 = 00
      WRITE @ A003 = FF
4:    LABEL 4
      WRITE @ A001 = REG1
      READ @ A000
      IF REG1 = REGE GOTO 5
      GOTO 2
      GOTO 5
5:    LABEL 5
      INC REG1
      IF 100 > REG1 GOTO 4
      DPY–VIA OK
```

Program 10.1   Test routine for user VIA

registers are given dedicated tasks by the 9010A. For example, register E stores the last piece of data used by the operator or generated by the 9010A. In this example REG1 is used to store the current value of the test pattern written to the output port and register E yields the data received at the input port after the read operation.

6520 (PIA) Display Test

The 20 character LED display is made up of five, four-digit display modules, each with their own internal memory and driver circuitry (Appendix 2). A 6520 PIA parallel port chip interfaces the complete array to the address, data and control buses. To display a character on the screen, port A of the PIA is used to select the display module and the individual character position within the module. The ASCII code for the desired character is then transmitted to the selected position through port B.

The test program begins by initializing both ports as outputs (Program 10.2). The character position is then selected on port A and the character code latched out through port B. The program enables all five modules together and uses a software loop to write the character on to each character position on each element. The next character code is then selected and the process repeats itself until the entire character set has been written into every position on the screen. The speed of the test procedure is slow enough for an observer to visually check that all character codes appear at every position.

6532 (RIOT) Keyboard Test

The matrix keyboard is interfaced to the processor through a 6532 RIOT. Port A is used as an output and strobes the matrix columns. Port B is configured as an input and monitors the matrix rows looking for a depressed key. The keyboard test routine shown in Program 10.3 begins by configuring the ports on the RIOT. It then continues by latching out the binary patterns shown below on port A and prompting the operator to press the relevant key.

Pattern on port A	Key requested
01111111	Space
10111111	LF
11011111	P
11101111	0
11110111	7
11111011	4
11111101	5
11111110	F1

```
PROGRAM 0      194 BYTES

      DPY-DISPLAY TEST###
      WRITE @ AC01 = 00
      WRITE @ AC03 = 00
      WRITE @ AC00 = FF
      WRITE @ AC02 = FF
      WRITE @ AC01 = 04
      WRITE @ AC03 = 04
      REG1 = A0
      REG2 = 00
1:    LABEL 1
      DPY-   AIM CHARACTER CODE
      DPY-+$1
2:    LABEL 2
      WRITE @ AC00 = REG2
      WRITE @ AC02 = REG1
      INC REG2
      IF 4 > REG2 GOTO 2
      REG3 = 0
3:    LABEL 3
      INC REG3
      IF 20 > REG3 GOTO 3
      REG2 = 0
      INC REG1
      IF E0 > REG1 GOTO 1
      DPY-FINISHED#
```

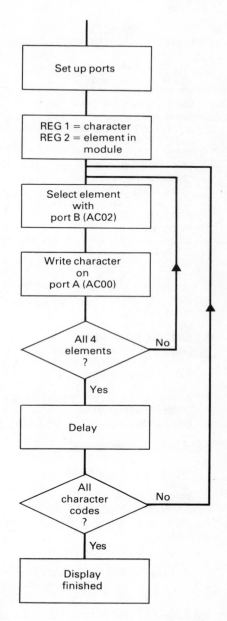

Program 10.2 Test routine for LED display

```
PROGRAM 3      319 BYTES

    WRITE @ A481 = FF
    WRITE @ A480 = FF
    WRITE @ A483 = OO
    WRITE @ A482 = OO
    REG8 = FE
    DPY-PRESS SPACE BAR ON AIM*
    EXECUTE PROGRAM 4
    REG8 = FD
    DPY-SPACE BAR OK - TRY LF KEY
    EXECUTE PROGRAM 4
    REG8 = FB
    DPY-LF KEY OK - TRY P*
    EXECUTE PROGRAM 4
    REG8 = F7
    DPY-P OK TRY O-AS IN OMNIPOTENT
    DPY-+*
    EXECUTE PROGRAM 4
    REG8 = EF
    DPY-O OK -TRY 7*
    EXECUTE PROGRAM 4
    REG8 = DF
    DPY-7 OK - TRY 4*
    EXECUTE PROGRAM 4
    REG8 = BF
    DPY-4 OK - TRY S-AS IN SENSUOUS*
    EXECUTE PROGRAM 4
    REG8 = 7F
    DPY-S OK - TRY F1 FUNCTION KEY*
    EXECUTE PROGRAM 4
    DPY-KEYBOARD TEST COMPLETE*

PROGRAM 4      37 BYTES

    WRITE @ A480 = REG8
1:  LABEL 1
    READ @ A482
    IF REGE = REG8 GOTO 2
    GOTO 1
2:  LABEL 2
```

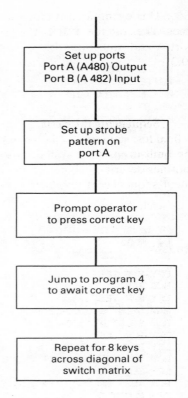

Program 10.3   Short test for matrix keyboard

By following this pattern, the program performs a short test of every row and column on the keyboard (obviously a more exhaustive test could be designed to monitor correct operation of every key and to detect possible shorts between rows or columns). When the correct key is pressed the program moves on to prompt the operator to press the next key in the sequence.

This example also illustrates how programs can be called as subroutines. The statement 'EXECUTE PROGRAM 4' calls a routine that reads port A and waits until the correct key is pressed before return to Program 10.3.

Sequencing the Tests

A final test sequence is shown in Program 10.4. The program links together the built-in tests for system buses, RAM and ROM with the special I/O routines described above. In this example the program is a straightforward linear sequence of tests. However, it is relatively simple to create a test

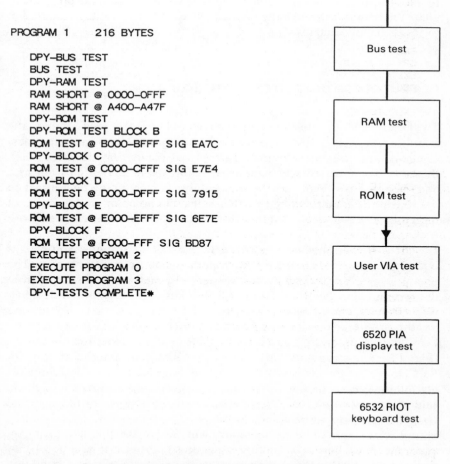

```
PROGRAM  1      216  BYTES

     DPY–BUS  TEST
     BUS  TEST
     DPY–RAM  TEST
     RAM  SHORT  @  0000–0FFF
     RAM  SHORT  @  A400–A47F
     DPY–ROM  TEST
     DPY–ROM  TEST  BLOCK  B
     ROM  TEST  @  B000–BFFF  SIG  EA7C
     DPY–BLOCK  C
     ROM  TEST  @  C000–CFFF  SIG  E7E4
     DPY–BLOCK  D
     ROM  TEST  @  D000–DFFF  SIG  7915
     DPY–BLOCK  E
     ROM  TEST  @  E000–EFFF  SIG  6E7E
     DPY–BLOCK  F
     ROM  TEST  @  F000–FFF  SIG  BD87
     EXECUTE  PROGRAM  2
     EXECUTE  PROGRAM  0
     EXECUTE  PROGRAM  3
     DPY–TESTS  COMPLETE*
```

Bus test

RAM test

ROM test

User VIA test

6520 PIA
display test

6532 RIOT
keyboard test

Program 10.4 Main program controlling test sequence

program that is sophisticated enough to call up more detailed tests if a failure is detected. The operator can thereby be guided to the root of the problem, when a message is displayed specifying what action has to be performed, e.g. replace IC number, etc.

Summary

The case study illustrates some of the features offered in the 9010A. Designing tests for specialist I/O devices and peripherals requires detailed knowledge of the system. This is aided by the simple programming language combined with the ability to read and write to individual memory locations. The real power of such instruments lies in the range of features required in the testing procedure, ranging from a main test program to guide the operator through the test sequence, to the stimulus software that forms each individual test.

COMPUTER CONTROLLED SIGNATURE ANALYSIS

The large amount of documentation combined with the need to guide the operator through a test sequence makes signature analysis the ideal candidate for computer control. Taking and comparing signatures with those on an annotated schematic or signature table is a tedious business and open to error. When a signature failure is detected the operator then has to consult a fault finding tree that helps him home in on the source of the fault. The following example shows how the computer can help with both these tasks.

The test arrangement is given in Fig. 10.4. Stimulus software is injected into the UUT using the Micropod emulator described earlier. The operator is guided through the test sequence by messages transmitted from the system controller (Fig. 10.5). All the messages, together with signatures from a known working system and configuration codes for the locator, are stored on tape in the file 'RECORDS' (Fig. 10.6.)

The test program begins by placing the analyzer under remote control (Fig. 10.7 and Program 10.5). Set-up codes stored in the first entry of RECORDS are then transmitted, selecting signature analysis and configuring the signature window, i.e. setting the polarity of start/stop and clock. Line 90 re-enters the RECORDS file to obtain the operator message and the good signature for the selected node.

The program employs a similar technique to the previous example, using the 'hold' button to capture signatures (subroutines at line 800). A further refinement to the routine is its ability to detect a 'timeout' condition arising from a faulty signature gate, i.e. no start, stop or clock signal. If this condition occurs the test stops with the message 'START/STOP/CLOCK PROBLEM' displayed on the HP85.

A further check for stable signatures is carried out at line 150, unstable signatures are characterized by a '#' character after the signature. Finally the logged signature is compared with its corresponding entry in RECORDS. If there is no match, the test stops with the message 'FAIL' displayed and a printout of the details of the failed node on the HP85 (Fig. 10.8). If they match, the test continues to the next circuit node and through the file RECORDS, until the last entry 'FINI' is detected.

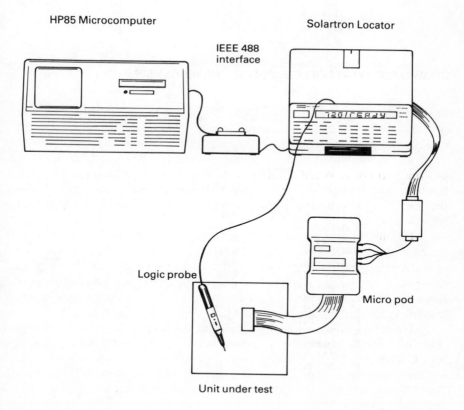

Fig. 10.4   Typical test arrangement; stimulus 'injected' by micropod emulator;
locator controlled over IEEE 488 by HP85 microcomputer

Fig. 10.5 Sample of messages sent to the display

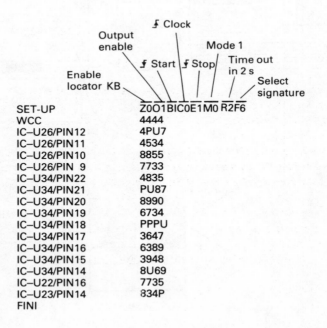

Fig. 10.6 Sample 'records' file; contains configuration codes; subsequent entries are made up of operator instructions and signatures from a known good system

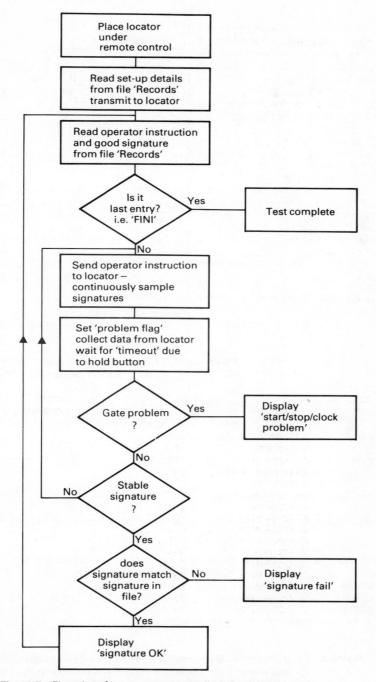

Fig. 10.7 Flowchart for computer controlled signature analysis

```
  1 ! **************************
  2 REM SIGNATURE CHECK PROGRAM
  3 ! **************************
  5 CLEAR
 10 REMOTE 716  ←──────────────Locator at Address 16
 20 DIM A$[25],B$[25]          placed under remote control
 30 ASSIGN# 1 TO "RECORDS"
 40 ON KEY# 1,"ABORT" GOTO 300
 45 KEY LABEL
 50 READ# 1 ; C$,D$
 60 OUTPUT 716 ;"TOP/";C$;"/"  ←──── First entry in file "RECORDS"
 70 WAIT 3000                  is used to set up Locator
 80 OUTPUT 716 ;D$
 90 READ# 1 ; C$,D$  ←──────── Subsequent entries contain
100 IF POS(C$,"FINI") THEN 300 operator instructions and
110 OUTPUT 716 ;"TOP/";C$;"/"  correct signatures
120 WAIT 2000
130 OUTPUT 716 ;"T1"  ←──────── Return to continuous sampling
140 GOSUB 800
145 IF POS(B$,"PROBLEM")=0 THEN ── Timeout without reading
150                               signature implies gate problem
147 PRINT B$ @ BEEP
148 GOTO 300
150 IF POS(B$[17],"*") THEN 110 ←── Is it a stable signature?
160 IF POS(B$,D$)=0 THEN 210  ←────Does it match signature on file?
170 OUTPUT 716 ;"TOP/ PASS
    /"
180 PRINT C$;"       SIGNATURE OK ←──If so onto next measurement
    "                             after 'PASS' message
190 WAIT 1000
200 GOTO 90
210 OUTPUT 716 ;"TOS2P/  FAIL ←────If signatures don't match
    /"                         display "FAIL MESSAGE"
220 PRINT "SIGNATURE FAIL ON ";C
    $
300 END
310 ! **************************
320 !
800 REM WAIT FOR HOLD BUTTON
805 !
807 B$="START/STOP/CLOCK PROBLEM ←─ Set "GATE PROBLEM" flag
    "
810 ENTER 716 ; A$  ←──────────────Read Locator
820 IF POS(A$,"TIMEOUT") THEN 85   Wait for Timeout due to
    0                              hold button (or gate problem)
830 B$=A$
840 GOTO 810  ←────────────────Store latest input in B$
850 RETURN
860 ! **************************
```

Program 10.5 Example program used to check signatures; routine configures
                signature analyzer, instructs operator through locator's display,
                gathers and compares signatures with those in file 'records'

```
        Vcc              SIGNATURE OK
        IC–U26/PIN12     SIGNATURE OK
        IC–U26/PIN11     SIGNATURE OK
        SIGNATURE FAIL ON  IC–U26/PIN10
```

Fig. 10.8 Sample printout from bus controller (HP85); in this test the fourth
logged signature fails to match record

SUMMARY

Computer control and documentation simplify and speed up testing by
signature analysis. In this example the program flow was simplified to
illustrate the technique. However, practical test programs can be made
more efficient by making logical decisions based on the location of the
faulty node, thereby leading the operator to the source of the fault.

PART III

Servicing on a Shoestring

11

Microcomputer Based Testers

Without doubt the easiest and widest road into debugging any microprocessor based system is through the processor socket. Emulation techniques, where the microprocessor is removed and a second microcomputer
system (host) is linked to the unit under test (target) through the processor
socket, offer the most powerful diagnostic aids available to date.

Emulators are usually associated with expensive microprocessor
development systems or equally expensive purpose-built troubleshooting
tools. However, it is possible to convert a micro into a host computer for
emulation, allowing it to test hardware and evaluate software in a target
system. This section describes a simple circuit that can be used with the
Apple II micro, turning it into a troubleshooter capable of testing other
micros using the same processor.

The Apple II in-circuit emulator (ICE) is carried on a single Apple
card. A 40-way ribbon cable terminated in a dual in-line plug connects the
ICE to the target micro (Fig. 11.1). In operation the ICE card gives the

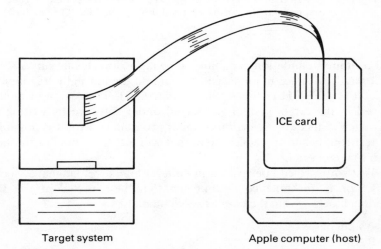

Target system   Apple computer (host)

Fig. 11.1   The processor is removed from the target system which is then
connected to the host via a 40-way ribbon cable

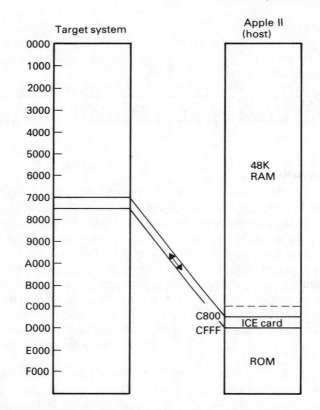

Fig. 11.2 Any 2K byte block of memory space in the target system can be mapped into the normal empty memory slot C800–CFFF in the Apple

micro a limited emulation capability allowing it to relocate any 2K byte block of address space in the target system into the normally free memory slot C800 H–CFFF H in the Apple II (Fig. 11.2). The region of memory observed in the target system is selected under software by writing to a 'select latch'. Since this selection is under program control it is possible to write test routines in the host system that will test the whole of the target system's memory map.

Test software can be written in either a high level language, such as BASIC, or in machine code, and can then be directed at the main functional blocks within the target system, namely:

−   system buses
−   RAM
−   ROM
−   input/output devices

Routines written in BASIC tend to be slow for even the simplest of tests. A better philosophy is to write standard test modules in machine code and use a BASIC program to form an overall test strategy that sequences the tests and guides the operator should a fault be detected.

This chapter describes test modules for exercising the system buses, testing RAM and ROM and concludes by presenting a case study illustrating how the Apple ICE can be used to test a typical single board computer.

ICE HARDWARE

Fig. 11.3 shows a circuit diagram of the ICE card. Address lines A0 to A10 together with control lines R/$\overline{\text{W}}$, ϕo, and $\overline{\text{RES}}$ and SYNC pass directly from the host to the target system via octal driver chips U4 and U5. However, address lines A11 to A15 in the target system are not obtained from their Apple II equivalents but are instead generated by the block select latch U3. To select the five most significant lines in the target system a control word is first written to this latch which is 'clocked' by the Apple II 'I/O select' line. Hence, if the ICE were in slot 5 the following short program would set A11 to A15 in the target system to zero.

```
LDA #00      \ sets A11 to A15 to zero
STA C500     \ activates I/O select line in slot 5
```

After configuring the block select latch, any read or write operations to memory locations between C800 H and CFFF H in the Apple II would activate the address decoder chip U1, and enable the output of latch U3, establishing corresponding addresses between 0000 H and 07FF H in the target system.

Address decoder (U1) also enables the octal transceiver (U2), allowing data to be either written to or received from the target system. Those familiar with the Apple I/O connector might feel the decoder U1 is redundant since 'I/O strobe' is active low for addresses between C800 H and CFFF H. However, close examination of its timing shows that it appears too late in the timing cycle to enable slow memory or I/O devices in the target system (Fig. 11.4).

TEST SOFTWARE

The test software falls into two categories:

–   Routines that exercise and test the different functional areas of the target micro, namely its system buses, RAM, ROM and input/output devices.

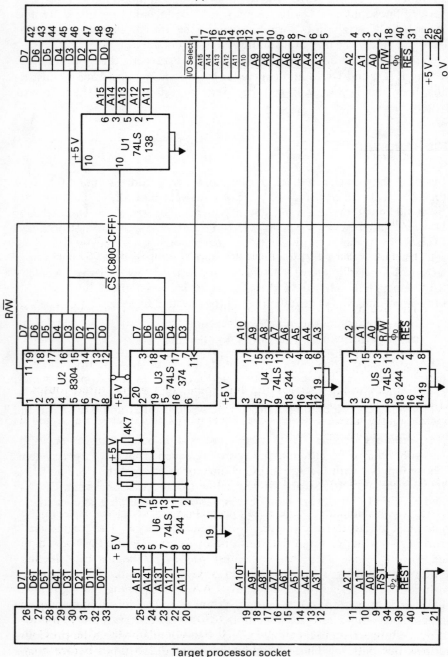

Fig. 11.3 Apple ICE circuit diagram

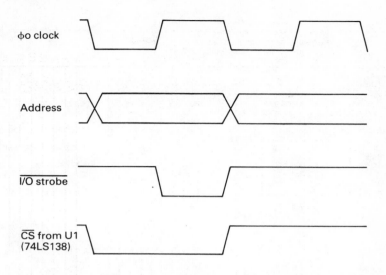

Fig. 11.4   Relative timing of Apple slot signal I/O strobe and the CS signal
from U1

–   The overall test program that guides the operator through the test
    sequence calling the functional tests and performing the tasks nor-
    mally performed by a 'fault-finding tree', i.e. pin pointing the source
    of the fault with a suggested remedy (e.g. replace IC28), or initiating
    a new test to gather more information.

The following describes the functional tests giving three routines
written in 6502 assembly language. Each program has been designed to
operate on the 'memory window' (C800 H–CFFF H) between the Apple II
and the target system.

(a) Address and Data Bus Toggle Test

A sensible preliminary check before launching into complex tests of the
systems ICs is to test the integrity of the system buses. The 'toggle test'
exercises each address and data bus line by alternately driving them high
and low. Program 11.1 shows the test routine. It begins by selecting
addresses beginning with (10101xxxxxxxxxxx binary) in the target system.
A dummy read is then made to address AAAA H placing the high, low,
high, low, etc. pattern on the target system bus. The select latch is again
accessed selecting addresses beginning (01010xxxxxxxxxxx binary) followed by a dummy read to location 5555 H, thus complementing the previous
address bus pattern. This procedure is repeated 256 times before com-
mencing a similar test pattern on the target systems data bus.

```
SOURCE FILE: APPTOG
0000:              1  ;••••••••••••••••••••••••••••••••••••••••••••••••••••••••••••••••
0000:              2  ;ADDRESS AND DATA BUS TEST
0000:              3  ; TOGGLE ADDRESS BUS AAAA-5555
0000:              4  ; 256 TIMES
0000:              5  ; TOGGLE DATA BUS AA-55
0000:              6  ; 256 TIMES
0000:              7  ;••••••••••••••••••••••••••••••••••••••••••••••••••••••••••••••••
0000:              8  ;
C500:              9  SELECT        EQU       $C500        ;2K SELECT LATCH
———— NEXT OBJECT FILE NAME IS APPTOG.OBJ0
2100:             10                ORG       $2100
2100:A2 00        11                LDX       #00          ;SET COUNTER TO ZERO
2102:             12  ;EXERCISE ADDRESS BUS
2102:A9 AA        13  ABUS          LDA       #$AA         ;SELECT ADDRESSES 10101XXX
2104:8D 00 C5     14                STA       SELECT
2107:AD AA CA     15                LDA       $CAAA        ;IE AAAA ON TARGET BUS
210A:A9 55        16                LDA       #$55         ;SELECT ADDRESSES 01010XXX
210C:8D 00 C5     17                STA       SELECT
210F:AD 55 CD     18                LDA       $CD55        ;IE 5555 ON TARGET BUS
2112:CA           19                DEX
2113:D0 ED        20                BNE       ABUS         ;REPEAT 256 TIMES
2115:             21  ;EXERCISE DATA BUS
2115:A9 00        22  DBUS          LDA       #$00         ;SELECT ADDRESSES 00000XXX
2117:8D 00 C5     23                STA       SELECT
211A:A9 55        24                LDA       #$55         ;01010101 ON DATA BUS
211C:8D 00 C9     25                STA       $C900        ;0100 IN TARGET SYSTEM
211F:A9 AA        26                LDA       #$AA         ;10101010 ON DATA BUS
2121:8D 00 C9     27                STA       $C900        ;0100 IN TARGET SYSTEM
2124:CA           28                DEX
2125:D0 EE        29                BNE       DBUS         ;REPEAT 256 TIMES
2127:60           30                RTS                    ;TOGGLING COMPLETE

*** SUCCESSFUL ASSEMBLY: NO ERRORS


2102 ABUS                  2115 DBUS                 C500 SELECT                2102 ABUS
2115 DBUS                  C500 SELECT
```

Program 11.1 Program to 'toggle' all address and data bus lines

Exercising the system buses with this pattern allows the operator to check, using an oscilloscope or logic probe that:

1 each line is drivable in the target system, i.e. no lines are stuck high or low;
2 each line is continuous from its source, at the processor socket, to its destination on each chip.

A more complex test could also check for shorts between lines by setting up a characteristic frequency or pattern on each line. A frequency meter or oscilloscope could then be used to check for corruption between lines.

Obviously toggling the system buses 256 times will not give the operator enough time to check even one circuit node. The short routine below illustrates how the bus test (BTEST) is used in the test sequencing program.

180 PRINT "BUS TESTING – PROBE TARGET SYSTEM BUSES"
190 PRINT "(PRESS SPACE FOR NEXT TEST)"
200 CALL BTEST
210 IF PEEK (−16384)<=127 THEN 200

By placing the test within a loop that also checks the keyboard, the test will be repeated until the operator signals he is satisfied by pressing the spacing bar.

(b) RAM 'Checkerboard' Test

The basic strategy for testing RAM involves writing some test pattern into memory, reading it back and checking that both the write and read operations are successful. Many different test patterns can be used, each sensitive to particular failure modes of the memory. One useful pattern providing a test of the read/write capability of every bit in the RAM in a reasonable time, is the checkerboard test pattern. Some more complex tests take several hours.

The RAM test program is shown as Program 11.2. A RAM location is selected and 55 Hex (01010101 binary) is stored in the location and then read back and compared. If the comparison fails, the test terminates with the Apple II displaying a RAM failure message. If the comparison passes, the location is then tested with the complementary pattern AA Hex (10101010 binary). The test then moves on to the next location until all locations within the window (C800 H–CFFF H) have been exercised and tested.

Before calling the RAM test in the main test program, the memory select latch should be written to, moving the RAM to be exercised into the ICE test window. For example the following program would test RAM from 0800 H to 0FFF H in the target system.

    250 PRINT "RAM TESTING 0800 – 0FFF"
    260 POKE SELECT, 08:CALL RAMTEST

ROM SIGNATURES

The normal method for testing ROMs involves forming a checksum byte based on a sum of all the data within the ROM. However, there always remains a chance that faults are concealed by several errors cancelling each other out. A more sensitive technique, less likely to mask errors involves forming a cyclic redundancy check (CRC) on the ROM contents. The technique has its origin in data communications but more recently finds itself at the heart of signature analysis. The cyclic redundancy check can be performed either by hardware or software, but the hardware model is perhaps the easiest to explain.

The circuit of Fig. 9.4 shows a 16-bit linear shift register with feedback. Each bit of data is fed serially into the register. When the data

```
SOURCE FILE: APPRAM
0000:                    1  ;•••••••••••••••••••••••••••••••••••••••••••••••••••••••••••••••••
0000:                    2  ;PROGRAM TO CHECKERBOARD TEST RAM
0000:                    3  ; (C800-CFFF)
0000:                    4  ;•••••••••••••••••••••••••••••••••••••••••••••••••••••••••••••••••
0000:                    5  ;
FDED:                    6  COUT       EQU      $FDED        ;CHARACTER TO SCREEN
FD8E:                    7  CROUT      EQU      $FD8E        ;C-RETURN TO SCREEN
FDE3:                    8  PRHEX      EQU      $FDE3        ;OUTPUT HEX DIGIT
0008:                    9  POINT      EQU      08           ;POINTER
0000:                   10  ;
----- NEXT OBJECT FILE NAME IS APPRAM.OBJ0
2090:                   11             ORG      $2090
2090:                   12  ;
2090:A9 00              13             LDA      #00          ;POINT TO C800
2092:85 08              14             STA      POINT
2094:A8                 15             TAY
2095:A9 C8              16             LDA      #$C8
2097:85 09              17             STA      POINT + 1
2099:A9 55              18  START      LDA      #$55         ;START TEST WITH 55
209B:91 08              19             STA      (POINT),Y    ;STORE
209D:D1 08              20             CMP      (POINT),Y    ;READ BACK AND COMPARE
209F:F0 03              21             BEQ      OK
20A1:4C BC 20           22             JMP      ERROR        ;DISPLAY ERROR MESSAGE AND END
20A4:A9 AA              23  OK         LDA      #$AA         ;NOW TRY AA
20A6:91 08              24             STA      (POINT),Y    ;STORE
20A8:D1 08              25             CMP      (POINT),Y    ;READ BACK AND COMPARE
20AA:F0 03              26             BEQ      OK1
20AC:4C BC 20           27             JMP      ERROR        ;DISPLAY ERROR MESSAGE AND END
20AF:E6 08              28  OK1        INC      POINT        ;NEXT LOCATION
20B1:D0 E6              29             BNE      START
20B3:E6 09              30             INC      POINT + 1
20B5:A5 09              31             LDA      POINT + 1
20B7:C9 D0              32             CMP      #$D0
20B9:D0 DE              33             BNE      START        ;END OF BLOCK?(CFFF)
20BB:60                 34             RTS                   ;TEST COMPLETE
20BC:                   35  ;
20BC:                   36  ;ERROR DISPLAY ROUTINE
20BC:                   37  ;
20BC:A2 00              38  ERROR      LDX      #00          ;POINTER FOR MESSAGE
20BE:BD D5 20           39  NEXT1      LDA      MESS,X
20C1:20 ED FD           40             JSR      COUT         ;MESSAGE TO SCREEN
20C4:E8                 41             INX                   ;NEXT CHARACTER
20C5:E0 0F              42             CPX      #$0F         ;MESSAGE COMPLETE?
20C7:D0 F5              43             BNE      NEXT1
20C9:A5 09              44             LDA      09           ;FAIL ADDRESS TO SCREEN
20CB:38                 45             SEC
20CC:E9 C8              46             SBC      #$C8
20CE:20 E3 FD           47             JSR      PRHEX
20D1:20 8E FD           48             JSR      CROUT        ;C-RETURN TO SCREEN
20D4:60                 49             RTS                   ; AND FINISHED
20D5:                   50  ;ERROR MESSAGE
20D5:A0 C5 D2           51  MESS       ASC      "            ERROR ON PAGE "
20D8:D2 CF D2
20DB:A0 CF CE
20DE:A0 D0 C1
20E1:C7 C5 A0

••• SUCCESSFUL ASSEMBLY: NO ERRORS
```

Program 11.2 Program to 'checkerboard' test RAM

stream ends, the final binary pattern remaining in the register forms the 4-digit cyclic redundancy check. The feedback paths effectively form a sum to the base 2 between the data fedback and the new data entering and ensure that every bit entering the register contributes towards the final CRC or signature.

An equivalent software routine is shown in Program 11.3. Each byte from the ROM under test is fed serially (bit 0 to bit 7) to the subroutine

```
SOURCE FILE: APPSIG
0000:                              1  ;••••••••••••••••••••••••••••••••••••••••••••••••••••••••••••••••••••••••••••••
0000:                              2  ; PROGRAM TO EVALUATE SIGNATURE
0000:                              3  ;OF 2KBYTE BLOCK (C800-CFFF)
0000:                              4  ;EACH BYTE IS SERIALIZED BIT0-BIT7
0000:                              5  ;••••••••••••••••••••••••••••••••••••••••••••••••••••••••••••••••••••••••••••••
0000:                              6  ;
0000:                              7  ;
0000:                              8  ;
————— NEXT OBJECT FILE NAME IS APPSIG.OBJ0
2000:                              9               ORG       $2000
1900:                             10  COUNT        EQU       $1900        ;STORE FOR SUM
1901:                             11  SIGL         EQU       $1901        ;CURRENT SIGNATURE LOW BYTE
1902:                             12  SIGH         EQU       $1902        ;CURRENT SIGNATURE HIGH BYTE
0008:                             13  POINT        EQU       $0008        ;BYTE COUNTER
1903:                             14  TEMP         EQU       SIGH + 1     ;TEMPORARY STORE
FDDA:                             15  PRBYTE       EQU       $FDDA        ;PRINT A HEX BYTE
FD8E:                             16  CROUT        EQU       $FD8E        ;GENERATE C-RETURN
2000:                             17  ;
2000:A9 00                        18  START        LDA       #00          ;ZERO SHIFT REGISTER
2002:8D 01 19                     19               STA       SIGL
2005:8D 02 19                     20               STA       SIGH
2008:A9 00                        21  WSTART       LDA       #00          ;WARM START
200A:85 08                        22               STA       POINT
200C:A8                           23               TAY
200D:A9 C8                        24               LDA       #$C8         ;START OF BLOCK C800
200F:85 09                        25               STA       POINT + 1
2011:B1 08                        26  NBYTE        LDA       (POINT),Y    ;GET BYTE
2013:8D 03 19                     27               STA       TEMP
2016:A2 08                        28               LDX       #08          ;FOR 8 BITS
2018:AD 03 19                     29  NBIT         LDA       TEMP
201B:29 01                        30               AND       #01          ;BIT0 INTO COUNT
201D:8D 00 19                     31               STA       COUNT
2020:20 36 20                     32               JSR       FEEDBACK     ;APPLY FEEDBACK
2023:6E 03 19                     33               ROR       TEMP         ;READY FOR NEXT BIT
2026:CA                           34               DEX
2027:D0 EF                        35               BNE       NBIT         ;BACK FOR NEXT BIT
2029:E6 08                        36               INC       POINT        ;NEXT BYTE
202B:D0 E4                        37               BNE       NBYTE
202D:E6 09                        38               INC       POINT + 1
202F:A5 09                        39               LDA       POINT + 1
2031:C9 D0                        40               CMP       #$D0
2033:D0 DC                        41               BNE       NBYTE        ;END OF BLOCK? CFFF
2035:60                           42               RTS
2036:                             43  ;
2036:                             44  ;
2036:                             45  ;FEEDBACK ALGORITHM—SUMS BITS
2036:                             46  ;15,11,8 AND 6 WITH INCOMING BIT
2036:                             47  ;ON ENTRY 'COUNT' CONTAINS INPUT BIT
2036:                             48  ;
2036:AD 02 19                     49  FEEDBACK     LDA       SIGH         ;TOP HALF OF SIG
2039:10 03                        50               BPL       NEX1         ;TEST BIT15
203B:EE 00 19                     51               INC       COUNT
203E:6A                           52  NEX1         ROR       A
203F:90 03                        53               BCC       NEX2         ;TEST BIT 8
2041:EE 00 19                     54               INC       COUNT
2044:6A                           55  NEX2         ROR       A
2045:6A                           56               ROR       A
2046:6A                           57               ROR       A
2047:90 03                        58               BCC       NEX3         ;TEST BIT 11
2049:EE 00 19                     59               INC       COUNT
204C:AD 01 19                     60  NEX3         LDA       SIGL         ;BOTTOM HALF OF SIG
204F:2A                           61               ROL       A
2050:2A                           62               ROL       A
2051:90 03                        63               BCC       NEX4         ;TEST BIT 6
2053:EE 00 19                     64               INC       COUNT
2056:6E 00 19                     65  NEX4         ROR       COUNT        ;SUM INTO CARRY
2059:2E 01 19                     66               ROL       SIGL         ;CARRY INTO BIT0 LBYTE
205C:2E 02 19                     67               ROL       SIGH         ;CARRY INTO BIT0 HBYTE
205F:60                           68               RTS
2060:AD 02 19                     69  DISPLAY      LDA       SIGH         ;MSB TO DISPLAY
2063:20 DA FD                     70               JSR       PRBYTE       ;ONTO APPLE DISPLAY
2066:AD 01 19                     71               LDA       SIGL         ;LSB TO DISPLAY
2069:20 DA FD                     72               JSR       PRBYTE       ;ONTO APPLE DISPLAY
206C:20 8E FD                     73               JSR       CROUT        ;C-RETURN
206F:60                           74               RTS
```

Program 11.3 Program to evaluate ROM signatures

FEEDBACK which performs a sum to the base 2 between bits 15, 11, 8 and 6 within the register and the incoming bit. When 2K × 8 bits of data have entered the feedback algorithm, the pattern remaining in locations SIGH, SIGL forms the final CRC or signature.

To enable checks to be made on ROMs containing more than 2K bytes, three routines are used:

Title	*Function*
NSIG (New signature)	Resets the 'shift register' SIGH, SIGL to zero and forms a signature on 2K bytes of ROM
CSIG (Continue Signature)	As above but the 'shift register' is *not* reset to zero at the start, thus allowing a continuation of a signature for ROMs greater than 2K bytes.
DISPLAY	Displays the contents of the 'shift register' SIGH, SIGL in Hex.

The following program shows how all three routines can be used to evaluate the signature of a 4K byte ROM located at B000 Hex to BFFF Hex in the target system.

```
320 REM    BO HEX IS 176 DECIMAL
330 POKE  SELECT, 176
340 CALL  NSIG:REM FIRST 2K BYTES
350 REM    B8 HEX IS 184 DECIMAL
360 POKE  SELECT, 184
370 CALL  CSIG:REM CONTINUE WITH NEXT 2K BYTES
380 CALL  DISPLAY:REM DISPLAY FINAL SIGNATURE
```

IMPLEMENTING A TEST PROGRAM – AN EXAMPLE

The Apple ICE can be used with a wide range of 6500 microcomputers designed to run at 1 MHz, provided that all the circuitry on board is controlled by the processor's ϕ_2 clock. As an example the AIM 65 provides the ideal target system, containing up to 4K bytes of RAM, 20K bytes of ROM and a wide range of input/output devices – 2 × 6522 VIAs, 6520 PIA, 6532 RIOT. An overview and a memory map are given in Appendix 2.

A test sequence is shown in Program 11.4. The program begins by testing the system buses, followed by a RAM test on the 4K bytes of RAM, and a ROM test that forms signatures for each of the five system ROMs. Finally the test sequence concludes with a check on the user 6522 VIA. For this test the ports are linked together with a hardwired fixture connecting

```
50      REM AIM65 TEST ROUTINE
60      HOME
70      REM DEFINE SYSTEM ADDRESSES
80      SELECT = − 15100
90      DISPLAY = 8288
100     NSIG = 8192
110     CSIG = 8200
120     BTEST = 8448
130     RAMTEST = 8336
140     PRINT " "
150     PRINT "LOADING MACHINE CODE TESTS"
160     PRINT "BLOAD APPTESTS"
170     PRINT " "
180     PRINT "BUS TESTING-PROBE TARGET SYSTEM BUSES"
190     PRINT "(PRESS SPACE FOR NEXT TEST)"
200     CALL BTEST
210     IF PEEK ( − 16384) < = 127 THEN 200
220     PRINT " "
230     PRINT "RAM TESTING 0000-07FF"
240     POKE SELECT,0: CALL RAMTEST
250     PRINT "RAM TESTING 0800-0FFF"
260     POKE SELECT,08: CALL RAMTEST
270     PRINT " ": PRINT " RAM TESTS COMPLETE "
280     PRINT " "
290     PRINT "ROM SIGNATURES BLOCKS B,C,D,E,F "
300     PRINT " "
310     FOR N = 176 TO 240 STEP 16
320     POKE SELECT,N: CALL NSIG
330     POKE SELECT,(N + 8): CALL CSIG
340     CALL DISPLAY
350     NEXT N
360     PRINT " ": PRINT " ROM SIGNATURES COMPLETE"
370     PRINT " "
380     PRINT " VIA TEST"
390     POKE SELECT,160: REM SELECT BLOCK AXXX
400     APRT = 51201:BPRT = 51200
405     ADIR = 51203:BDIR = 51202
410     POKE ADIR,0: POKE BDIR,255
415     REM A INPUT − B OUTPUT
420     FOR N = 0 TO 255
430     POKE BPRT,N
440     IF PEEK(APRT) < > N THEN PRINT "VIA ERROR"
450     NEXT N
460     POKE BDIR,0: POKE ADIR,255
465     REM BINPUT − A OUTPUT
470     FOR N = 0 TO 255
480     POKE APRT,N
490     IF PEEK (BPRT) < > N THEN PRINT "VIA ERROR"
500     NEXT N
510     PRINT " ": PRINT " TEST COMPLETE"
520     END
```

Program 11.4   Applesoft program sequencing tests

PA0 to PB0, PA1 to PB1, . . ., etc. The routine starts by configuring port A as an input and port B as an output. A 'ramping' test pattern is then written out to port B and read and checked at port A. The role of the ports is then reversed and the test repeated (Fig. 11.5).

The example illustrates some of the techniques that can be used with the Apple ICE. A more detailed program would test the remaining I/O devices to the display, printer, keyboard, etc. and present more guidance to the operator. However, the ideas presented here help to illustrate the principles behind the techniques and mirror those found in commercial instruments, making the Apple ICE not only a practical fault-finding tool but also an ideal low-cost educational aid.

```
]RUN

LOADING MACHINE CODE TESTS

BUS TESTING-PROBE TARGET SYSTEM BUSES
(PRESS SPACE FOR NEXT TEST)

RAM TESTING 0000–07FF
RAM TESTING 0800–0FFF

RAM TESTS COMPLETE

ROM SIGNATURES BLOCKS B,C,D,E,F

B89C
A181
F727
B072
8ABE

ROM SIGNATURES COMPLETE

UIA TEST

TEST COMPLETE

]
```

Fig. 11.5   Typical result of test run on working board

SUMMARY

The cost of a piece of test equipment can be dominated by the display, input and control devices rather than the electronics carrying out the fault identification itself. A microcomputer can be adopted to provide these functions, reducing the test equipment to a single low-cost card. The example uses software running on a standard microcomputer to control an in-circuit emulation card for testing the ROM and RAM of a target system. The system is a good training aid as well as being a practical tool for straightforward testing.

12

Single Board Analyzers

A SIGNATURE ANALYZER

Commercial instruments incorporating signature analysis may have a range of other features such as frequency meters, event counters and logic analyzers. This makes them comprehensive test instruments but also complicated and expensive. A low cost design based only on signature analysis can, however, be accommodated on a small board. With suitable display decoders to produce the letters A,C,F,H,P and U instead of the more usual hexadecimal characters A,B,C,D,E and F respectively, it is possible to obtain a stand-alone design. It is also attractive, if a suitable low-cost microcomputer is available, to supply the signature data to this and make use of a software routine to convert and display the signature using the built-in display or screen. This arrangement would also be suitable for use in computer-assisted fault finding.

The single-board analyzer described here has most of the features of commercial analyzers and is designed to be extended to include a micro-computer interface. For ease of testing, however, this initial design uses four LED displays with integral decoding logic (TIL308), so the unit operates as a stand-alone signature analyzer. The TIL308 decoding logic gives a unique character for each 4-bit binary number. The data bits can also be latched into the display if an appropriate signal is provided. The displayed characters, unfortunately, do not conform to either the hexadecimal or signature analysis character sets, so a conversion table is required when comparing the signatures obtained using this device with those obtained using commercial instruments. This is not a serious disadvantage when a new system is being documented using the unit. The control inputs to this unit have been limited to:

1 a start signal
2 a stop signal
3 a clock signal

and three signals which can be set using switches to select the active edge of the above signals. The essential feature of the start/stop inputs is that it must be possible to connect them both to the same signal on the test unit and maintain correct operation of the analyzer with any combination of positive or negative edges selected.

The signature analyzer circuit of this unit consists of a 16-bit shift register with feedback to a modulo–2 adder, to which the data is also an input. Bits 6, 8, 11 and 15 of the shift register are the feedback points, bit 0, the least significant bit of the shift-register, being the bit closest to the serial input. The data in the shift register at the stop condition provides the signature.

Two 74LS164, 8-bit shift registers are used with a quad exclusive-OR gate to make up the modulo-2 adder, as shown in Fig. 12.1.

The sequence of operation requires the shift register to be set to zero, and no clock signal to be applied to it prior to the start condition. At the start of the signature window, the clock signal can be switched to the register and the signature generated from the input data. At the end of the window period, the shift register data can be latched to the displays (or to 8-bit latches if the computer interface is being used). The system can now be reset to be ready for the next start condition.

It is imperative that the data present on the stop edge is not clocked into the shift register or one too many bits will be clocked in and the signature will be incorrect.

The situation is best explained in terms of the signatures of a 16-bit counter, for example, as indicated in Fig. 12.2. (The free-run address bus signatures for most 8-bit microprocessors will be the same as those for a 16-bit counter.)

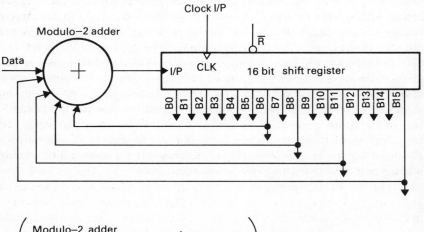

Fig. 12.1   The central element of a signature analyzer

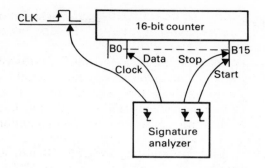

Fig. 12.2 Using a signature analyzer with a 16-bit counter

If the counter is clocked on a rising edge then the data will be stable on the falling edge of the clock. One complete cycle of operation of the counter will require 64K clock pulses and the falling edge of bit 15 of the counter can be used as both start and stop signals for the signature recording process.

The first data item which must, therefore, be clocked into the shift register is that which occurs when all counter outputs are '0'. The last data must be clocked in when all counter outputs are '1'. This means that the signature analyzer shift register must not be allowed to shift on the clock edge which occurs after Q15 on the counter goes low for the first time after a start condition. This is shown in the timing diagram in Fig. 12.3.

The approach to this problem in the design has been to introduce a short delay betwen the test unit clock signal and that which causes the shift action in the shift register. This delay permits the start/stop circuitry to change state and thus allow or inhibit the clock signal to the shift register in advance of the active edge of the clock at the shift register clock input.

The data being input has, therefore, to be latched using the nondelayed clock to ensure that the correct information is input to the analyzer circuit. A J–K flip-flop connected as a D-type latch is used for this purpose, as indicated in Fig. 12.4. A J–K flip-flop is used because the hold time for the data inputs is shorter than that required for most D-types. The introduction of the delay limits the maximum frequency of operation of this analyzer to about 8 MHz. This is satisfactory for testing 8-bit systems and for general educational and training purposes.

Fig. 12.4 also shows the start/stop circuitry which also makes use of J–K flip-flops, clocked on the undelayed clock signal. This clocking is necessary since some microprocessors, like the 8085, do not have stable address lines at all parts of the processor cycle. If A15 is being used in such a system to trigger the start and stop of the signature analyzer, then an incorrect window will be obtained. Using circuitry which clocks the start and stop signals with the test clock signal ensures that the circuit is only

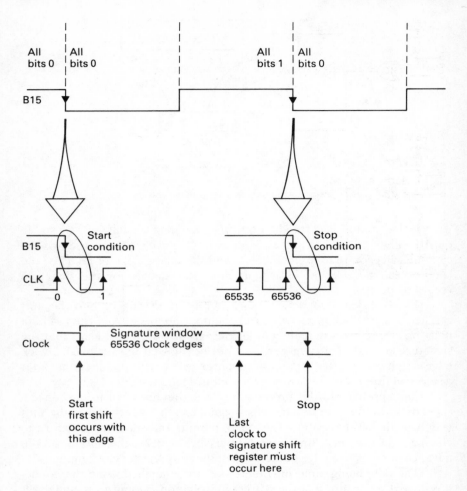

Fig. 12.3   Timing diagram for Fig. 12.2

affected by data states which are detected on the clock transition. The operating edges of start, stop and clock are selected using exclusive-OR gates as controlled inverters. The edges can be selected using single pole switches (or by logic signals derived from a microcomputer interface).

The stop signal has no effect until the two flip-flops associated with 'start' have been set. Both signals require to be at their pretrigger condition for at least one active clock edge and must have changed state on the next active edge for them to operate as indicated earlier. The RUN signal is high for the signature window period and the delayed clock ensures that the correct data is clocked into the signature analyzer circuitry. The falling edge of RUN triggers two one-shots, one of which produces a reset pulse to

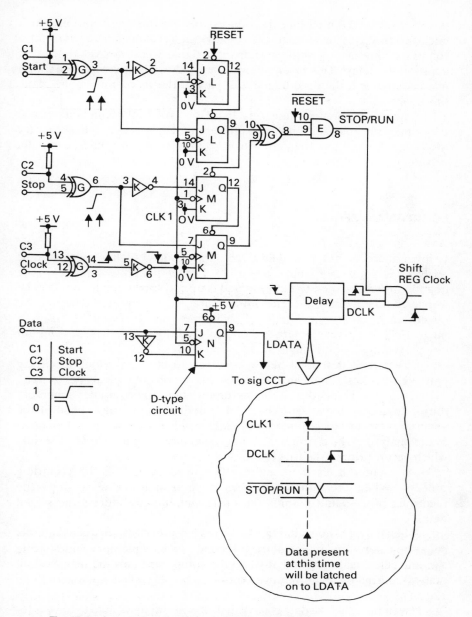

Fig. 12.4 A start-stop circuit for a signature analyzer

the start/stop circuitry while the other starts a sequence of pulses which latch the shift register data to the displays and/or 8-bit latches used for a computer interface. A shift register reset signal is also provided after an appropriate delay. This reset can also be used as an interrupt signal to a microcomputer if the decoding and display of the signature is being done this way.

The reset signal is shown as $\overline{R}$ in Fig. A4.1, the complete circuit diagram of the analyzer, and is of sufficient length to prevent flicker on the display and avoid too frequent interrupt in the case of a microcomputer driven system.

LOGIC ANALYZER

Using a microcomputer to handle the data obtained with a low-cost logic analyzer is even more attractive than with a signature analyzer. The quantity of information to be presented is usually much greater and can be displayed on a monitor screen with advantage. The captured data may be needed in hexadecimal, binary or sometimes ASCII format, so using a microcomputer to manipulate and display the information cuts the amount of logic required on the single board.

The circuit described below is given in outline, without specifying particular devices; it indicates the design philosophy of typical analyzers.

To avoid the need to store captured data in the computer's memory during the recording stage (which could limit the operating speed of the analyzer) a small block of read-write memory is made the central element of the analyzer. The circuit has also been simplified by not storing the data which occurs prior to the trigger event.

A counter is used to address this memory during the recording process. When the counter reaches its maximum value it stops the recording process and permits the microcomputer to address the stored data.

The analyzer shown in Fig. A4.1 uses 8-bit memory. Sixteen data bits could be catered for by including a second block of memory and altering the chip select circuitry so that when the computer reads the data bytes it does so alternately from the two blocks of memory. This is shown in Fig. 12.5.

Even though 8-bit data is recorded, it is useful to be able to have a 16-bit trigger word. The circuit, therefore, shows four 4-bit comparators connected to the data lines and the additional trigger lines. The outputs of the comparators are connected to an AND gate to produce a trigger output. Blocks of four bits can be disabled using the switches shown, to cause a '1' on the AND gate input.

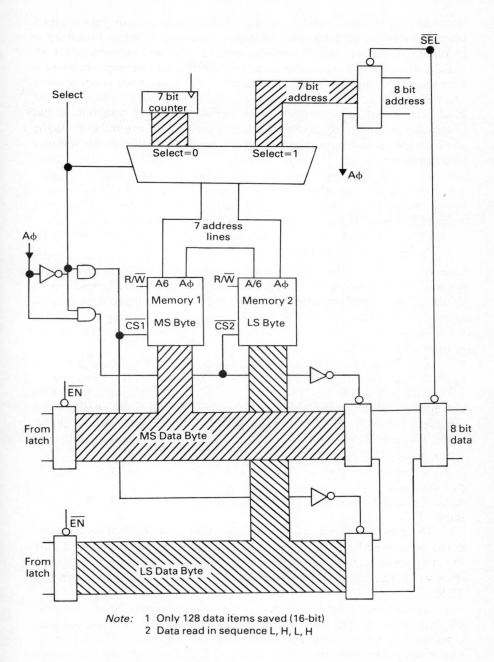

Fig. 12.5 An alternative address – logic circuit for a 16-bit analyzer

Additional comparators can be used to increase the number of trigger bits, and a trigger qualifier can be added if desired. The qualifier circuit would be the same as that shown for the clock qualifier, and its output and the signal labelled T would be connected to an AND gate, the output of which would be the qualified trigger signal.

The input data bits are latched into the input latches by the qualified clock signal and loaded into the first memory location if the analyzer has been armed. The rising edge of the R/$\overline{\text{W}}$ signal is delayed from the input clock edge to allow for propagation delays from the latches to the memory location itself.

The address counter is prevented from advancing until the trigger condition is met. When this occurs, a further delay occurs and a clock pulse is allowed through to the counter to advance it. On reaching the final count, the carry-out signal is used to set a flip-flop which disconnects the counter outputs from the memory, making the addresss lines accessible from the microcomputer circuit.

A 'data available' signal is supplied. The complement output from this flip-flop is used to force the R/$\overline{\text{W}}$ line high so that no data can be written into the memory while the microcomputer is reading the data.

SUMMARY

Two single-board analyzers are discussed: a signature analyzer using low-cost display and with simplified triggering, and an outline design for a logic analyzer. The emphasis is on the underlying principles but with information provided to allow the user to develop further designs.

13

Communications Tools

AN INTERFACE CONVERTER

The variety of interface standards used in serial data communications can give rise to problems when fault finding. Test equipment may be designed to be used only with RS232 signals and not cover current-loop operation.

In those cases where the interface board is separate from the microprocessor board under test, it can be convenient to generate the interface signals to drive a VDU or printer directly from the logic signal outputs and thus avoid having to use a board which may have a fault. The low-cost circuit described below is intended for use in any situation where it is necessary to convert from one signal level to another, without the need to use a supply voltage other than 5 V. It can be used for conversion between current loop and RS232 (or RS423), and can generate signals to these standards from logic levels, and vice versa. Although the circuit provides a number of options, these are selectable via links rather than switches to keep the cost and complexity down. The circuit is shown in Fig. 13.1. The description below illustrates some of the applications.

RS232 AND RS423 SIGNALS

To generate true RS232 signals requires a negative supply. Though ±12V supplies are normally used for such outputs, ±5 V will suffice when the transmission line is short. For RS423 systems, 5 V levels are correct. A negative 5 V supply can be obtained from a +5 V supply using a diode pump circuit or one of the integrated circuit converters such as the 7660. Fig. 13.2 shows the Logic-to-RS232 circuits with a receiver using a CMOS gate with diode clamps to protect it from the normal RS232 signal levels. There are special purpose interface devices such as the 75152 and 75150, which are normally used to perform such conversions. This circuit was, however, developed to show how standard components can be used for these functions if such interface circuits are not available.

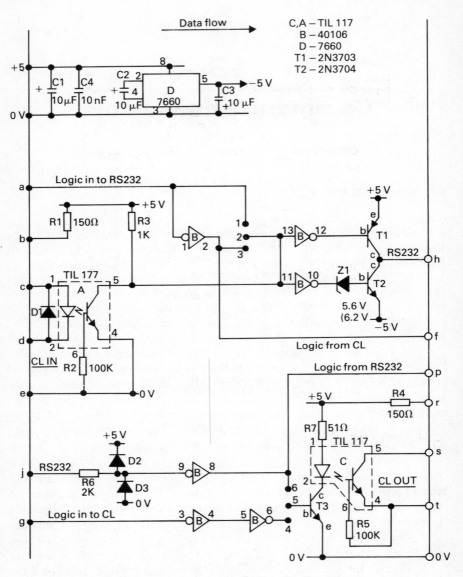

Fig. 13.1   General purpose interface level converter

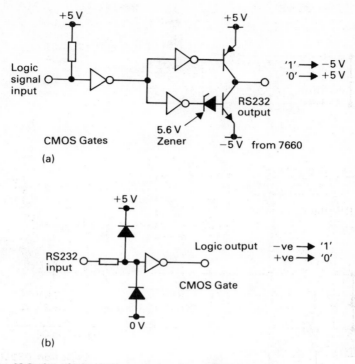

Fig. 13.2 Interfacing logic level signals to RS232 lines
(a) Logic to RS232   (b) RS232 to logic

CURRENT LOOP SIGNALS

Opto-isolators are commonly used in current-loop receive circuits, and the circuit of Fig. 13.3 is a typical example. Care is required over the choice of the collector resistor R_c since too high a value limits the frequency response of the circuit. The value of 1K prevents the output transistor going into saturation, while maintaining a reasonably low collector voltage for diode forward currents in the range 15–22 mA. The diode across the opto-isolator input provides protection against accidental reverse voltages. The current-loop transmitter of Fig. 13.1 also has an opto-isolator which can provide isolation at the transmitter end of the circuit. The current source would in such a case be at the receiving end of the system.

Converter ICs such as the HCPL–4100 and HCPL–4200 can provide logic to current-loop and current-loop to logic conversion with a minimum of additional components. The receiver and transmitter voltage drops are, however, about 2.4 volts compared with 1.6 volts and almost zero in the case of the circuit described here.

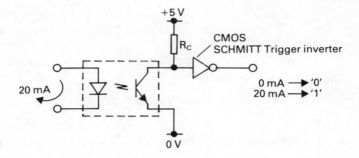

Fig. 13.3   Current loop – logic level conversion

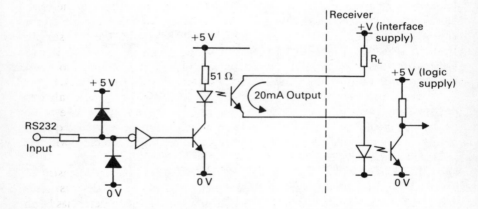

Fig. 13.4   RS232 to current loop with current source in receiver

Configuration	Components	Links	Input	Output	Other comments
LOGIC → RS232	B, D, T1, T2, Z1, R6, D2, D3, C2, C3, C1,	2–3, ab	a	h	R3 must be out
RS232 → LOGIC	C4, R1 = 100K	gov	j	p	
C LOOP → LOGIC	R1, R2, R3, D1, R5,	1–2, de	b c	f	Active
	R7, A, B, C, R4, T3,	1–2	c d	f	Passive
LOGIC → C LOOP	C1, C4, D3 = 100K	5–4, t-ov	g	r s	Active
	RES	5–4	g	s t	Passive
C LOOP → RS232	All components	d-e, 1–2	b c	h	Active
	g linked to 0 V	1–2	c d	h	Passive
RS 232 → C LOOP		6–5, t-ov	j	r s	Active
		6–5	j	s t	Passive

Table 13.1   Configurations for level converter

Fig. 13.4 shows a RS232 to current-loop circuit and Table 13.1 indicates how the components and links should be arranged for a number of different applications.

SERIAL ANALYZER ADD-ON FOR LOGIC ANALYZER

A number of low-cost logic analyzers are available, with capacity to handle up to 16 channels. A front end card able to convert serial data to parallel, and provide a clock pulse to the analyzer on each conversion, can extend its functions to tracing faults in serial transmission systems.

The circuit provided here can be used with any analyzer which has at least eight channels and the facility to set a trigger word using only the least significant eight channels. The particular analyzer in this example has a ribbon cable connector at the rear for the test cable with the 5 V supply brought out. Although not designed to supply external circuitry, it can cope with the serial–parallel converter if CMOS devices are used to keep the current to a minimum. (The prototype circuit draws about 12 mA.)

The facilities which would normally be available on serial analyzers for selecting baud rate and word format via keys and a display have to be switch selectable. A baud-rate generator which produces all the required frequencies simultaneously is an advantage, since only a selector switch is required for the outputs.

The 6402 UART is a stand-alone device, and is therefore easier to interface to discrete logic than bus-oriented programmable devices. This UART produces a data ready (DR) signal when a serial character has been received. This signal can act as a clock input to the logic analyzer. It requires to be reset by a negative going pulse on the input $\overline{DRR}$ (data ready reset). This signal is produced by a counter circuit which is held reset while DR is low. This is shown in Fig. 13.5 and is more satisfactory than a circuit using capacitors to generate a delay, since the $\overline{DRR}$ pulse will always occur after the same number of baud-rate clock pulses. The baud-rate generator is the MC14411, and is wired to produce a clock frequency 16 times that of the required baud rate, as required by the 6402. The complete functional block diagram for the add-on unit is shown in Fig. 13.6. The input selector permits the analyzer to be used to monitor any one of the four signal levels. The logic analyzer is set up by choosing the required trigger word – the hex value of the ASCII character. All trigger and clock qualifiers are switched out and the analyzer is armed after the serial input has been connected to the monitor point, and the expected word format and baud rate set. The serial output being monitored is activated, and after the required number of words have been stored, the first data captured will be displayed. This process can be repeated,

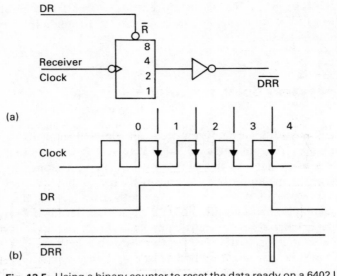

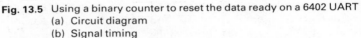

Fig. 13.5 Using a binary counter to reset the data ready on a 6402 UART
　　　　　(a) Circuit diagram
　　　　　(b) Signal timing

monitoring progressively from the signal source to the interface, to determine where the fault lies.

This circuit can of course be used directly with a microprocessor system if a suitable routine is available to examine the data bits provided by the UART, perform any checks required, and store the data in memory during the time between one character and the next. At 1200 baud the bit time is ~830 microseconds and with a 10-bit character there is sufficient time for a machine code routine to be employed to manipulate the data. When the required number of characters has been input, the microcomputer can display the information stored in the buffer area using a high level language, since execution time is no longer a restriction. In this case the most appropriate display format is of the ASCII characters received and some mnemonics to represent the control characters. Many serial data system 'faults' are caused by hidden control characters which are transmitted by the system, and this is one of the most common reasons to use a serial data analyzer.

A SERIAL CHARACTER GENERATOR

The system described below is based on the Z80 single board controller described in this book. The main features are determined by the program, the additional hardware required being minimal.

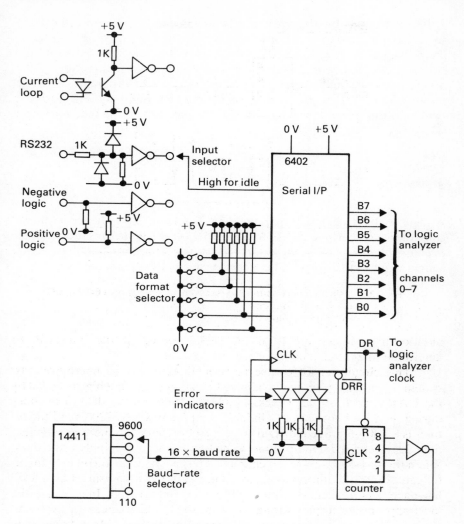

Fig. 13.6   A serial analyzer add-on for a logic analyzer

The program has been written for 1200 baud to simplify the presentation, and can easily be modified to cover other data rates. The PIO ports read switches and output the serial data to the interface card described above. Four functions are provided and are selected by a 4-way switch. The functions are:

1   U*U* . . . test
2   character set in ascending sequence
3   space! test (short line test)
4   selectable character test

A block diagram for the system is shown in Fig. 13.7, where the eight switches connected to port B are those for function 4. The program sets up the ports, checks the switches and then enters the selected routine until a switch is changed. The flowcharts in Fig. 13.8 show the structure of the program and its subroutines. The listing is given in Program 13.1. The system can be extended to cater for various data rates by introducing a switch for this purpose which is read in the same way as the function select switch.

SUMMARY

A logic analyzer deals with parallel data. Communication between micro-computers and peripherals is often in serial form and designs are outlined to convert between different serial formats, to convert into parallel data for a logic analyzer to display and to generate test patterns in serial form.

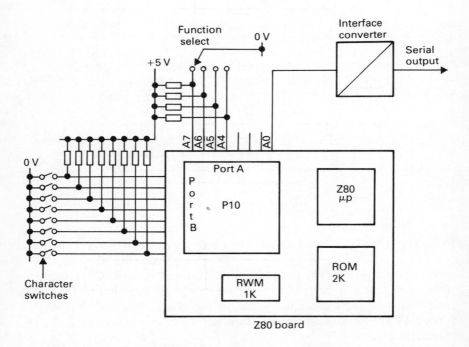

Fig. 13.7   A serial character generator for interface testing

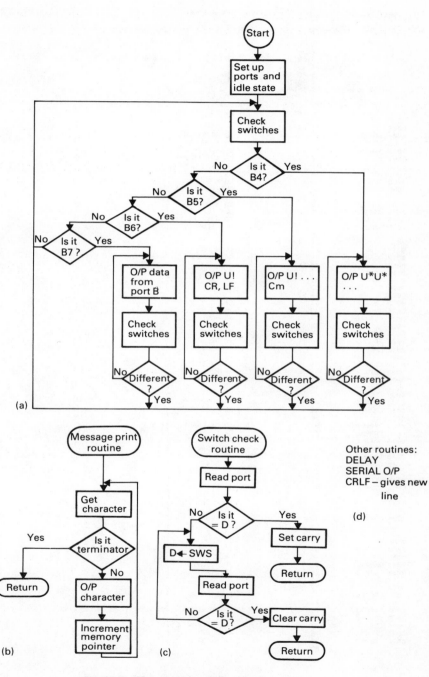

Fig. 13.8 Flowchart for character generator

MSS-H*

```
FILE: SERTSTZ:pLM        HEWLETT-PACKARD: Z80 Assembler                        PAGE   1

LOCATION OBJECT CODE LINE     SOURCE LINE

                           1  "Z80"
              <0002>       2  CLK          EQU      2                    ;MHZ
              <0041>       3  OBTIM        EQU      ((10000*CLK)/12-125)/24+1
              <0078>       4  STPTIM       EQU      120
              <0000>       5  PORTA        EQU      0
              <0001>       6  PORTB        EQU      1
              <0002>       7  CNTRLA       EQU      2
              <0003>       8  CNTRLB       EQU      3
              <00CF>       9  MODE3        EQU      0CFH
              <83FF>      10  SWSAV        EQU      83FFH
                          11
0000                      12  MAIN:
0000 3183FF               13               LD  SP,83FFH
0003 3ECF                 14               LD  A,MODE3
0005 D302                 15               OUT [CNTRLA],A
0007 3EF0                 16               LD  A,11110000B
0009 D302                 17               OUT [CNTRLA],A
                          18
000B 3E01                 19               LD  A,01
000D D300                 20               OUT [PORTA],A
                          21
000F 3ECF                 22               LD  A,MODE3
0011 D303                 23               OUT [CNTRLB],A
0013 3EFF                 24               LD  A,11111111B
0015 D303                 25               OUT [CNTRLB],A
                          26
0017                      27  START:
0017 1600                 28               LD  D,00
0019 CD008E               29               CALL SWCHK
001C                      30  B4:
001C CB62                 31               BIT 4,D
001E 2003                 32               JR  NZ,B5
0020 C30038               33               JP  ROUT1
0023                      34  B5:
0023 CB6A                 35               BIT 5,D
0025 2003                 36               JR  NZ,B6
0027 C3004E               37               JP  ROUT2
002A                      38  B6:
002A CB72                 39               BIT 6,D
002C 2003                 40               JR  NZ,B7
002E C30067               41               JP  ROUT3
0031                      42  B7:
0031 CB7A                 43               BIT 7,D
0033 20E2                 44               JR  NZ,START
0035 C30079               45               JP  ROUT4
                          46
0038                      47  ROUT1:
0038 CD00E9               48               CALL CRLF          ┐
003B 0627                 49               LD  B,39           │
003D                      50  R11:                            │
003D 2100F0               51               LD  HL,MESS1       │ U*........
0040 CD00A0               52               CALL PRMESS        │ OUTPUT.
0043 10F8                 53               DJNZ R11           │
0045 CD008E               54               CALL SWCHK         │
0048 DA0038               55               JP  C,ROUT1        │
004B C30017               56               JP  START          ┘
                          57
004E                      58  ROUT2:
004E CD00E9               59               CALL CRLF          ┐
0051 1E20                 60               LD  E,20H          │
0053                      61  R21:                            │
0053 4B                   62               LD  C,E            │
0054 CD00AC               63               CALL SEROP         │
0057 1C                   64               INC E              } CHARACTER SET O/P.
0058 7B                   65               LD  A,E            │
0059 FE6E                 66               CP  6EH            │
005B C20053               67               JP  NZ,R21         │
005E CD008E               68               CALL SWCHK         │
0061 DA004E               69               JP  C,ROUT2        │
0064 C30017               70               JP  START          ┘
                          71
0067                      72  ROUT3:
0067 CD00E9               73               CALL CRLF          ┐
006A                      74  R31:                            │
006A 2100F6               75               LD  HL,MESS4       } <SP> ! <CR> <LF>
006D CD00A0               76               CALL PRMESS        │
0070 CD008E               77               CALL SWCHK         │
0073 DA006A               78               JP  C,R31          │
0076 C30017               79               JP  START          ┘
                          80
```

Program 13.1   Program using Z80 board as serial character generator

FILE: SERTSTZ:pLM   HEWLETT—PACKARD: Z80 Assembler   PAGE   2

LOCATION OBJECT CODE LINE   SOURCE LINE

```
  0079                   81 ROUT4:
  0079 CD00E9            82              CALL CRLF              ⎤
  007C                   83 R41:                                │
  007C DB01              84              IN A,[PORTB]           │
  007E 4F                85              LD C,A                 ⎬ O/P CHARACTER SET ON
  007F CD00AC            86              CALL SEROP             │ PORT B SWITCHES.
  0082 CD008E            87              CALL SWCHK             │
  0085 DA007C            88              JP C,R41               │
  0088 CD00E9            89              CALL CRLF              │
  008B C30017            90              JP START               ⎦
                         91
                         92 ;THIS ROUTINE READS THE SWITCHES AND IF NOT ALTERED RETURNS WITH
                         93 ;CARRY FLAG SET.  IF ALTERED WAITS UNTIL SETTLED AND RETURNS
                         94 ;WITH CARRY CLEAR, AND SWS IN D
                         95
  008E                   96 SWCHK:
  008E DB00              97              IN A,[PORTA]      ;READ SWS
  0090 E6F0              98              AND 11110000B     ;ONLY INTERESTED IN MS HALF BYTE
  0092 BA                99              CP D
  0093 37               100              SCF               ;SET CARRY
  0094 C8               101              RET Z
                        102
  0095                  103 SWCHK0:
  0095 57               104              LD D,A            ;SWS IN D
  0096 DB00             105              IN A,[PORTA]      ;READ SWS
  0098 E6F0             106              AND 11110000B
  009A BA               107              CP D
  009B C20095          108              JP NZ,SWCHK0
  009E B7               109              OR A              ;CLEAR CARRY
  009F C9               110              RET
                        111
                        112
                        113
                        114
  00A0                  115 PRMESS:
  00A0 7E               116              LD A,[HL]              ⎤
  00A1 FE04             117              CP EM                  │
  00A3 C8               118              RET Z                  ⎬ MESSAGE PRINT
  00A4 4F               119              LD C,A                 │ ROUTINE.
  00A5 CD00AC          120              CALL SEROP             │
  00A8 23               121              INC HL                 │
  00A9 C300A0          122              JP PRMESS               ⎦
                        123
                        124 ;Z80 SERIAL O/P PROGRAM
                        125 ;USES BIT 0 OF PORT 0
                        126 ;IDLE STATE =1
                        127 ;CHARACTER TO BE PLACED IN C BY CALLER
                        128 ;LINE MUST BE SET TO 1 WHEN THIS IS CALLED
                        129 ;CHARACTER IS PLACED IN C-REG BY CALLER
                        130
  00AC                  131 SEROP:
  00AC F3               132              DI
  00AD C5               133              PUSH BC
  00AE D5               134              PUSH DE
                        135
  00AF 0608             136              LD B,08
  00B1 DB00             137              IN A,[PORTA]      ;READ PORT TO PRESERVE IT
  00B3 E6FE             138              AND 11111110B     ;SET BIT 0 TO START BIT
  00B5                  139 LOOP:
  00B5 D300             140              OUT [PORTA],A     ;OUTPUT BIT
  00B7 110041           141              LD DE,OBTIM       ;BIT DELAY IN DE
  00BA CD00E2          142              CALL DELAY         ;WAIT THIS TIME
                        143
  00BD 79               144              LD A,C            ;GET CHARACTER FROM C
  00BE 0F               145              RRCA              ;LSB INTO CARRY
  00BF 4F               146              LD C,A            ;SAVE ROTATED CHAR IN C
  00C0 3807             147              JR C,SET1
  00C2                  148 SET0:
  00C2 DB00             149              IN A,[PORTA]
  00C4 E6FE             150              AND 11111110B     ;SET B0 TO 0
  00C6 C300CE          151              JP CONT
  00C9                  152 SET1:
  00C9 00               153              NOP               ;TO EQUALISE TIME IN THE TWO PATHS
  00CA DB00             154              IN A,[PORTA]
  00CC F601             155              OR 00000001B      ;SET B0 TO 1
  00CE                  156 CONT:
  00CE 05               157              DEC B
  00CF F200B5          158              JP P,LOOP
                        159
```

Program 13.1 Program using Z80 board as serial character generator (continued)

```
      00D2 DB00        160                    IN A,[PORTA]
      00D4 F601        161                    OR 00000001B      ;STOP BIT SET
      00D6 D300        162                    OUT [PORTA],A     ;OUTPUT BIT
      00D8 110078      163                    LD DE,STPTIM
      00DB CD00E2      164                    CALL DELAY        ;WAIT
                       165
      00DE D1          166                    POP DE
      00DF C1          167                    POP BC
      00E0 FB          168                    EI
      00E1 C9          169                    RET
                       170
                       171
                       172 ;DELAY PROGRAM
                       173 ;DECREMENTS DE TILL ZERO
                       174 ;DE MUST BE LOADED WITH APPROPRIATE DELAY VALUE
      00E2             175 DELAY:                              ⌉
      00E2 1B          176                    DEC DE           |
      00E3 7A          177                    LD A,D             DELAY.
      00E4 B3          178                    OR E               ROUTINE.
      00E5 C200E2      179                    JP NZ,DELAY      |
      00E8 C9          180                    RET              ⌋
                       181
      00E9             182 CRLF:
      00E9 2100F3      183                    LD HL,MESS2      ⌉ O/P <CR> <LF>
      00EC CD00A0      184                    CALL PRMESS      |
      00EF C9          185                    RET              ⌋
                       186
           <000D>      187 CR        EQU    0DH               ⌉
           <000A>      188 LF        EQU    0AH               |
           <0004>      189 EM        EQU    04                |
      00F0 552A04      190 MESS1:    DEFB  'U*',EM              MESSAGES.
      00F3 0D0A04      191 MESS2:    DEFB  CR,LF,EM           |
      00F6 20210D0A04  192 MESS4:    DEFB  ' !',CR,LF,EM      ⌋
```

Appendices

A1

Microprocessor Comparison

MICROPROCESSOR DETAILS

Information is given here on the 6502, 8085 and Z80 microprocessors used in the examples in the text. Less detailed information on the 6800, NSC800 and 8086 is also included.

It has been collated from the different manufacturers' data sheets but rearranged in a more uniform way. The inputs and outputs have been grouped into categories which relate to the servicing aspects of the signals and emphasize the common features of different microprocessors. This is different from the manufacturers' approach where each gives emphasis to the special features of his own processor.

The signal groups are:

1   Processor control signals
2   Data transfer controls
3   Address and data bus signals
4   Processor status signals
5   Interrupt controls
6   Supplies
7   Clocks
8   Other signals – usually special functions

1 PROCESSOR CONTROL SIGNALS – These signals are designed to stop or slow down processor operation, e.g. the RESET, which ensures that the microprocessor can be set to a known state.

2 DATA TRANSFER CONTROLS – These signals control the transfer of data between the processor and memory or I/O devices, e.g. READ or WRITE lines.

3 ADDRESS AND DATA BUS SIGNALS – Address lines are set to values determined by the processor to permit it to select a device as a source or destination for data. The address lines are output lines from the microprocessor and must therefore not be controlled by another device unless it is possible for the microprocessor to relinquish control by making them high impedance (tristate).

The data lines are bidirectional and carry data to and from the processor. The two sets of lines have been grouped together since many processors use the address to carry data on a time multiplexed basis, as in the 8085, NSC800, and most 16-bit processors. In small systems where the most significant address lines are not all used, it is possible to have faults on these lines which do not cause system failure.

4 PROCESSOR STATUS SIGNALS – These provide information about the internal operation of the microprocessor and may sometimes provide control signals to devices in the system. They allow the designer to link to test equipment for a more complete analysis of machine operation, for example in logic analysis. Signals of this type, which are not used in the system, could in certain circumstances be faulty without causing system malfunction, e.g. an output stage could be blown and the status output held permanently low but the microprocessor might still function.

5 INTERRUPT CONTROLS – These signals are used when some external event requires the microprocessor to respond by breaking its normal sequence of execution. Some of the signals included in this section provide status to the interrupting device on the result of the interrupt request. Some may have no effect unless enabled in the program, and can therefore be in any state without causing a fault when disabled. Others are always active and will have to be in the off state if the microprocessor is not to respond to them all the time and fail to execute its desired program, e.g. NMI – nonmaskable interrupt–is always available.

6 SUPPLIES – Most modern microprocessors operate from a single supply but some existing equipment using, for example, the 8080 requires more than one supply on the processor chip. Faults on supply lines will obviously cause failure of the microprocessor and its system.

7 CLOCKS – These include clock signal inputs and outputs. Since the microprocessor circuits are clock driven, faults on clock lines will cause system failure. If a clock output is buffered and not connected to other system components, a fault there will not always cause system failure. Some microprocessors use dynamic memory for internal registers and will lose data if the clock frequency falls below a particular value.

8 OTHER SIGNALS – These are signals not included in the above categories and usually provide special features on the particular microprocessor.

THE 6502

The 6502 is an 8-bit microprocessor which is related in its structure to the 6800 having similar instruction types, and a similar register set. The signals and their pin numbers are shown in Fig. A1.1 and are described below.

6502 Signals

1 CPU Controls
RESET   This signal resets the processor, and when removed causes it to load the program counter with the contents of addresses FFFC and FFFD.

RDY   Causes the processor to enter wait states.

2 Data Transfer
R/$\overline{\text{W}}$ A single line is used to indicate when the processor is reading or writing data. '1' = read; '0' = write. This processor does not have the facility to address I/O separately from memory.

3 Address and Data Buses
D0–D7   These are standard nonmultiplexed buses.
A0–A15

4 CPU Status
SYNC   This indicates that the microprocessor is fetching an instruction.

5 Interrupt
$\overline{\text{NMI}}$ This is the nonmaskable interrupt. The program counter will be loaded from FFFA and FFFB and execution will proceed using this value.

$\overline{\text{IRQ}}$ This is the maskable interrupt. The program counter will be loaded from FFFE and FFFF.

6 Supplies
0 V, 5 V   A single 5 V supply, only, is required.

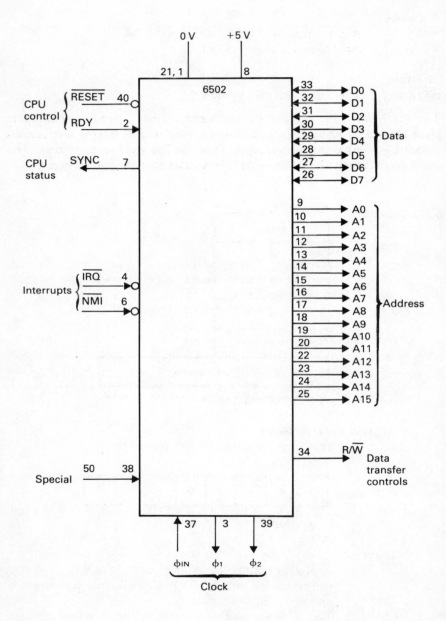

Fig. A1.1   6502 signals and pin connections

7 Clocks

ϕ_{IN} A clock input is required at this point.

ϕ_1, ϕ_2 Are the two phase clock outputs.

8 Other

$\overline{SO}$ This signal sets the overflow flag.

Fig. A1.2 shows the register set which has a smaller number of registers than most 8-bit processors, but makes up for this by having instructions which have fast access to addresses from 00H to FFH or page zero. The stack pointer register is 8 bits wide and assumes that the stack is in page 1.

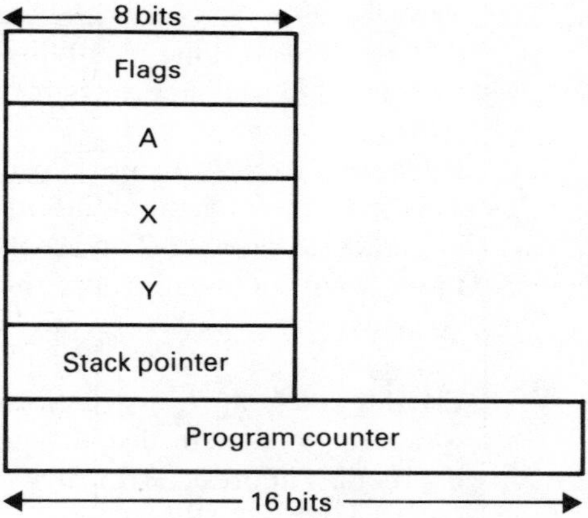

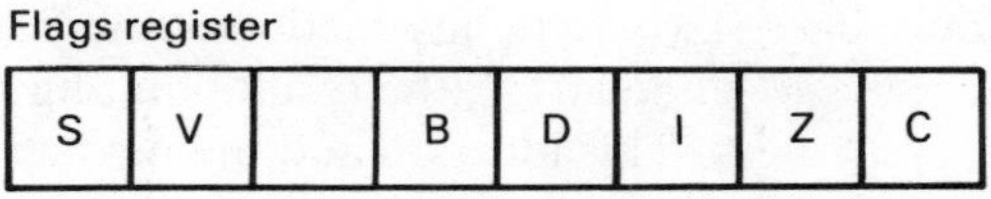

Flags register

S—Sign
V—Overflow
B—Break
D—Decimal
I—Interrupt
Z—Zero
C—Carry

Fig. A1.2   6502 register set

The processor has a number of addressing modes, some of which use data in two consecutive memory locations. In these cases the low order byte is always first and the high order one second.

1 Accumulator: The operation is on accumulator data.

2 Immediate: The data contained in the address following the instruction in memory is used for the operation.

3 Absolute: Three byte instructions where the address referred to forms the second and third bytes of the instruction.

4 Zero page: Similar to absolute addressing except that the instructions are two bytes long and the address referred to in the second byte is in page 0.

5 Zero page indexed: The registers X or Y are used to compute an address. This is done by adding the second instruction byte to the appropriate index register contents.

6 Absolute indexed: Registers X or Y are used to produce an address. This is formed by the addition of the 16-bit absolute address in bytes 2 and 3 of the instruction and the contents of the appropriate index register.

7 Implied: A particular register is implicitly stated in the instruction.

8 Relative: Conditional branch instructions use a second byte which is a signed displacement from the next instruction address. Branches can, therefore, only jump back by 128 locations or forward by 127.

9 Absolute indirect: The second and third bytes of an instruction form an address which, together with the next address in sequence, contain the two bytes of an address.

10 Indexed indirect: Two byte instructions where the second byte is added to X, the result pointing to a location in page 0. This location and the next contain the address to which the instruction refers.

11 Indirect indexed: A 2-byte instruction in which the second byte points to a location in page 0. The contents of this address and the next in sequence are treated as a 16-bit address to which the contents of the Y register are added to obtain the address to which the instruction refers.

6502 Instruction Mnemonics

Arithmetic and Logical
ADC   add to A register with carry

SBC	subtract with borrow
AND	logical AND
ORA	logical OR
EOR	logical EXCLUSIVE OR
CMP	compare with accumulator
CPX	compare with X
CPY	compare with Y
INC	increment contents of memory
DEC	decrement contents of memory
INX/INY	increment X/Y
DEX/DEY	decrement X/Y
ROL/ROR	rotate left/right through carry
ASL/LSR	left/right shift

Data Transfer

LDA	load accumulator
STA	store accumulator
LDX/LDY	load X/Y
STX/STY	store X/Y
TAX/TAY	transfer A to X/Y
TXA/TYA	transfer X/Y to A
TSX	transfer SP to X
TXS	transfer X to SP

Branching instructions

JMP	jump
JSR	jumpt to subroutine
RTI	return from interrupt
RTS	return from subroutine
BCC	branch on carry clear
BCS	branch on carry set
BEQ	branch on zero result
BMI	branch on negative result
BPL	branch on positive result
BVC	branch on overflow clear
BVS	branch on overflow set

Stack Operations

PHA/PHP	push A/flags to stack
PLA/PLP	load A/flags from stack

Interrupt

CLI	clear interrupt disable status bit
SEI	set interrupt disable bit
BRK	break

Miscellaneous

SEC	set carry flag
SED	set decimal status
NOP	no operation
CLC	clear carry flag
CLD	clear decimal status
CLV	clear overflow status
BIT	bit test

THE 8085

This is an improved version of the 8080 having two additional instructions, RIM and SIM; single supply; multiplexed address and data bus; and increased interrupt handling capacity. Fig. A1.3 shows the signals and their pin numbers.

8085 Signals

1 CPU Control

$\overline{\text{RESET IN}}$ This is the processor reset signal. The program counter is reset to 0000.

READY   Indicates that memory or I/O is ready to send or receive data. When taken low, the processor waits until ready goes high before completing read or write cycle.

HOLD   This is used by another device to request use of address and data bus. The processor relinquishes control when the current transfer is completed.

2 Data Transfer Controls

$\overline{\text{RD}}$ The read control signal.

$\overline{\text{WR}}$ The write control signal.

ALE   The demultiplexing control for the address bus. This signal is high when the lower 8 bits of the address bus are used to carry address information.

$\text{IO}/\overline{\text{M}}$ This line is low for memory and high for I/O transactions.

3 Address and Data Bus

AD0–AD7   The two buses are multiplexed in this processor.

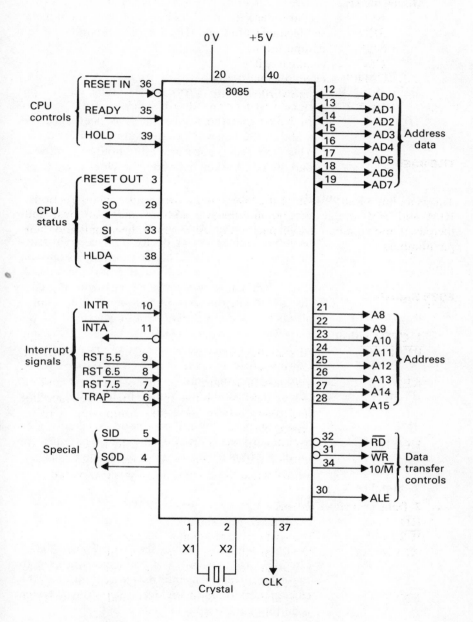

Fig. A1.3 8085 signals and pin connections

AD8–AD15   The lower 8 bits AD0–AD7 carry address informa-
                    tion during the first clock cycle of any memory or
                    I/O transaction and data for the remainder of the
                    time.

4 CPU Status
RESET OUT   Indicates that the processor is being reset. This
                    signal is synchronized with the clock.

HLDA   Indicates that the hold signal has been received
                    and that the bus will be released in the next cycle.
                    This signal also goes low after hold is removed,
                    and the bus is taken over one-half clock cycle later.

5 Interrupt Controls
INTR   This is the general purpose maskable interrupt
                    signal. It is acknowledged by INTA which can be
                    used by the interrupting device to place an instruc-
                    tion on the data bus. This instruction, usually an
                    RST or a CALL, is read as if from memory. A
                    CALL will cause two further reads from the data
                    bus to obtain the two address bytes which must
                    also be supplied by the interrupting device.

RST 5.5   Hardware interrupts which can be masked using
RST 6.5   SIM. They cause the processor to take up execu-
RST 7.5   tion at addresses 2C, 34, 3C respectively, if en-
                    abled and not masked.

TRAP   The nonmaskable interrupt. The interrupt routine
                    for this should start at 0024H.

INTA   This is provided by the processor to acknowledge
                    as interrupt on INTR and can be used by interrupt
                    hardware to place instructions on the data bus.

6 Supplies
0 V, 5 V   Single 5 V supply, only, required.

7 Clocks
X1, X2   A crystal with a frequency up to 6 MHz for 8085A
                    (10 MHz for 8085A–1) is connected directly to
                    these terminals. The internal circuit contains the
                    clock generator and a divider, one output of which
                    is buffered and output at CLK.

8 Others
SID   A single data input line which can be read into bit 7
                    of the A–reg by executing a RIM instruction.

SOD   A single data output line which takes the state of bit 7 of A when SIM is executed with bit 6 of A set to 1.

These lines can be used for serial input and output under software control.

Fig. A1.4 shows the register set of the processor which has an accumulator and six general purpose 8-bit registers which can also be treated in pairs as 16-bit registers. The stack pointer and program counter are 16-bit registers.

Operations can address data in a number of different ways as listed below. 16-bit data stored in memory is always stored least significant byte first.

1 Register: One of two registers are implicitly referred to in the single byte instruction code.

2 Immediate: The data in the second byte of a 2-byte instruction is used for the operation.

3 Extended immediate: The second and third bytes of a 3-byte instruction are used for the 16-bit operation.

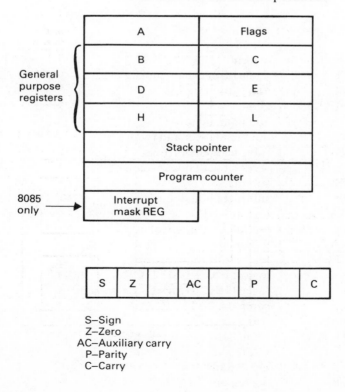

S–Sign
Z–Zero
AC–Auxiliary carry
P–Parity
C–Carry

Fig. A1.4 8080/8085 register set

4 Absolute: The address referred to by the instruction is contained in the second and third bytes of the 3-byte instruction.

5 Register indirect: The address referred to by the instruction is contained in a register pair. The common register indirect instructions use the HL pair as the memory pointer.

6 Double register: One or two register pairs are referred to in the single byte code.

7 Port mode: Two instructions use the address bus and control line IO/$\overline{\text{M}}$ in such a way that memory is not selected.

The instruction set is given below in summary form. Note that all branching instructions are absolute branches, and can thus jump to any location in memory.

8080/8085 Instruction Mnemonics

Arithmetic and Logical
ACI	add with carry immediate
ADC	add with carry
ADD	add
ADI	add immediate
DAD	double register add (with HL)
SBB	subtract with borrow
SBI	subtract with borrow immediate
SUB	subtract
SUI	subtract immediate
ANA	logical AND
ANI	logical AND immediate
ORA	logical OR
ORI	logical OR immediate
XRA	logical EXCLUSIVE OR
XRI	logical EXCLUSIVE OR immediate
CMP	compare
CPI	compare immediate
RAL/RAR	rotate left/right through carry
RLC/RRC	rotate left/right circular
INR	increment
DCR	decrement
INX	increment register pair
DCX	decrement register pair

Data Transfers

MOV	transfer data
MVI	load immediate
LXI	load register pair immediate
LDA	load accumulator direct from memory
LDAX	load accumulator indirect from memory
STA	store accumulator direct
STAX	store accumulator indirect
XCHG	exchange DE, HL

Branching Instructions

CALL/RET/JMP	call/return/jump	absolute
CNZ/RNC/JNZ	call/return/jump	if not zero
CZ/RZ/JZ	call/return/jump	if zero
CNC/RNC/JNC	call/return/jump	if no carry
CC/RC/JC	call/return/jump	if carry
CPO/RPO/JPO	call/return/jump	on odd parity
CPE/RPE/JPE	call/return/jump	on even parity
CP/RP/JP	call/return/jump	on positive result
CM/RM/JM	call/return/jump	on negative result
RST	restart	
PCHL	transfer HL to PC	

Stack Operations

PUSH	store on stack
POP	load from stack
XTHL	exchange top of stack with HL

Interrupt

EI	enable interrupts
DI	disable interrupts

Input/Output

IN	input from port to A register
OUT	output to port from A register

Miscellaneous

NOP	do nothing	
HLT	halt	
CMA	complement accumulator	
CMC	complement carry	
STC	set carry flag	
DAA	decimal adjust accumulator	
RIM	read interrupt mask to A register	} 8085 only
SIM	set interrupt mask from A register	

THE Z80

This microprocessor is an extended version of the 8080 with additional registers, instructions and facilities. It requires only a single-phase clock and 5 V power supply but does not produce an interrupt acknowledge, which has to be generated externally if required. The memory/IO select signals are separate. All control signal inputs and outputs are active–low. The signals and their pin numbers are shown in Fig. A1.5 and are described below.

Z80 Signals

1 CPU Control

$\overline{\text{RESET}}$ — An active low input which resets the processor. The program counter is reset to 0000.

$\overline{\text{WAIT}}$ — Indicates that the processor is required to enter wait states.

$\overline{\text{BUSRQ}}$ — An active low input which can be supplied by a device requiring access to the system bus.

2 Data Transfer Controls

$\overline{\text{RD}}$ — Used when the processor wishes to read data from memory or I/O.

$\overline{\text{WR}}$ — The write control.

$\overline{\text{MREQ}}$ — Active when memory transactions are taking place.

$\overline{\text{IORQ}}$ — Active when I/O transactions take place, i.e. during IN and OUT instructions.

3 Address and Data Bus

D0–D7 — Eight data lines and 16 address lines are used on the Z80. When buses are relinquished as response to BUSRQ these lines are high impedance.

4 CPU Status

$\overline{\text{MI}}$ — An active low output indicating that an instruction fetch is taking place.

$\overline{\text{HALT}}$ — An active low output indicating that an HLT instruction has been executed and that, as a result, the processor has stopped.

$\overline{\text{BUSAK}}$ — This signal indicates that the processor has relinquished control of the buses.

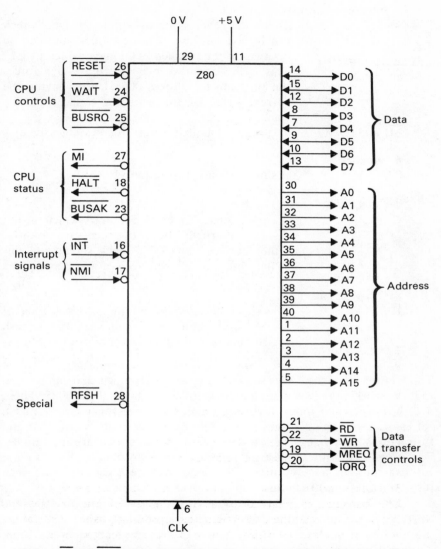

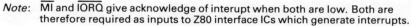

Note: $\overline{MI}$ and $\overline{IORQ}$ give acknowledge of interupt when both are low. Both are therefore required as inputs to Z80 interface ICs which generate interrupts.

$\overline{INTA}$ can be generated:

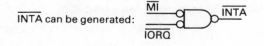

Fig. A1.5 Z80 signals and pin connections

5 Interrupt Controls

$\overline{\text{INT}}$ This is the general purpose interrupt signal which can be used in one of three modes, and can be disabled by the instruction DI and enabled by EI.

$\overline{\text{NMI}}$ This is the nonmaskable interrupt which forces the program to address 0066H after saving the current value of the program counter on the stack.

$\overline{\text{M1}}$ and $\overline{\text{IORQ}}$ Together act as an interrupt acknowledge signal.

6 Supplies

0 V, 5 V   A single 5 V supply is required.

7 Clocks

CLK   A single phase clock is required which is not divided internally by the processor circuitry. Other devices requiring a clock should use this signal, since no buffered clock output is available.

8 Other Signals

$\overline{\text{RFSH}}$ This signal is active during the last clock cycle of an M1 cycle and the contents of the refresh register are placed on the lower bits of the address bus.

The register set of the Z80 is shown in Fig. A1.6, from which it can be seen that the working registers are almost identical to those of the 8085. There are, however, two index registers, an interrupt vector register, and a refresh register. In addition to these there is an alternate register set and instructions to exchange the contents of the working registers and this set. This provides a fast way of saving registers when new data has to be set up, for example, in a subroutine. The index registers can be used with displacements in instructions to obtain values from tables.

The instruction set contains that of the 8085 (except for RIM and SIM) so all the 8085 addressing modes are appropriate to the Z80. There are additional modes which use relative addressing techniques for branching instructions.

Z80 Instruction Mnemonics (also NSC 800)

Arithmetic and Logical

ADC	add with carry (8 bit and 16 bit)
ADD	add (8 bit and 16 bit)
SBC	subtract with carry (8 bit and 16 bit)
SUB	subtract
AND	logical AND

OR	logical OR
XOR	logical EXCLUSIVE OR
CP	compare
INC	increment
DEC	decrement
RLA	rotate A left through carry
RRA	rotate A right through carry
RLCA	rotate A left circular
RRCA	rotate A right circular
RL	rotate left through carry
RLC	rotate left circular
RR	rotate right through carry
RRC	rotate right circular
RLD	decimal rotate left
RRD	decimal rotate right
SLA	shift left
SRA	arithmetic shift right
SRL	logic shift right

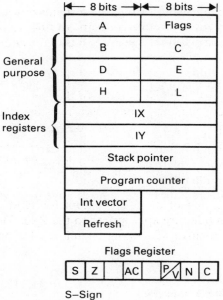

Flags Register

S–Sign
Z–Zero
AC–Auxiliary carry
P–Parity
V–Overflow
N–Subtract
C–Carry

Fig. A1.6 Z80 register set

Data Transfers
LD a,b   load a from b

where

1   a is any one of A, B, C, D, E, H, L
    b is any one of A, B, C, D, E, H, L, (HL), (IX+disp), (IY+disp), 8-bit
    number
2   a is A
    b is (BC), (DE), (address), R, or I
3   a is (BC), (DE), (address), R, or I
4   a is one of (HL), (IX+disp), (ZY+disp)
    b is one of A,B,C,D,E,H,L, 8-bit number
5   a is (address)
    b is A,BC,DE,HL,IX,IY,SP
6   a is BC,DE,HL
    b is (address), 16-bit number
7   a is SP
    b is (address), HL,IX,IY, 16-bit number

Branching instructions
JP/CALL/RET	jump/call/return	absolute
JP/CALL/RET NZ	jump/call/return	if not zero
JP/CALL/RET Z	jump/call/return	if zero
JP/CALL/RET NC	jump/call/return	if no carry
JP/CALL/RET C	jump/call/return	if carry
JP/CALL/RET PE	jump/call/return	if parity even
JP/CALL/RET PO	jump/call/return	if parity odd
JR displacement	jump relative	
JR C, displacement	jump relative	if carry
JR NC, displacement	jump relative	if no carry
JR NZ, displacement	jump relative	if not zero
JR Z, displacement	jump relative	if zero
DJNZ	decrement B and jump relative if not zero	
RETI	return from interrupt	
RETN	return from nonmaskable interrupt	

Stack Operations
PUSH   Store on stack   }
POP   load from stack   } AF,BC,DE,HL,IX,IY

Bit Operations
BIT   bit test   }
SET   set bit   } Any bit of A,B,C,D,E,H,L, (HL),
RES   reset bit   } (IX+disp),(IY+disp)

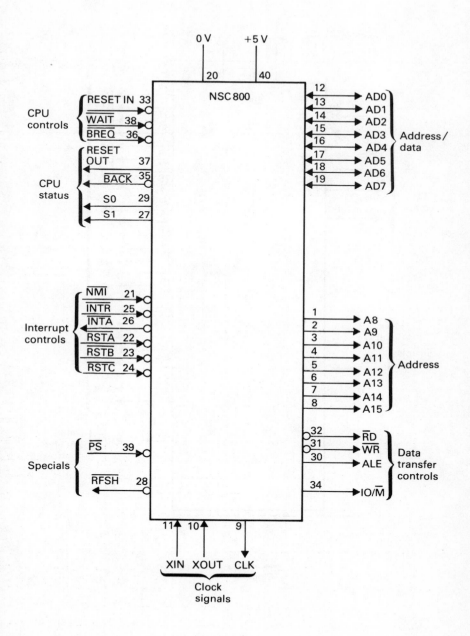

Fig. A1.7 NSC800 signals and pin connections

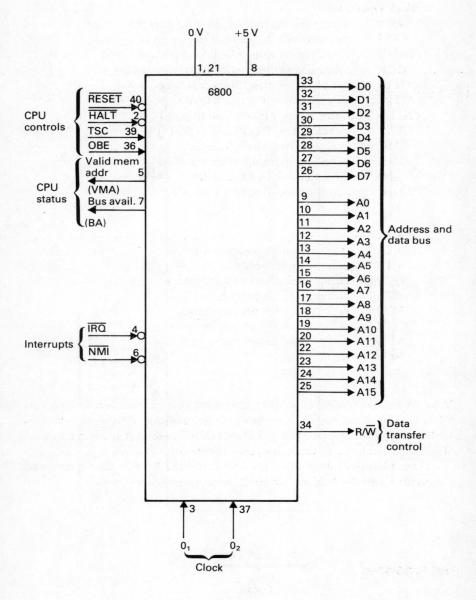

Fig. A1.8   6800 signals and pin connections

Block Operations

IND	decrementing block load from port (C)
INI	incrementing block load from port (C)
INDR	autodecrementing block load from port (C)
INIR	autoincrementing block load from port (C)
OTDR	autodecrementing block load to port (C)
OTIR	autoincrementing block load to port (C)
OUTD	decrementing block load to port (C)
OUTI	incrementing block load to port (C)
LDD	decrementing block transfer
LDDR	autodecrementing block transfer
LDI	incrementing block transfer
LDIR	autoincrementing block transfer

Miscellaneous

DAA	decimal adjust accumulator
CFF	complement carry flag
CPD	compare decrementing memory
CPL	complement A register
CPDR	search decrementing memory
CPIR	compare incrementing memory
NEG	obtain twos complement of A register
NOP	do nothing
SCF	set carry flag

Note: When using Z80 assembler mnemonics, an expression in brackets refers to the contents of a memory location, the address of which is evaluated by the expression, e.g. LD A, (IX +5) – load A from the address obtained by adding 5 to the index register contents.

The additional diagrams Figs. A1.7 and A1.8 show the signals and pin numbers for the NSC800 and 6800 microprocessors.

THE 8088/8086

The 8086 was introduced in 1978 as Intel's first 16-bit microprocessor. It was designed to be upward compatible with the 8080 at assembly language level (i.e. the 8080 mnemonics are a subset of the 8086) but not at machine code level.

Like the 8080 the 8086 is only one chip in a multiprocessor system. In addition to the 8086 the following chips are normally used:

– 8284: clock generator/driver
– 8288: bus controller – used in applications where the processor is configured in MAXIMUM MODE for use with coprocessors.

The 8088 is an 8086 with an 8-bit data bus. The two processors are identical in many respects (Fig. A1.9). Any external differences are highlighted in the following discussion.

8088/8086 Signals

Note: Minimum mode signals are indicated by being enclosed in brackets, e.g. (HOLD)

1 CPU Control

RESET

System reset positive edge triggered. Interrupts and single stepping mode are disabled. Program execution after reset begins from location FFFF0H with DS, ES, SS and PC = 0000H.

READY

Used to indicate to processor that a memory or I/O device is ready to send or receive data. If ready is low, then 8086 executes 'wait' states until READY goes high. Again this signal is usually passed to the processor via the 8284.

(HOLD)

Other devices use this line to request use of the system buses. When set high, 8086 enters a hold state after completing its current bus cycle and then acknowledges this state by setting HLDA high.

$\overline{\text{TEST}}$

When the 8086 meets a WAIT instruction it will idle if $\overline{\text{TEST}}$ is high.

MN/$\overline{\text{MX}}$

Used to configure the processor in either:

(a) Minimum mode – MN/$\overline{\text{MX}}$ pin connected to Vcc sets the 8086 into minimum mode and sets processor pins 24 to 31 to the following:
$\overline{\text{INTA}}$, ALE, $\overline{\text{DEN}}$, DT/$\overline{\text{R}}$, $\overline{\text{IO}}$/M, $\overline{\text{WR}}$, HLDA, HOLD

(b) Maximum mode – MN/$\overline{\text{MX}}$ pin tied to Vss selects maximum mode. In this mode the 8086 is normally used along with the 8288 bus controller to operate coprocessor options. In maximum mode pins 24 to 31 take on the following roles:
QS1, QS0, $\overline{\text{S0}}$, $\overline{\text{S1}}$, $\overline{\text{S2}}$, $\overline{\text{LOCK}}$, $\overline{\text{RQ}}$/$\overline{\text{GT0}}$, $\overline{\text{RQ}}$/$\overline{\text{GT1}}$

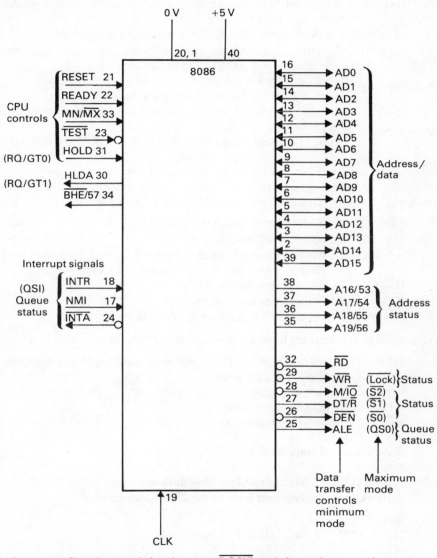

Fig. A1.9 8086 signals and pin connections

Notes: 1 Signal names in brackets, e.g. $\overline{\text{(LOCK)}}$ apply in maximum mode.
2 Status signals S0–S7 are multiplexed.

2 Data Transfer Controls

$\overline{RD}$	The read control signal
$(\overline{WR})$	The write control signal
(ALE)	A high ALE pulse signifies a valid memory address on the address/data bus
$(\overline{DEN})$	Used to enable 8286/8287 transceivers on data bus
$(DT/\overline{R})$	Controls direction of flow of data through data bus transceivers. Similar to $\overline{S1}$ in maximum mode
	High – data flows from processor onto system bus
	Low – data from buses passes to processor
$(M/\overline{IO})$	Driven low by instructions directed at I/O devices and high for memory (output)
	Note: on 8088 signal is inverted, i.e. $IO/\overline{M}$ to maintain compatibility with 8085.

Most of the signals described above are generated directly by the processor when in minimum mode. In a maximum mode system the 8288 bus controller uses the S0, S1, S2 status signals to generate the following.

$\overline{MRDC}$	Memory read command
$\overline{MWTC}$	Memory write command
$\overline{AMWC}$	Advanced memory write command. Signal gives memory an earlier indication of a write instruction than MWTC
$\overline{IORC}$	I/O read command (output)
$\overline{IOWC}$	I/O write command (output)
$\overline{AIOWC}$	Advanced I/O write command (output)

Note: 8288 also generates for maximum mode configuration:

DEN	(Data enable) as $\overline{DEN}$ on processor but with opposite polarity, i.e. active high
$DT/\overline{R}$	Data transmit/receive
ALE	Address latch enable
$\overline{INTA}$	Interrupt acknowledge

3 Address and Data Bus

8086

AD0–AD15	Multiplexed address/data bus
A16–A19	Top four lines of the 20-bit address bus

8088

AD0–AD7	Multiplexed address/data bus
A8–A19	Top 12 lines of the 20-bit address bus

4 CPU Status

(HLDA)	Output set high to acknowledge a hold request made on HOLD input. When high, processor floats its tristate outputs.

A19/S6
A18/S5
A17/S4
A16/S3

These dual purpose pins carry the most significant address bits during the first clock period on an instruction cycle. Throughout other clock cycles they provide status information. They are held low during I/O operations.

S4   S3

0	0	Extra segment
0	1	Stack segment
1	0	Code segment or no segment
1	1	Data segment

S5 – reflects state of interrupt enable flag
S6 – held low if 8086 is controlling system bus

When the processor is in maximum mode, pins $\overline{S0}$, $\overline{S1}$ and $\overline{S2}$ are used to provide status information for the 8288 bus controller as follows:

$\overline{S2}$ $\overline{S1}$ $\overline{S0}$

0	0	0	Interrupt acknowledge
0	0	1	I/O read
0	1	0	I/O write
0	1	1	Halt
1	0	0	Instruction fetch
1	0	1	Memory read
1	1	0	Memory write
1	1	1	Inactive

Further pins QS0 and QS1 provide details of the processor's instruction queue status.

QS0   QS1

0	0	No operation
0	1	The first byte of an instruction is being executed
1	0	The queue is being emptied
1	1	A subsequent instruction byte is being taken from the queue

$\overline{RQ}/\overline{GT0}$ Request/grant line used to obtain control of the tristate buses. The 8088/86 acknowledges a request by outputting a low going pulse on the same line. When the new bus master is finished it returns control by passing a second low going pulse to the 8088/86.

$\overline{RQ}/\overline{GT1}$ Same as RQ/GT0 but with a lower priority (i.e. request grant sequence only carried out with this line provided that RQ/GT0 is not already in progress).

LOCK   Used to indicate that other system bus masters are not to obtain control of the system bus. This is actuated by software.

5 Interrupt Controls

INTR   Interrupt request input level triggered. If the interrupt enable bit is set (1) and INTR is high, then the 8088/86 will first enter an interrupt acknowledge sequence before transferring control to interrupt routine.

(INTA)   Output held low while 8088/86 is performing interrupt acknowledge sequence. For maximum mode system INTA is generated by the 8288 bus controller.

NMI   Nonmaskable interrupt input pin rising edge triggered. Control is passed to SERVICE routine starting at 00008.

6 Supplies

0 V, 5 V Single 5 V supply (+10 percent).

7 Clocks

CLK   Clock signal is usually generated by 8284 clock generator (2–5 Mhz) (crystal frequency = 3X CPU frequency, e.g. 15 MHz crystal for 5 MHz CLK).

8088/8086 Programming Model

Fig. A1.10 shows a programming model for the 8088/86. The register set is made up of four 16-bit general purpose registers, two 16-bit pointer registers, two 16-bit index registers, a 16-bit program counter, four 16-bit segment registers and a 16-bit processor status register.

Address and Addressing Modes

All 8088/8086 addresses are computed by summing the contents of a segment register with an 'effective' or offset address. The segment address always has four zeros added, resulting in the final or 'actual' 20-bit address, e.g.

segment register contains 20000H
effective or offset register 2800H

        20000H
    +   2800H
        ―――――
Actual address = 2280H

The 8088/8086 supports the following addressing modes:

1 Register
2 Immediate
3 Direct
4 Indirect
5 Base
6 Indexed
7 Based indexed
8 String
9 Port

The instruction set contains all the 8080 and most of the 8085 mnemonics as a subset. For the extra instructions the reader is referred to the Intel data sheet or a suitable text (e.g. *The 8086 Book* by Russell Rector and George Alexy, Osborne/McGrawHill, 1980).

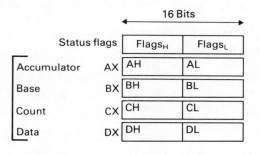

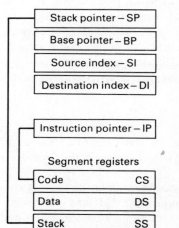

Fig. A1.10   Programming model of 8088/86

A2

Technical Details of Three Single Board Microcomputers

This section contains background information on three popular single board microcomputers referred to in the main text. The systems were chosen as examples illustrating the use of three major microprocessor families, namely 6502, Intel 8085 and the Zilog Z80.

AIM 65 DESCRIPTION

(Reprinted from the *AIM 65 User Guide* by kind permission of The Rockwell International Corporation.)

This section describes the AIM 65 hardware and software. The hardware is segmented into logical functional areas for ease of description. The AIM 65 Monitor, Editor and Assembler software are also described. User available subroutines are described along with the calling procedures and conditions.

Overview

AIM 65 is a complete microcomputer system. It contains an R6502 CPU, programmed instructions in ROM, RAM and peripheral equipment in the form of a display, a printer and a keyboard. On- and off-board expansion capabilities enhance the usability of the AIM 65. True application ease is provided by a user dedicated R6522 Versatile Interface Adapter.

The major components are shown on the AIM 65 block diagram in Fig. A2.1.

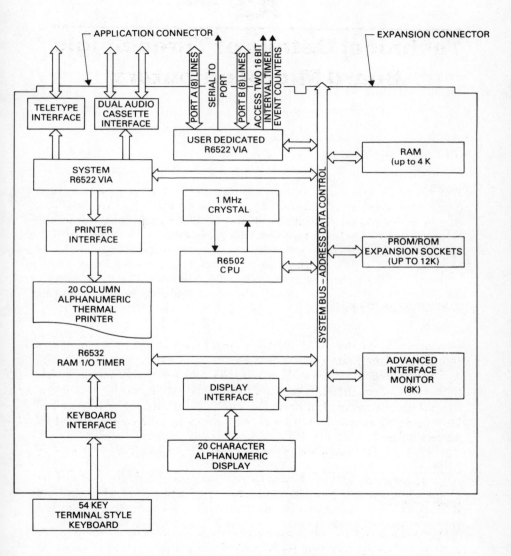

Fig. A2.1 Major components in AIM 65

Functional Areas

The hardware functional areas are:

Power distribution
Chip select
RAM
ROM
Printer interface
Display interface
Keyboard interface
User R6522 interface
Audio cassette recorder interface
TTY and serial interface

R6502

The R6502 8-bit microprocessor, the central processing unit (CPU) of the AIM 65, provides the overall control and monitoring of all AIM 65 operations. The R6502 communicates with other AIM 65 elements on three separate buses. A 16-bit address bus allows the CPU to directly address 65,536 memory locations. An 8-bit bidirectional data bus carries data from the R6502 CPU to/from memory and interface devices. The control bus carries various timing and control signals between the R6502 CPU and interfacing peripherals, devices and off-board elements.

R6502 Clock
The R6502 on AIM 65 operates at 1 MHz. The frequency reference is a 4 MHz crystal controlled oscillator. A dual D-type flip-flop Z10 divides the 4 MHz signal by four to drive the R6502 phase 0 (ϕ0) input with a 1 MHz clock.
    The R6502 generates the phase 1 (ϕ1) and phase 2 (ϕ2) clock outputs based on the phase 0 input clock. The ϕ1 (OUT) is routed to J3-3 for external use.
    The ϕ2 (OUT) from the R6502 is routed to J1-C and to inverter J16-9. A ϕ2 signal provided by J16-8 is routed to J3-Y and Z16-11. A buffered ϕ clock (SYS ϕ) generated by inverter Z16-10 provides the system level timing reference for on-board and expansion use (at J3-U).

R/W
The read/write (R/W) signal controls the direction of data transfers between the R6502 and interfacing devices. The R/W signal is routed to J1-D and inverter Z16-3. A buffered R/W signal from Z16-6 provides the system level R/W signal (SYS R/W) for on-board and expansion use (at J3-V).

Control Switches

RESET

Pushbutton switch S1 initiates RESET of the AIM 65 hardware and software. Timer Z4 holds the RES low for at least 15 ms from the time the pushbutton is released. RES is routed to the R6502 CPU, the monitor R6522 (Z32), the monitor R6532 RIOT (Z33), the user R6522 VIA (Z1), and the display R6520 PIA (U1). To initiate the device, RESET function is also routed to the expansion connector for off-board RESET functions. The monitor performs a software reset when the RES line goes high.

KB/TTY

The position of switch S3 (KB/TTY) tells AIM 65 to accept commands from either the AIM 65 or the TTY keyboard. This switch is sampled through the monitor R6522.

Printer Interface

The printer prints on heat sensitive roll paper by means of ten thermal elements, each of which can print two 5 × 7 matrix dot characters. The 10 thermal elements are mounted in fixed positions on a movable thermal head. During a print cycle, the thermal head is driven back and forth horizontally allowing a row of dots to be printed during movement in each direction. The individual thermal elements are turned on for discrete intervals during the thermal head movement to form partial characters. After a row of dots has been printed, the motor driven platen advances the paper vertically by one dot row. A full line of printed characters is complete after seven dot rows are printed. The printed characters are formed by dot patterns stored in the AIM 65 monitor. The print cycle set-up, sequencing and timing is also controlled by the AIM 65 monitor.

Display Interface

Tha AIM 65 display consists of five 4-digit 16-segment alphanumeric displays. Each display (DS1–DS5) contains internal memory, decoder and driver circuitry. The displays interface with the AIM 65 address, data and control bus lines through the R6520 PIA (U1) mounted on the display module. Each display is controlled by seven data lines (D0–D6), two address lines (A0 and A1), two control lines (W and CW) and a chip select (CE) (Fig. A2.2).

There are five separate chip-select lines (CE1–CE5), one to drive each display. To load data, CE is held low to the desired display. The

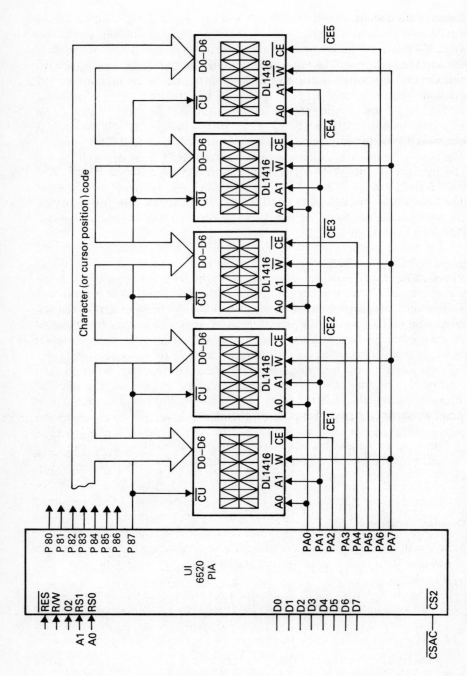

Fig. A2.2 Display interface

desired data code is placed on D0–D6 and the selected digit address (0–3) is placed on A0 and A1. The cursor line (CU) is held in the high state. The write (W) line is driven low to store and display the data. After W is returned to high, the data will continue to be displayed until replaced with new data or the cursor is displayed. Data entry may be asynchronous and random.

Keyboard Interface

The interface to the AIM 65 keyboard is through the R6532 RIOT. Z33 R6532 peripheral I/O lines PA0 through PA7 are assigned to keyboard input lines K11 through K18 respectively. R6532 lines PB0 through PB7 are wired to the keyboard output lines K01 through K08, respectively (Fig. A2.3).

When scanning for key depression, a logic 0 is placed in the R6532 output register A (ORA) in one bit position at a time corresponding to one KI line. The logic 0 provides a low output to the KI line key switches. Each key depressed of the switches connected to the selected KI line will present a closed circuit output from K01–K08 causing a logic 0 to be present in the respective bit position of R6532 output register B (ORB). Each unpressed key presents an open circuit to PB0–PB7 causing a logic 1 to be present in the respective R6532 ORB bit position.

SDK-85 SINGLE BOARD DEVELOPMENT KIT

This single board development kit makes use of the Intel 8085 microprocessor and a number of the support chips specifically for use with this microprocessor. The basic kit consists of the 8085 processor, a 2K monitor program in an 8355 ROM device, which also has two 8-bit I/O ports, and a 256-byte RAM with two 8-bit ports and one 6-bit port.

The monitor program is in two sections: one which permits communication with the system using the built-in keyboard, the other is designed for communication with a serial device at 110 baud, e.g. a teletype or a VDU and keyboard.

The SDK kit provided in this package is an extended version of the basic kit with an additional 8155 ROM, thus giving a total of 512 bytes for program and data storage. An additional ROM with a line-by-line assembler program is also on the board. This assembler can only be used in the teletype mode of the monitor. The addition of these two memory devices extends the number of I/O ports to eight of 8-bit length and two of 6-bit length.

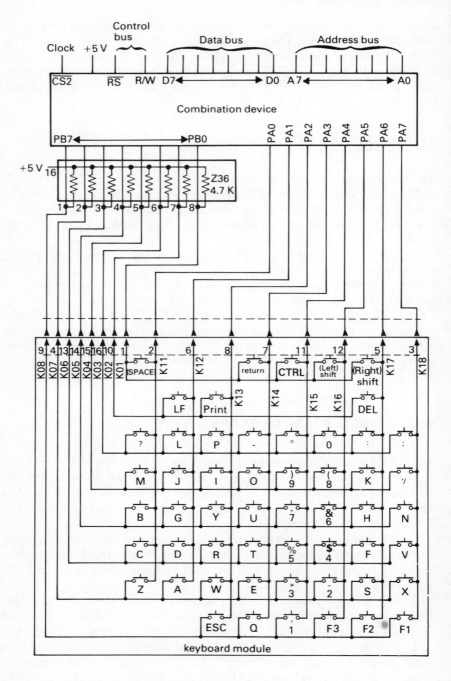

Fig. A2.3　Keyboard interface

The serial communications facilities on the basic kit required an additional −10 V supply. This kit has been modified so that this supply is no longer required, and the receive circuit has been made passive 20 mA with opto-isolation. The memory map for the system is:

0000–07FF Monitor ROM
0800–0FFF Assembler ROM
1800–1FFF Keyboard/display functions
2000–20FF Read–write memory
2800–28FF Read-write memory

(See Figs. A2.4–A2.6). For further details see the *SDK–85 User Manual*.

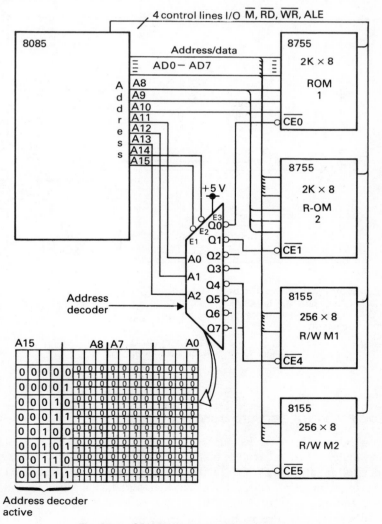

Fig. A2.4 SDK 85 memory addressing

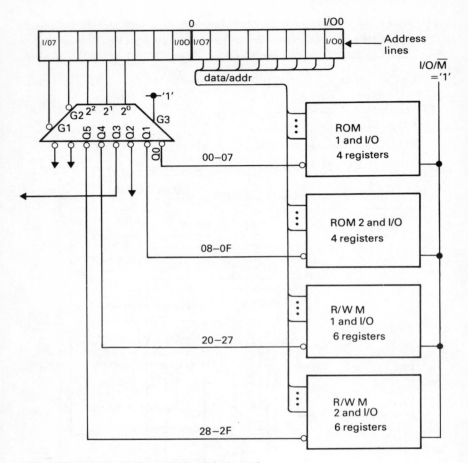

I/O addresses are duplicated on both halves of
address/data bus. In SDK 85 A8–A15 are used
for I/O selection using same decoding as for
memory selection.

Fig. A2.5   SDK 85 I/O addressing

MEDC Z80 SINGLE BOARD CONTROLLER

This single board controller is based on the Z80 microprocessor and
associated family of I/O devices. The board circuitry has all that is needed
for a small microprocessor based system and has a suitable connector
which can be used to make the board part of a larger system. The
controller was designed with the aim of facilitating the implementation of

small projects and also as a small Z80 system to be used in the teaching of in-circuit emulation techniques using a microprocessor development system.

The circuit can be considered in three sections as indicated below:

1   The Z80 processor and associated memory with decoding and control circuitry
2   The input/output section
3   The general purpose interface.

	Addresses	Device
Memory	0000–07FF	Monitor ROM
	0800–OFFF	Assembler ROM
	1800, 1900	KB/display controller
	2000–27FF	R/W M1 selected
	2000–20FF	1st appearance of RWM1
	2100–21FF	2nd appearance of RWM1
	.	
	.	
	.	
	2700–27FF	8th appearance of RWM1
	2800–2FFF	RWM2 selected
	2800–28FF	1st appearance of RWM2
	2900–29FF	2nd appearance of RWM2
	.	
	.	
	2F00–2FFF	8th appearance of RWM2

I/O map	8755 I/O addresses		I/O port register
	Monitor ROM { 00	Ass. ROM { 08	Port A
	01	09	Port B
	02	0A	DDR A
	03	0B	DDR B

8155 I/O addresses

	R/W 1 { 20	R/W 2 { 28	Control/status
	21	29	A
	22	2A	B
	23	2B	C
	24	2C	Counter L
	25	2D	Counter H

Fig. A2.6   SDK 85 memory and I/O map

The Processor and Associated Circuitry

The Z80 microprocessor is an enhanced version of INTEL's 8080 with an extended instruction set and improved hardware requiring only a single 0–5 V supply and a single phase clock. Programs written for the 8080 will run on the Z80 but, at assembly level, 8080 programs would have to be converted to Z80 mnemonics before they could be assembled using a Z80 assembler.

The clock generator consists of two inverters and a crystal oscillator, the output of which is buffered using an additional inverter before being distributed to the various components on the board (Fig. A2.7).

A reset switch is provided on board which in addition to resetting the Z80 will also reset the I/O devices by activating the $\overline{M1}$ inputs. The read-write memory consists of two 21/4 ICs arranged to form 1K × 8 bits of R/W memory. The read only memory socket can support either a 2716, 2K × 8 bit, or a 2532, 4K × 8 bit EPROM. The memory selection logic places the R/O memory at the bottom end of the address space while the R/W memory is placed at the top (Fig. A2.8).

Memory read or write action will activate the processor control line $\overline{MEMRQ}$, so this signal is used to control the output of the two NAND gates connected to the memory select lines. The outputs can only be active when $\overline{MEMRQ}$ is active (low).

The control line $\overline{R/OSEL}$ will be in its active state only when the Z80 is reading data ($\overline{RD}$='0') and address line A15 is '0' M (addresses 0000–7FFF). Processor addresses 0000–07FF (or 0000–0FFF for 4K memory) will cover each location of the R/O memory. The next 2K(4K) addresses will activate the 11 (12) memory address lines over the full range. Thus the R/O memory will appear repeatedly over the range of processor addresses from 0000–7FFF. Only when an address with A15='1' is selected by the processor will the R/O memory be deselected. It is usual to consider that the R/O memory appears from 0000 to 07FF (0FFF). The R/W select line $\overline{R/WSEL}$ will be active (low) when A15='1' with $\overline{MEMRQ}$='0' for both read and write operations. The W line is connected directly to the 2114 memories to control direction of data transfer between the Z80 and the memory.

The $\overline{R/WSEL}$ line is active for addresses from 8000–FFFF, but since the R/W memory is only 1K in size the memory will appear repeatedly in this address range (32 times). The start of R/W memory can be considered as 8000, 8400, 8800, ... ,FC00. The R/W memory can be considered for the purpose of programming the board, to exist from FC00 to FFFF (or 8000 to 88FF – the first appearance if desired).

This appearance of the same memory at different microprocessor addresses is a feature of systems where the address decoding is simple and the select line for a particular memory device is active for a processor

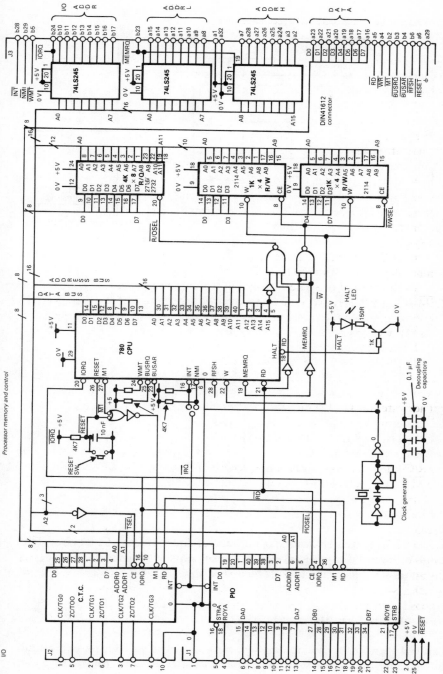

Fig. A2.7 Z80 single board controller – circuit diagram

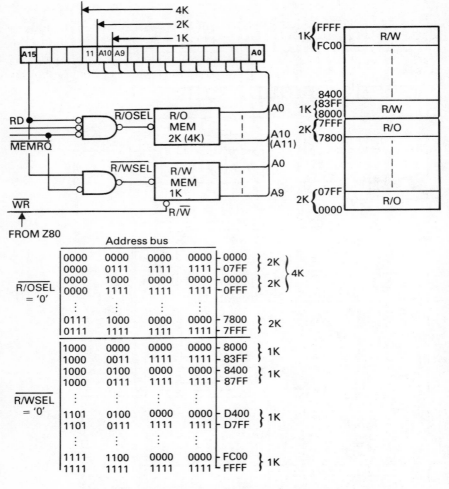

Fig. A2.8 Memory select circuitry and memory map

address range greater than the number of locations in the device. This rough on-board decoding gives rise to problems when external memory is required since bus conflicts must be avoided.

Input/Output Circuits

The I/O facilities provided on the board consist of a PIO, parallel input/output chip, and a CTC, counter/timer circuit. These are designed to be used with the port addressing mode of the Z80 which transfers data to and from the processor on the execution of IN and OUT instructions. These two instructions activate the $\overline{\text{IORQ}}$ output and leave $\overline{\text{MEMRQ}}$ off, so memory is disabled. The 8-bit address of the port appears on the lower 8 bits of the address bus. Both the PIO and CTC have four addressable registers and have, therefore, two address lines. These address lines are connected to A0 and A1 on the processor. Read and write operations are controlled by the single line $\overline{\text{RD}}$ from the processor (Fig. A2.9).

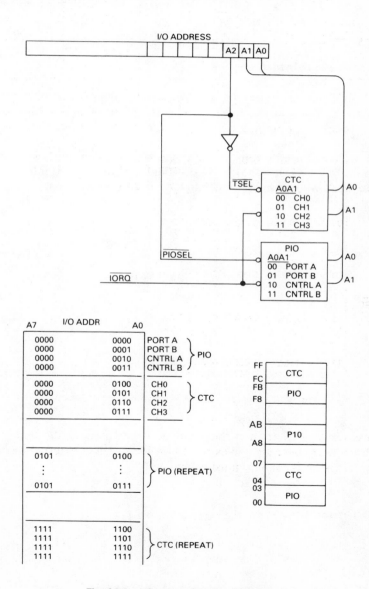

Fig. A2.9 I/O select circuitry and I/O map

Address line A2 is used in the I/O select circuitry to ensure that the PIO is selected when A2='0' and the CTC when A2='1'. I/O addresses 00, 01, 02, 03 and 08, 09, 0A, 0B, ... , F8, F9, FA, FB will select the PIO registers for port A, port B, control A and control B, i.e. the same registers appear repeatedly in the I/O map. Similarly the CTC channels CH0, CH1, CH2 and CH3 will appear first at 04, 05, 06, 07 then 0C, 0D, 0E, 0F, and so on up to FC, FD, FE and FF. The first appearance of the ports in the I/O map are used as the addresses of these ports in any program.

General Purpose Interface

The general purpose interface can be rearranged to suit most 6500/6800 bus systems. The address lines are buffered using 74LS245 chips and the I/O addresses are obtained by gating the bottom nine address lines with IORQ.

Care is required when extending the system using this bus connector to avoid conflicts with the on-board memory, e.g. to extend the R/W memory the on-board memory would have to be removed.

A3

Power Supplies and Regulators

POWER SUPPLIES

The major part of microprocessor systems involves digital circuits which operate within specifications over a supply range of, say, ± 5 percent about the nominal value. In addition to the standard +5 V supply there may be other voltages, including −5 V, ±12 V, etc. These are needed either by some of the integrated circuits, the data transfer processes (RS232 serial ports) or by peripheral devices such as displays or printers.

Some form of regulation is required both against the slow variations in the input and any changes of load current as the microprocessor system carries out its tasks. In addition there must be some means of absorbing or attenuating any transient voltages on the line. To see how servicing of this part of the system can proceed, consider first the basic circuits – experienced engineers and technicians may want to skip this section.

The simplest arrangement has a center-tapped transformer driving a full-wave rectifier (Fig. A3.1). (A half-wave is simpler, with a single untapped winding and diode, but halving the number of voltage peaks markedly worsens the ripple voltage.) The preferred version reduces the cost of the transformer by accepting a single secondary winding, with a bridge rectifier to keep the full-wave action (Fig. A3.2). The peak reverse voltage on each diode is reduced but a disadvantage is that there are two diodes conducting during each charging period. As a reminder of the action, Fig. A3.3 shows some typical waveforms.

THE OUTPUT VOLTAGE (Fig. A3.3(a)) – The peak value is just less than the peak winding voltage, reduced by the forward voltage drops of two diodes. At low currents the diode voltage drop is a logarithmic function of the current, increasing only by about 18 mV for each doubling of current. It is usual, then, to assume a constant drop of ~0.7 V for silicon diodes.

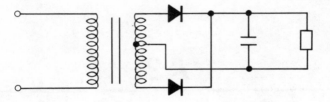

Fig. A3.1   Full-wave rectifier with center-tapped transformer

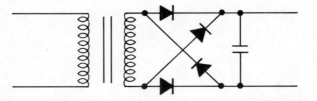

Fig. A3.2   Bridge rectilier uses more diodes

Higher currents, as at the peak of the charging cycle, produce additional voltage drops in the bulk resistance of the diodes and these are proportional to the current. This makes it hard to predict the effect of current increases without knowing more about the current ratings of the diodes. A conservative estimate of 1 V per diode seems safe in most cases.

DIODE CURRENTS (Fig. A3.3(b), (c)) – The capacitor is charged for a brief time during each positive peak and discharges steadily into the load between peaks. The shorter the charging time, the higher that peak current has to be, and the current is proportional to the rate of increase of input voltage. A larger capacitance will cause an increased current flow, shorten the charging time and reduce the ensuing fall in voltage. It is a designer's compromise to get the least fall in voltage without exceeding the peak current ratings of capacitor or diodes. The current flows in diodes 1 and 4 on the first half cycle and in 2 and 3 on the second.

If any of these diodes go open circuit the mean output voltage may not be greatly affected – the power supply may have been designed to deliver a much larger current than is being drawn. However, the capacitor will now charge at half the frequency (corresponding to either Fig. A3.3(b) or A3.3(c)) and will have twice as long to discharge.

Ripple Voltages

This roughly doubles the magnitude of the ripple voltage. The following regulator can attenuate this ripple by a large factor, but there comes a

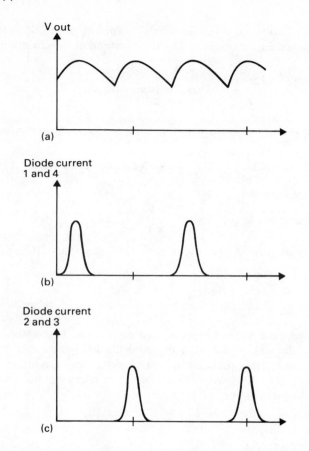

Fig. A3.3 (a) Output voltage peaks twice per cycle
(b),(c) Each diode pair carries high peak currents on alternate half
cycles

minimum instantaneous voltage at which the regulator is driven below its linear range. It then transmits any further input falls almost without attenuation. The onset of this condition is sharp and, for example, a ripple voltage on the capacitor of 2 V peak–peak might be attenuated to a few millivolts, while 3 V peak–peak could result in about 1 V of ripple (Fig. A3.4). The critical parameter is the 'input/output differential voltage', which for many regulators is about 2 V, i.e. for a nominal 5 V out, the input voltage must never fall below 7 V under any circumstances at any point in its cycle. To estimate the ripple voltage we can assume:

1 that the load current is substantially constant, at a value equal to the peak voltage divided by the load resistance;
2 that the fall in voltage continues for a complete half cycle.

These give a pessimistic estimate of the resulting ripple, and for a first guess the nominal capacitance may be used instead of its minimum value.

$$\text{Discharge current } (I) \approx \frac{\text{peak voltage}}{\text{load resistance}} = \frac{V}{R}$$

$$\text{Rate of fall of voltage } \frac{dV}{dt} = \frac{\text{charge lost/time}}{\text{capacitance}} = \frac{I}{C}$$

This continues for time 't' where

$$t \approx \begin{cases} 10 \text{ ms at 50 Hz} \\ 8 \text{ ms at 60 Hz} \end{cases}$$

$$\text{Peak–peak ripple voltage} \approx \frac{V}{R \times C \times t}$$

If this ripple is expressed as a fraction of the peak voltage, it becomes even simpler

$$\frac{\text{Peak–peak ripple voltage}}{\text{Peak voltage}} \approx t$$

where t is the time between successive peaks and is the time constant composed of the smoothing capacitor and the load resistance. These are not intended as design equations, which would in any case involve rigorous statistical analyses; they are intended as a shorthand guide to check for likely sources of problems.

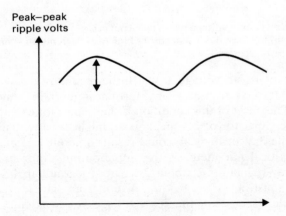

Fig. A3.4   Peak-peak ripple voltage reduced by large capacticance at expense of high peak currents

The regulator is shown in Fig. A3.5 as a three-terminal device having a common point between input and output. This point will normally be connected to the chassis which may in turn be grounded. (This is not necessarily so and the problems of linking equipment, each of which is locally grounded, are well known, often requiring optically-coupled signal paths to cope.) It is common to find capacitors across both input and output of a regulator in addition to the main smoothing or reservoir capacitor across the rectifier. In Fig. A3.6 both C_1 and C_2 should be placed physically close to the regulator. They may be relatively small in value (<1 μF) and serve to provide low-impedance paths at high frequencies, inhibiting the high frequency oscillators that can result from line and load inductances. For example, the reservoir capacitor is designed for high capacitance and ripple-current capability in the smallest possible volume. It has substantial inductive terms at high frequencies where the regulator behavior is complex and liable to burst into high-frequency oscillation.

If a direct-voltage measurement on a nominally regulated supply is out of specification, and particularly if it shows signs of instability, a quick check with an oscilloscope may reveal oscillations in the MHz range that could be due to a failure in the hf decoupling. In the absence of an oscilloscope, a 0.1–1.0 μF capacitor across the C_1 or C_2 locations may produce an observable change in the measured voltage by modifying or removing these oscillations. Any such change points to inadequate decoupling as a possible source of the problem.

The three-terminal regulator was initially produced as a fixed-voltage device particularly for on-board regulation of 5 V logic systems. It has replaced most of the circuits based on discrete transistors and operational amplifiers. The exceptions are where the voltages, currents or other parameters of the circuit are extreme. Once the simplicity of the three-terminal regulator was matched by the low cost stemming from mass production, designers looked to expand its role. In place of a fixed voltage, the configuration of Fig. A3.7 allows variation to any value lying between the following limits:

$$V_o > V_{ref}$$
$$V_o < V_s - V_{diff}$$

where V_{diff} is the minimum input/output differential voltage noted above. In theory, the circuit itself is subject only to the difference between the supply and output voltages. A 5 V regulator with a normal supply-voltage rating of 20 or 30 volts *could* be used to regulate an output of 100 V from an input of, say, 110–120 V. This can be risky, since even a temporary short circuit across the output would place the whole supply voltage across the regulator. The idea is widely used to produce regulated outputs up to a few tens of volts, either fixed or variable as in Fig. A3.7. More recent ICs using the so-called band-gap technique to generate very low but stable reference voltages have extended the range down to 1.2 V. Such a three-terminal regulator can provide output voltages from 1.2 V to above 20 V given the appropriate supply.

Equally important, they have a considerable measure of internal protection against fault conditions. That should not be taken as encouragement to misuse them, but with both current and thermal limiting they are better protected than many older circuits. The thermal sensing uses a pn junction on the chip to pull the regulator down into a low voltage state. As it cools, this limit can be removed, restoring the original voltage. If this symptom – a voltage rising and falling over a period of seconds – is observed, it may signify a severe overload.

An unusual fault to which some versions of regulators were prone required the addition of an external diode as in Fig. A3.8. The cause was any short circuit across the *input* circuitry, e.g. an intermittent short in the reservoir capacitor. Energy stored in the output capacitor could now be discharged through internal junctions in the regulator. To avoid this there may be an external diode to bypass the regulator under such a fault condition. Short circuits across the output are less of a problem with the in-built current and thermal limiting.

Another extension much requested by users was increased output current capability without loss of regulation. An added transistor takes the regulator current as base drive, supplying its collector current to the load (Fig. A3.9). This scales the current up by a large but variable factor depending on the transistor current gain, i.e. the precise current limiting action is lost, and to be restored needs more transistors.

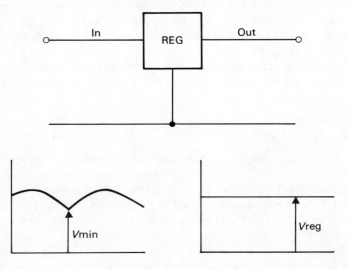

Fig. A3.5   Three-terminal regulator stabilizes output voltage provided $V_{min} > (V_{reg}+2)V$

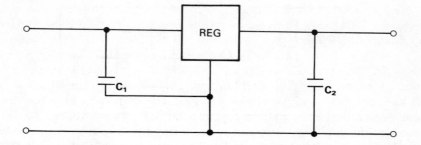

Fig. A3.6 Low-inductance capacitors suppress high-frequency instability

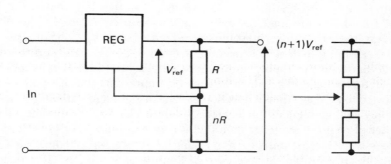

Fig. A3.7 Output voltage set by potential divider ratio which can be varied

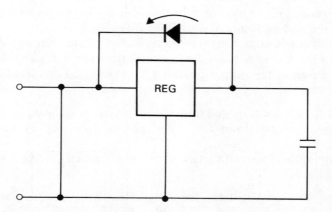

Fig. A3.8 Shunt diode discharges output capacitance protecting regulator if input has transient short circuit

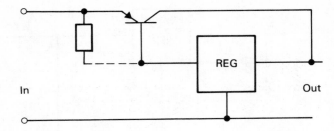

Fig. A3.9   Additional transistor boosts output current without changing voltage

A quick visual indication of the dissipation characteristics is provided in Fig. A3.10. A simple regulator with no current limiting has an output voltage V_o that remains constant up to the design limit current I_o (Fig. A3.10(a)). As the load resistance falls to zero corresponding to a short circuit, the current rises to some much higher current I_s. The dissipation in the series power device at maximum rated output depends on the difference between the supply and output voltages and is shown as a heavily-shaded rectangle. The much larger area represents the dissipation under short circuit conditions. It is somewhat exaggerated, assuming that the supply voltage remains unchanged. None the less, the dissipation can be an order of magnitude higher than that for normal full-power out. Neither an excessively large transistor nor taking a chance on avoiding such short circuits are sensible. Simple current limiting as in Fig. A3.10(b) cuts the excessive dissipation by a large factor – the short-circuit current need only be 10 or 20 percent above the rated output current. Even better is the characteristic of Fig. A3.10(c). This is the so-called foldback or re-entrant effect where multiple feedback loops pull the short-circuit current back towards zero. The shaded areas representing dissipation under normal rated output and short-circuit conditions are comparable.

The principle underlying regulators, including three-terminal devices, is shown in Fig. A3.11. A zener diode or other reference device is compared with a fraction of the output provided by a potential divider. Sources of error include:

–   voltage changes injected from the supply into the zener;
–   currents drawn from zener and potential divider by the sensing circuits;
–   temperature-induced variations in the reference voltage and sensing amplifiers.

The three-terminal regulator has these elements embedded within the chip, i.e. they are not user alterable. The current is boosted by the arrangement of Fig. A3.12. Emitter followers are inserted between the regulator and the load. The potential divider is shifted to the new output

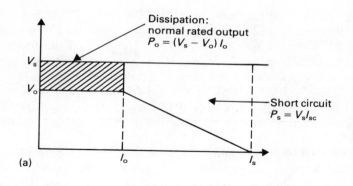

(a)

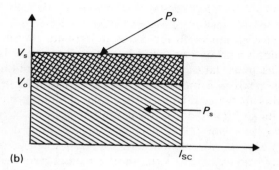

(b)

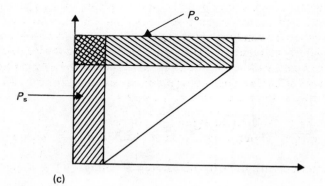

(c)

Fig. A3.10 (a) Areas represent power dissipated under normal and short
circuit conditions
(b) Current limit cuts excessive dissipation
(c) Foldback limiting reduces short-circuit current and dissipation

with the reference circuit unchanged. Additional voltage drops in the base-emitter junctions raise the minimum supply voltage for a given output by about 1.4 V in the example shown, assuming relatively high currents.

Current-limiting ability depends on sensing the current as in Fig. A3.13(a). A series resistor R_s develops a voltage proportional to the load current. This voltage is compared with a reference voltage in the same way as for voltage sensing. It is not usually necessary to achieve such accuracy and the base-emitter voltage of a transistor offers adequate performance (Fig. A3.13(b)).

The onset of current limiting may be only 10 or 20 percent above the peak rated output of a regulator. A low output voltage could be the result of a relatively small increase in current due to the addition of some peripheral, or the substitution of ICs of higher than specified current drain.

A difficult fault to trace can occur when there are several regulated voltages in a system with common or derived reference voltages. An excessive load on one can then produce unexpected results on the others. The discussion has concentrated on the static behavior of these circuits,

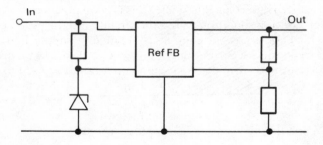

Fig. A3.11   Fraction of output is compared with reference voltage, to control the output

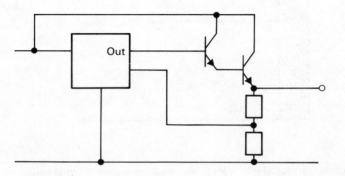

Fig. A3.12   Additional transistors boost the current with potential divider still sensing load voltage

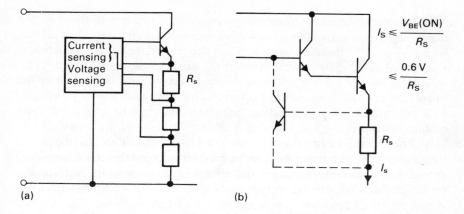

Fig. A3.13 (a) Current sensing resistor used with integrated-circuit regulator
(b) Similar function added to existing regulator

partly because it is more predictable. Any such faults are then fairly straightforward to detect and eliminate; this is good practice.

Under working conditions, both the circuits and the peripherals draw currents with large transient content. A regulated supply that can cope with a given continuous current may experience a distinct fall in voltage at much lower transient currents. An oscilloscope should be used to check for such spikes on both supply and ground lines. Local decoupling of TTL logic circuits is common to minimize this effect: TTL is prone to this problem because at logic transitions both transistors in a series pair come into conduction briefly, drawing a high pulse current.

SWITCHING REGULATORS

Linear regulators apply a control signal to the power device continuously readjusting the output to compensate for changes in external conditions. The power device has to dissipate a large proportion of the total power corresponding to the difference between supply and output voltages.

A totally different approach places an electronic switch between supply and load, varying the proportion of time for which the two are connected. In some cases no other components are needed – the mean power to a resistive load can be controlled with a theoretical efficiency of 100 percent in that an ideal switch carries no current in its off state and experiences no voltage drop in its on state. The general principle of this pulse width modulation is shown in Fig. A3.14.

Most loads need the voltage to be subject to as little instantaneous variation as possible. The first step is to add a series inductor (Fig. A3.15).

Again assuming ideal components, no power is dissipated in the inductor which releases energy when the applied voltage is zero. The ripple on the load voltage is reduced by raising either the frequency or the inductance. Additional filtering by a parallel capacitor further reduces the ripple (Fig. A3.16), though a further linear regulator is usualy provided to bring the ripple down to millivolt level. This implies some small loss in efficiency, with the output of the switching regulator set slightly above the final required output.

The switched output could be derived from a direct voltage supply via a changeover switch but these cannot be implemented directly in semiconductor form. Simply to switch the supply into an open-circuit state is unacceptable when driving an inductor – the back emf would be excessive. A pair of on-off switches driven antiphase is one possibility (Fig. A3.17).

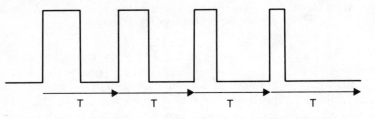

Fig. A3.14   Mean voltage controlled by mark-space ratio

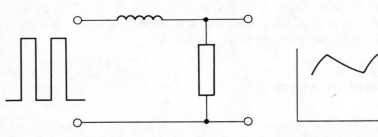

Fig. A3.15   An inductor reduces the ac component without significantly changing the mean voltage

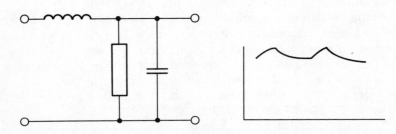

Fig. A3.16   Capacitive filtering lowers the ripple still further .

Timing is critical: if the conducting states were to overlap the supply would be short circuited. If they are both off at any instant the inductor current is again interrupted. The usual solution is to replace one switch by a diode (Fig. A3.18). This so-called fly-wheel diode sustains the current flow when the switch goes off. A disadvantage is that the diode voltage drop

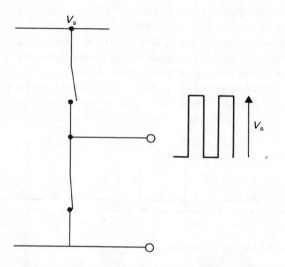

Fig. A3.17 The output can be provided by antiphase switches

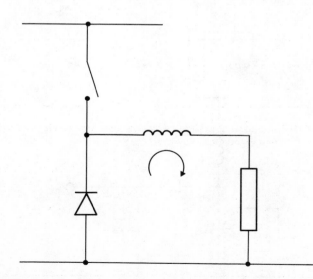

Fig. A3.18 To avoid overlap in the switches that would short circuit supply, a diode sustains the current flow

contributes to the power losses. The overall efficiency can still be well above 80 percent, even where the output voltage is only a fraction of the supply voltage and a linear regulator would be limited to < 50 percent. The current flow is in the same sense for both parts of the cycle. Either pnp or npn transistors can be used as switches (Fig. A3.19). In the on condition the voltage drop can be ≪ 1 V but the base current can reduce the efficiency by several percent. Field-effect transistors have no corresponding gate currents but cannot usually be driven so hard into conduction.

Switching outputs are not even restricted to reducing the supply voltage (Fig. A3.20). In this configuration the inductor cannot smooth the output, and capacitive smoothing has to suffice.

In all these examples only the output stage of a regulator is shown. The control sections have two jobs to do. As in all regulators, one stage compares the output with a reference voltage, amplifying the difference.

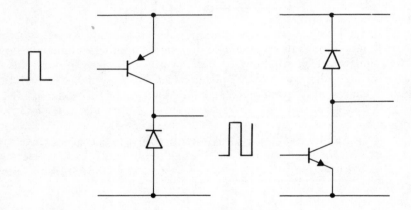

Fig. A3.19 A bipolar transistor acts as a controlled switch

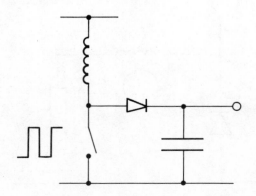

Fig. A3.20 Other configurations can increase output voltage

This error voltage has then to produce a pulse train of variable mark-space ratio. One way of achieving this (Fig. A3.21) is to compare this error signal with a sawtooth voltage. If the comparator has a high gain, a pulse waveform is produced that can activate the electron switch. The overall feedback, if properly designed, will hold the comparator input at just that level on the sawtooth to produce the required mark-space ratio.

The stress on such devices is particularly high in switching mains power supplies. These have increased in popularity because they are far smaller for a given output, but the switching devices have to withstand the full mains voltage while switching rapidly. The transient voltages generated by the inductive elements in the system must also be protected against, the basic principle is shown in Fig. A3.22. There are two rectifier/smoothing sections. The first produces a high direct voltage from the mains input, the second from the transformer coupled output. The switching frequency is high allowing low capacitance smoothing circuits and physically small transformers and inductors.

The fault conditions in switching regulators can differ from those in linear circuits, though as noted above there are a number of linear sections to the regulator. The switching frequency varies from tens to hundreds of kilohertz, and radiation and stray pickup is always a problem. Though this should be cured at the design stage, other sections of the system may be unexpectedly sensitive, e.g. any A/D converter at an input. The ferrite-cored transformers and indicators change characteristics sharply if loose or stressed due to faulty mounting or vibration. This can lead to overheating. The switching devices could be driven into a permanently conducting state on failure of the drive circuitry and over-voltage detection and shut-down would normally be expected.

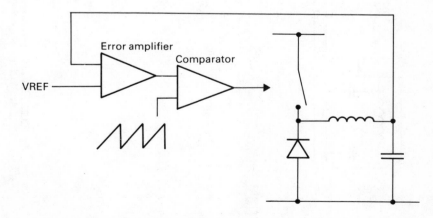

Fig. A3.21 Overall feedback compares the output with a reference voltage, adjusting the switching time via a comparator

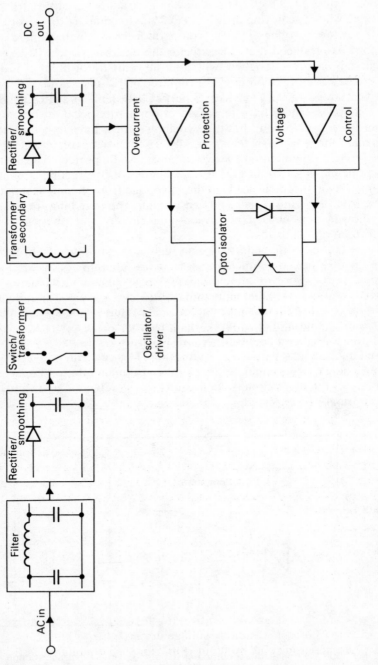

Fig. A3.22 Switching power supplies combine power switches and linear control circuitry

A4

Signature and Logic Analyzers — Suggested Circuits

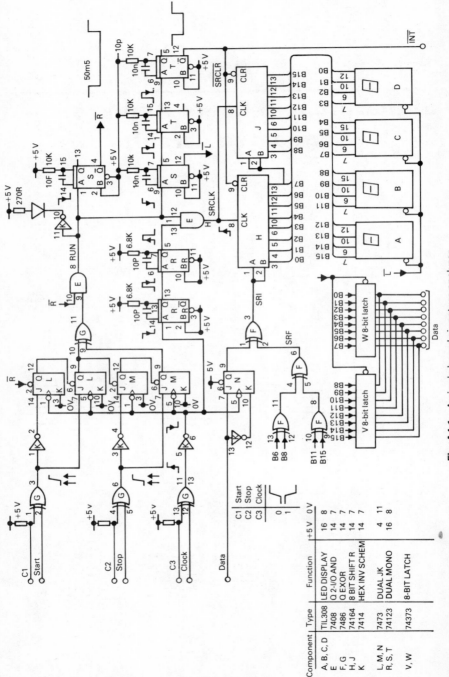

Fig. A4.1 A single board signature analyzer

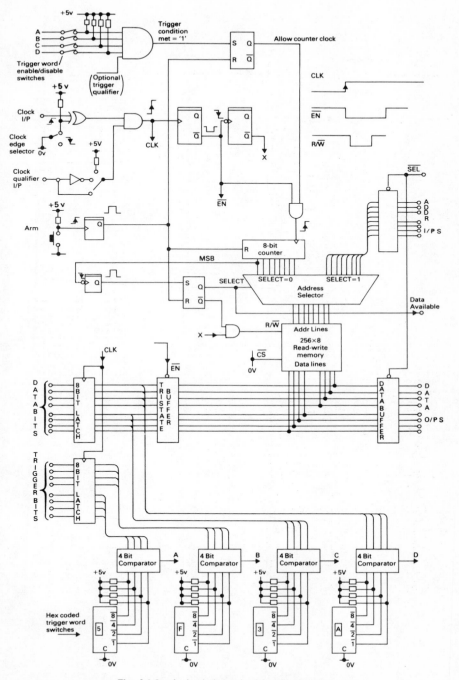

Fig. A4.2 A single board add-on logic analyzer

Index